EDITORS
MAKE WAR

EDITORS MAKE WAR

Southern Newspapers in the Secession Crisis

DONALD E. REYNOLDS

VANDERBILT UNIVERSITY PRESS
Nashville

International Standard Book Number 0–8265–1164–3
Library of Congress Catalogue Card Number 71–129050

Printed in the United States of America by
Kingsport Press, Inc., Kingsport, Tennessee

To Martha

Preface

IF a newspaper of today were to publish its product in the makeup of a typical Southern paper of 1860, it would probably plunge into bankruptcy. Journals published in the period before the Civil War lacked the visual appeal necessary to attract sophisticated twentieth-century readers. They were skimpy in size, and they carried no large headlines, photographs, color, comic strips, or even cartoons. Editors usually relegated news and editorials to inside pages, devoting the front page to drab advertisements.

Unappealing as they are to the modern eye, the newspapers of 1860 were the most popular form of literature available to Southerners—or to all Americans, for that matter. Many read nothing else. The Director of the Census of 1860 said that newspapers and periodicals "furnish nearly the whole of the reading which the greater number, whether from inclination or necessity, permit themselves to enjoy." Newspapers constituted the only true mass news medium available to Southerners in 1860. In the absence of radio, television, and weekly news magazines to supplement their knowledge of current events and to give them a better understanding of people in other regions of the country, Southerners learned from newspapers virtually everything they knew of events outside their own communities. Thus, the way in which news was selected and interpreted exerted a tremendous influence in molding the viewpoints of Southerners on many subjects.

On the eve of the Civil War, Southern newspapers were

particularly influential in altering Southern attitudes toward the Union. Newspapers unquestionably provide one of the most important sources for a clear understanding of why the South seceded. Recognizing the value of contemporary journals, historians of the secession period have relied heavily upon newspapers. Avery Craven, in *The Growth of Southern Nationalism, 1848–1861,* explained that he used newspapers extensively because the press was "both an expression and a molder of public opinion." James G. Randall, in *The Civil War and Reconstruction,* called newspapers "an exceedingly important body of sources." Newspapers, "and not private correspondence, were the sources of information for the people at large," wrote Dwight L. Dumond, in *The Secession Movement, 1860–1861.*

Nevertheless, no historian has made a study of the press itself during the secession crisis. Dumond's *Southern Editorials on Secession* is the only book dealing with the press during this critical period. It consists of chronologically arranged editorials taken from various Southern journals between January 6, 1860, and May 9, 1861. Except for a brief and unilluminating introduction, Dumond's collection is devoid of interpretation. Moreover, Professor Dumond selected his 183 editorials from only thirty different newspapers, almost all of which were published in the larger towns and cities of the South. Neither he nor any other Southern historian has attempted to ascertain the views and attitudes of any appreciable number of Southern rural weeklies on the secession question. This neglect is unfortunate, for the country editor frequently had an opinion all his own and a pithy way of expressing it.

I have not attempted to write a history of all aspects of the Southern press during the secession crisis. For example, I have ignored the business and technical sides of the press; those facets are admirably treated in Frank L. Mott, *American Journalism: A History, 1690–1960.* I have omitted periodicals because, with few exceptions, they were relatively unimportant in the South.

This study attempts simply to analyze the evolution of newspaper opinion in the eleven Confederate states from a generally unionist position in early 1860 to a predominantly secessionist viewpoint a year later. In tracing the evolving views of the Southern press I have concentrated mainly upon editorial matter. This is not to imply that news reporting was unimportant in reflecting a paper's political attitudes. Editors carefully selected news that reflected their own viewpoints. But most Southern papers clipped much of their news from the dozens of other journals which they regularly received in exchange for their own. Therefore, for a large majority of Southern newspapers—particularly rural journals, which often were one-man operations—"news" was usually material that had been lifted bodily and, sometimes, without acknowledgment from other journals.

In my survey of the Southern press I have looked for geographical and political patterns; I have tried to determine the issues which most concerned the press of all parties in the states that would compose the Confederacy; and I have examined the techniques which editors used in dramatizing those issues. In the research for this study I relied primarily upon the newspapers themselves. I examined partial or complete holdings of nearly 200 newspapers, many of them in the libraries of the University of Texas, Tulane University, Duke University, the University of North Carolina, the University of South Carolina, and Louisiana State University. Other important repositories visited were the state archives of Texas, Mississippi, and Alabama. In addition, I studied newspaper files in several courthouses and municipal libraries.

Many of the newspapers used in this study were borrowed on microfilm via interlibrary loan. In addition, a grant from the Judah P. Benjamin Fund, Tulane University, enabled me to purchase microfilm both from commercial companies and from repositories which I was unable to visit personally, such as the Alderman Library of the University of Virginia and the Library of Congress. East Texas State University expedited the revision of my original manuscript by providing generously through its Faculty Development Leave program.

I owe personal debts of gratitude to literally dozens of librarians in the above-mentioned repositories for making my task easier. I especially wish to thank Miss Betty Maihles and Mrs. Dorothy Whittemore of the Howard Tilton Library for facilitating my use of the interlibrary loan service at Tulane University.

Professors Charles P. Roland, William R. Hogan, Gerald M. Capers, Frank H. Smyrl, and Dale A. Somers all read the manuscript at some stage of its development and offered helpful suggestions. I am especially grateful to Professor Roland for reading the manuscript both in its original and revised forms and for supplying advice and encouragement without which my task would have been infinitely more difficult. Mrs. Gale Nelson did an excellent job of typing and proofreading the final manuscript.

I owe the largest debt to my wife, Martha Ann Reynolds, who not only acted as an invaluable helpmate in the usual sense during the preparation of this manuscript, but who also performed the duties of research assistant, secretary, proofreader, critic, and, sometimes, chaplain.

Commerce, Texas   Donald E. Reynolds
February 26, 1970

Contents

EDITORS
MAKE WAR

Introduction

THROUGHOUT the decade preceding the Civil War, Southern newspapers, like those in the rest of the nation, were growing rapidly both in numbers and in circulation. A rapidly expanding population, a declining illiteracy rate, and a steady reduction in the price of papers all contributed to the great strides which Southern journalism made during the period. In 1850 the eleven states of the future Confederacy possessed only 503 newspapers and periodicals, with a combined annual circulation of about 11 issues per white person. Ten years later the number of journals in the same states had increased to 847, and their per capita circulation had grown to approximately 19 per white person.[1]

Although the growth of Southern journalism was impressive, the circulation figures of Southern papers and periodicals scarcely compared with those in certain other sections of the nation. The newspaper and periodical circulation of the entire future Confederacy in 1860 was 103,041,436; that of the remainder of the nation 824,910,112. The eleven states which would soon fly the "stars and bars" thus produced about one of every eight newspapers and periodicals sold in the country—not a very good record, considering that one of every three Americans lived in the same states. The greatest contrast was between the Southern states and the more urban states of the North. New York had a circulation of newspapers and periodicals which was more than three times as great as that of all the future Confederate states combined. Pennsylvania also boasted a circulation greater than that of all of the Confederate states in 1860. Massachusetts could make nearly the same claim: the Bay State's newspapers and periodicals annually sold over 102,000,000 copies.[2]

Southern states fared little better when they compared the per capita circulation of their publications with those of the more heavily populated Northern states. Alabama's annual per capita circulation in 1860 was fourteen; Arkansas's, seven; Florida's, thirteen; Georgia's, twenty-three; Louisiana's, forty-seven; Mississippi's, twenty-five; North Carolina's, seven; South Carolina's, twelve; Tennessee's, twelve; Texas's, eighteen; and Virginia's, twenty-five. But Massachusetts's was ninety; New York's, eighty-four; and Pennsylvania's, forty-one. The Southern states appeared in a better light, however, when compared to many of the predominantly rural states of the North; for example, Connecticut's per capita circulation of newspapers and periodicals was twenty-one; Maine's, thirteen; Wisconsin's, ten; Michigan's, sixteen; and Iowa's, ten.[3]

As the above figures suggest, the more successful Northern journals had much larger subscription lists than did their Southern counterparts. The New York *Herald* was the largest daily paper in the country in 1860. Its circulation of 77,000 was about half that of all sixty-six dailies of the future Confederate states combined. Horace Greeley's New York *Weekly Tribune* sold an average of 200,000 copies every week.[4] In the South, where cities were fewer, population less dense, and illiteracy rates higher, editors had to be satisfied with substantially fewer subscribers. The Richmond *Dispatch,* one of the most successful penny papers in the South, announced a circulation of about 8,000 for its daily, 2,000 for its semiweekly, and 5,500 for its weekly editions. Greeley would have found such figures far from impressive, but the *Dispatch* bragged that its "business results are not equalled by any paper in the Union, South of the Potomac, save the New Orleans *Picayune* and, perhaps, one other paper in that city." The influential Charleston *Courier* had a circulation of only about 3,000, but, even more surprisingly, its widely quoted neighbor, the *Mercury,* boasted only about 550 paid subscriptions and, reportedly, cost the Rhett family $8,000 a year to keep it in business.[5] Apparently no paper of the future Confederate states sold as many as 10,000 copies of any single edition. The great majority of Southern newspapers numbered their readers by the hundreds rather than thousands.

Despite their limited circulation, Southern journals were extremely important as sources of information. In the absence of other media, the newspapers of 1860 had a virtual monopoly on news distribution. Moreover, journalism was more narrowly political in its emphasis than it is today, and this was especially true of Southern journalism. Papers usually classified themselves as either political, religious, or literary journals. According to the Census of 1860, the eleven future Confederate states had 703 political to only 47 religious, 64 literary, and 30 miscellaneous publications. Thus, more than 83 percent of the South's publications were political in nature. By contrast, 74 percent of Northern publications were devoted primarily to politics.[6]

Northern journals posed no threat to the hegemony of the native political press in the South. Although Southern readers still imported Northern publications of general interest, most preferred to feed upon indigenous editorial products when it came to politics. Northern papers considered dangerous to Southern interests, such as William L.

Garrison's *Liberator*, had long been proscribed from the South. During the secession period, other Northern newspapers which were critical of Southern institutions had very little circulation in the South. Greeley's *Tribune*, with its combined daily and weekly circulation of 287,750 in early April of 1861, was possibly the most widely influential newspaper that America had ever produced. Not only did the *Tribune* have a circulation in New York of over 100,000, in each of eight other Northern states it had a distribution of over 10,000 copies. Its circulation figures for the South, however, show how far that section had isolated itself from such Northern publications. Greeley's paper had 35 subscribers in Texas, 52 in North Carolina, 42 in Alabama, 35 in Georgia, 23 in South Carolina, 21 in Mississippi, and 10 in Florida.[7]

A few of the South's most influential journals were independent papers, which sought to appeal to large reading publics by avoiding partisan politics. In practice, however, the independent newspapers usually were far from impartial politically. The New Orleans press best exemplified the partisanship of these "independent" papers. The *Picayune* never endorsed a candidate in the presidential campaign of 1860, but it clearly leaned toward John Bell and was intensely anti-Breckinridge. The *Bee* also disclaimed partisanship, but it clearly preferred Stephen A. Douglas and, like the *Picayune*, abhorred John C. Breckinridge. The *Delta*, on the other hand, proclaimed its impartiality but scarcely attempted to hide either its strong Southern-rights position or its high regard for Breckinridge. Moreover, virtually all of the so-called independent Southern newspapers expressed as much dislike for Lincoln and his party as the political sheets. Thus, in the strictest sense, these papers could hardly be labeled "nonpolitical." The relatively few journals which adhered strictly to an independent course during the election campaign were generally inconsequential. As the Montgomery *Advertiser* said of two neutral Alabama papers, they were "on the fence, and hardly worth shoving off."[8]

Newspapers had various sources of income. A political party sometimes gave financial support to a paper, in return for which it expected the journal to act as its "organ," faithfully representing the party's views and candidates. A favored few received state and city printing contracts, and job printing gave publishers some income. Most journals depended heavily upon advertising to keep them in the black.

Subscription fees often spelled the difference between success and bankruptcy. Even a casual reading of Southern papers during the secession crisis reveals how important and how difficult it was for papers to collect back debts owed them by their readers. A business recession struck the South in 1860, brought on in part by drouth and in part by the talk of secession. No one felt the effects of stringent times more quickly than editors, whose collections from both advertisers and subscribers dwindled. Journals frequently printed appeals for the payment of arrears by their readers. The Milledgeville *Federal Union,* the State Printer for Georgia, admitted in February of 1861 that the business slump had caused it to lose eight columns of advertising in the previous six months and appealed to its subscribers to pay their debts. An Alabama paper wrote: "We have not for months collected half enough to pay for the paper we print on, and if our patrons do not wish to put it utterly out of our power to furnish them with the important news of the day, they must come to our relief." In a long front-page editorial, the San Antonio *Ledger and Texan* said that only one tenth of its subscribers were paid up and warned those who had taken the paper "for years" without paying that their names must soon be erased from its list of subscribers. Even the religious press had problems with recalcitrant debtors. On January 1, 1861, the Montgomery *Universalist Herald* wished its patrons a happy New Year, admonished them to trust in God for help during the difficult days ahead, and then sought more worldly succor for itself: "And let all who are owing for the *Herald* please send us a remittance. *We greatly need aid.*"⁹

When appeals failed to bring results, some journals attempted to intimidate readers who owed them money. Virginia's Charlestown *Register* began publishing a list of subscribers who refused to pay their debts, prompting another Virginia paper to comment: "We know of some papers that would have to print *extras,* if they attempted to edify the public in like manner." The editor of the Wadesborough *North Carolina Argus,* observing that almost a hundred readers had owed the *Argus* for two and a half years, threatened to sue the delinquents, in which case he would demand both "interest and advance."¹⁰

It clearly was easier to start a newspaper than to keep it solvent, yet, curiously, hard times failed to discourage would-be publishers. Indeed the presidential campaign accelerated the already rapid increase in the numbers of Southern newspapers. A Georgia journal commented: "If we fail to notice the appearance of any new paper it is not from an intentional discourtesy, but simply because we can scarcely keep up with the list, they increase so fast." Newspapers were springing up as "thick as hops" in North Carolina, observed one paper in that state; every village was said to require at least one journal, courthouse towns two or three, "and some have been established where there were neither towns nor villages." A Texas newspaper announced the establishment of several new papers in the Lone Star State and said: "Newspapers in Texas are continually on the increase. We doubt whether there is another State in the South, in which there are so many, compared with the number of population."¹¹

The phenomenal increase in Southern newspapers, despite unhealthy business conditions, inevitably led to an increase in failures. There simply were not enough potential customers to support all of the new publications. A Virginia paper reported in January of 1861 that many papers in the Old Dominion recently had suspended operations and that others had found it necessary to curtail their size and cut down on reading matter. The same paper asserted: "The publishing business is much overdone, and there are too many newspapers printed, either for use or profit." A Georgia editor thus satirized the rush of aspiring publishers to establish new journals: "The great number of papers now printed in Georgia and the *immense fortunes* that all of them are making, is the best indication of the increased intelligence of the State. We are now receiving so much money that it will be necessary for us to employ sixteen bank officers to count the weekly receipts. The field of newspaper enterprise is an inviting one to those who desire to amass rapid and princely fortunes, and we hope it will not be long ere every town and X roads in the State will have its newspaper."[12] The general impecuniosity of Southern journals may suggest one reason why editors so often resorted to dueling pistols instead of legal proceedings to settle their disagreements. "Sueing a newspaper editor for libel," said a Virginia paper, "is about as sensible as to boil a brick-bat to get lamp-oil out of it."[13]

It seems likely that the lack of affluence among the Southern newspaper-publishing fraternity forced editors to be more mindful of readers' tastes and prejudices than they might otherwise have been, had their subscribers and advertisers been more numerous and politically more cosmopolitan. Newspapers may well have reflected public opinion on political issues even more than they created it, a possibility widely recognized by the press itself. A Little Rock editor said: "Newspapers as a general thing reflect the sentiment of the country." "The popular theory is that the press is free," a Raleigh journal wrote: "The fact is, that no man has less freedom allowed him to express his opinions than an Editor. His patrons regard him as a penny trumpet through which not a note is to be sounded, unless it accords precisely with their own music."[14]

Still, many editors undoubtedly entered the crowded publishing field, not because they wished to act simply as "penny trumpets," but because they expected to help shape the public mind on political issues. Some editors were prominent political figures in their own right. William Woods Holden of the *North Carolina Standard* was one of the most powerful Democrats in North Carolina. Parson William G. Brownlow, editor of the Knoxville *Whig*, had once run for Congress against Andrew Johnson and would later serve Tennessee both as senator and governor. John Marshall of the Austin *State Gazette* was state chairman of the Democratic party in Texas from 1858 to 1861. A. B. Norton, editor of the Austin *Southern Intelligencer* and Fort Worth *Chief*, placed Governor Sam Houston's name in nomination at the Constitutional Union party's convention in Baltimore. Ethelbert E. Barksdale, editor of the Jackson *Mississippian* and one of the most militant secessionists in his state, served his party as a delegate to the Democratic national convention at Charleston. As the official spokesman of a key delegation, Barksdale stood out prominently among the leading fire-eaters at Charleston. After the Mississippi editor had addressed the convention on April 27, Murat Halstead said of him: "His personal appearance is much in his favor; but he is full of fire and prone to fly off the handle. Some expressions of his countenance are very amiable; but there is a dangerous glitter in his eye, and his thin white lips are, when in repose, shut like the jaws of a steel clasp."[15] At the other end of the political spectrum, A. W. Campbell, who edited the pro-Republican Wheeling *Intelligencer,* attended the Republican convention in Chicago as a delegate fromVirginia. Such direct editorial participation in high-level politics was exceptional. Most editors apparently were too busy to take the extended leaves of absence necessary to attend party conventions or to assume time-consuming political responsibilities. They were content to make their influence felt with their pens. It is hardly surprising, therefore, that an analysis of the membership of the secession convention in the Confederate states showed that lawyers and farmers, not editors, predominated. Indeed, a total of only four editors attended as members of those eleven conventions.[16] But whether editors actively participated in politics or confined their activities to the writing of highly partisan editorials, they composed a force of considerable power during the election of 1860 and the ensuing secession crisis.

I

"The Fire Will Glow Brighter and Brighter"

IT was small wonder that Southern newspapers in early 1860 already were expressing grave doubts about the continuation of the Union. The recent raid on Harper's Ferry by John Brown, and his apotheosis by Northern abolitionists, had struck fear and rage into the hearts of Southerners and had revived the talk of secession that had all but died out in 1859. Every flag lowered, every poem published, every speech intoned, and every bell rung in honor of the hoary-headed abolitionist confirmed the suspicion of many Southerners that the North wished to destroy the South. Why else would it glorify in death a man whose life had been dedicated to the destruction of slavery—the cornerstone of Southern civilization? And if Northerners now eulogized Brown because of what he stood for, would they not favor the sending of other Browns into the South to accomplish that which he had left undone?[1]

A two-month-long Congressional struggle that culminated in the election of the Republican William Pennington as Speaker of the House of Representatives further angered Southerners. Neither the Republican nor the Democratic party had enough votes to secure the speakership, without help from the twenty-seven splinter-party members in the House. In the ensuing battle for uncommitted votes, Republicans and Democrats had ample opportunity to vent old sectional hatreds which now reached new peaks of intensity in the aftermath of Brown's raid. So acrimonious were the verbal encounters that violence almost broke out on the House floor; at one point, Crawford of Georgia nearly grappled with Thaddeus Stevens of Pennsylvania, and, on another occasion, Illinois representatives Kellogg and Logan squared off. The excitement spread to the Senate, and men in both houses of Congress armed themselves, fearing that words would give way to combat. Senator Hammond of South Carolina said, "the only persons who do not have a revolver and a knife are those who have two revolvers." Using obstructionist tactics, the House Democrats managed to prevent the election of the first Republican candidate for Speaker, John Sherman of Ohio, whom the Southerners regarded as an abolitionist; but they lacked sufficient votes to elect their own candidate, Thomas S. Bocock of Virginia. After nearly two months of virulent debate, the deadlock was finally broken on February 1, after Sherman withdrew in favor of the more moderate Pennington, an ex-Whig from New Jersey, who then attracted enough uncommitted votes to be elected.[2]

The sectional malevolence so apparent in Congress was further reflected by events which occurred in the slaveholding states. Communities formed vigilance committees to ferret out and punish any abolitionists who might be found conspiring against slavery. Ominously, the lower South flaunted its growing martial spirit. Men in several states shouldered rifles and drilled in expectation of a sectional confrontation which many of them considered inevitable. South Carolina appropriated $100,000, Mississippi $150,000, and Alabama $200,000 for organizing and equipping their militias. And there was talk that a Southern convention would soon meet to discuss ways of uniting the slave states to resist Northern encroachment upon their rights.[3]

Newspapers in the South reacted variously to these and other danger signals. Indeed, regarding the nature and condition of the Union, there were almost as many points of view in the Southern press as there were Southern newspapers. To generalize, therefore, on the opinion of Southern journals is risky. Notwithstanding the constant shifting and overlapping of viewpoints among Southern newspapers, certain categories were discernible in their editorial attitudes.

First, there were the secessionist newspapers—those Southern journals which despaired of maintaining Southern equality with the North within the Union, and which therefore actively urged withdrawal in the winter and spring of 1860. A second and much larger group were the radical Southern-rights papers—which also believed that the South's grievances were great and differed with the secessionist journals only in that they thought that secession should depend upon some future Northern aggression, not upon past outrages. Many radical Southern-rights papers contended that the election of a Republican President would justify secession. A third group of papers may be termed moderate Southern-rights. Like the radical Southern-rights journals, these sheets frequently editorialized on the need to defend Southern rights generally, and especially on the necessity of preventing the election of a Republican President. Nevertheless, such papers were more moderate in tone than radical Southern-rights journals, and, at least before the election of 1860, they often were ambiguous, even self-contradictory, on whether the South should secede in the event of a Republican victory. Unionist papers constituted a fourth category. They were marked by a tendency to minimize the apparent dangers to the Republic, and they praised the Union extravagantly, while placing few conditions upon its continuation.

Although attitudes on the South's position in relation to the Union were not strictly identifiable by political party, secessionist and Southern-rights papers tended to be Democratic, while Unionist views were most often held by journals of the nebulous Opposition party,[4] which in the presidential election of 1860 coalesced to form the Constitutional Union party.

Those papers which favored secession in early 1860 believed that the North had continually violated the constitutional rights of the South and that the emergence of the Republican party constituted a clear and present danger to "Southern institutions," not only in the territories, but in the Southern states as well. But secessionist journals went further. They saw no hope of a peaceful adjustment of the existing differences between North and South. The phenomenal, unbroken rise of antislavery sentiment in the North, coupled with the rapid growth and extension of Northern population, had convinced them that anti-Southern elements would increasingly dominate the national government.

Once the Republicans had gained power, secessionist journals asserted, the South would appeal in vain for concessions. "We might as well sing Psalms over the dead carcas of a buzzard, as to appeal to the Union for *rights* and *justice*," declared the Albany (Georgia) *Patriot,* after the election of Pennington as speaker.[5] It was "perfectly useless," asserted the Camden (South Carolina) *Weekly Journal,* "to attempt anything like constitutional argument with the Black Republican leaders." The only alternative left to the South was "a dissolution of the Union, and *entire independence* of their peculiar views as touching the institution of slavery."[6]

In short, the more extreme "fire-eating" papers of the
lower South accepted the abolitionist view that there was
indeed an irrepressible conflict in the land. Moreover, in
the view of these journals, this conflict could be resolved
only by a dissolution of the Union, or by a shameful "submission" to the Northern majority.[7] Therefore, it did not
matter in the long run whether or not the Republicans
won the White House in 1860. The trend clearly indicated
a future Republican hegemony over the national government. The South must act while it yet could; its only reward for clinging to the Union would be further defama-
tion by the North now, with much worse to come. "Insult
upon insult has been heaped upon the South," complained
a Georgia journal, "and we are daily informed that these
wrongs and aggressions are to be repeated. . . . For our part
we would prefer to strike the blow this very hour than
to wait for the morrow."[8]

Most radical Southern-rights papers took a somewhat less
aggressive position than the secessionist journals of the
lower South. Some were content to reaffirm their belief in
the abstract right of secession, like the Spartanburg *Carolina Spartan* which warned: "We stand upon secession as a
cardinal doctrine—the ultima ratio—in reference to Northern aggressions."[9] Other sheets, while not openly advocating secession, demonstrated by dire predictions and veiled
threats that they had but little faith in the Union and not
much desire to maintain it. Many concurred with the False
River (Louisiana) *Pointe Coupée Democrat,* whose masthead motto ironically recalled Jackson's famous phrase,
"The Union—It must be preserved," when it confided to
its readers a fear that the growing strength of abolitionism
shortly would compel Southerners "to show the people of
the North and West, that we can do very well without them.
As to the terms of parting, whether as friends or foes, let
them choose."[10]

In preparation for the crisis which they thought inevitable, secessionist papers and many Southern-rights papers hoped to create a degree of Southern unity that would enable all of the slave states to leave the Union together when the time was right. In late December of 1859 the South Carolina legislature, acting at the behest of Governor William H. Gist, resolved to call a conference of the Southern states as a means of uniting the South "in measures of defense." Gist sent Christopher Memminger to Virginia to secure the co-operation of that key state, but, although Mississippi and Alabama promptly endorsed the proposal and sent out emissaries of their own, Virginia and the other Southern states refused to take part.[11]

The more radical Southern-rights papers supported this proposed conference and were miffed by the border states' refusal to participate. As a result of this failure to achieve united action, radical Southern-rights sheets began to regard separate action by the individual states as the proper means of dissolving the Union. The Charleston *Mercury* spoke for this segment of the press when it declared: "Whenever the South is delivered from her present condition of inferiority and peril, we believe it will be by the resolute action of one or a few states."[12]

Failing to achieve headway toward political separation in early 1860, many "fire-eating" editors supported an old Southern shibboleth—economic independence. Southern nationalists long had protested the South's colonial subservience to the North. In 1852 the Committee on Commerce of the Alabama legislature had asserted that, by means of direct trade with Europe and a "commercial and manufacturing revolution," the South not only would advance its "aggregate wealth by millions," but also would "secure political liberty." But no progress was made in achieving these lofty goals. A commercial convention of all the Southern states convened in Montgomery in 1858 to

discuss possible ways of achieving economic independence
from the North, but it accomplished little more than to
give William Lowndes Yancey a forum for his secessionist
ideas.[13] Yet the siren song of economic independence continued to attract Southern-rights editors. The South must
develop its own manufactures, they insisted, if it were to
reap its proper share of the nation's economic fruit. "The
South imports almost everything from the North—from
her professors to her ax-helves," observed a Texas paper:
"Can the South manufacture nothing for home consumption? Our resources are sufficient. All we need is earnest,
practical energy, to build up our own manufacturers all
over the South."[14]

If the South could only develop economic self-sufficiency
and the North be made to realize its dependence upon
Southern markets, the masses of Northerners would turn
against the fanatics who fostered sectional misunderstand-
ing and hatred. The key to political equality was economic
equality, and even the formation of a Southern Confederacy
would not alone insure Southern independence. "We may
talk about Southern independence as much as we please,"
declared the Atlanta *Daily Intelligencer,* "but until Southern merchants shake off the dependence upon Northern
merchants, we shall ever be 'hewers of wood and drawers of
water' to the 'Yankee nation.' "[15]

In the pursuit of commercial independence, Southern
papers had few concrete suggestions. They argued that the
South must develop its own manufactures, but did not say
how this was to be done. The only practical measure suggested was a negative one: the South should refuse all commercial traffic with the North. In the manner of their
revolutionary forefathers, Southerners ought to resort to a
policy of "nonintercourse." Like Britain, the North would
be grievously damaged, would repent, and would seek the
South's favor by repudiating antislavery fanaticism. It was

a rather naïve, romantic view, but many Southern-rights and secessionist papers[16] and some Unionist journals[17] subscribed to it. Secessionist sheets seem to have regarded "nonintercourse" as a step toward the creation of a Southern nation. At any rate, it was respectable in early 1860 to advocate a commercial "secession" from the North, but outside of South Carolina it remained unpopular to propose disunion for existing causes.[18]

A large body of Opposition papers and some Democratic journals opposed the idea of secession in the early months of 1860. These Unionist papers refused to take seriously the alarms raised by the more militant Southern sheets. They usually discountenanced all agitation of the slavery question, and they particularly disapproved of the Southern Conference proposed by South Carolina.[19] The most dedicated among them praised the Union with an almost religious fervor. They laid the blame for the talk of disunion at the doors of time-serving politicians, who sought to arouse the people needlessly for their own ulterior purposes. "The Union has to be *saved* every four years, and [we] must '*vote the ticket,*' or the country will go to the Devil," complained the San Antonio *Daily Herald.*[20]

The more ardent Unionist journals expressed an unshakable faith that the masses of people, both Northern and Southern, soon would rise up and smite the demagogues who preached disunion. A Mississippi paper confidently predicted: "The fire of Unionism will glow brighter and brighter, and spread over every city and village and hamlet in this broad Union, until every vestige of disunion shall be consumed." A Texas paper dismissed the current disunion agitation as "a part and parcel of the humbug of the present age, the patent medicines with which quack politicians of the day expects [*sic*] to physic the people." Citizens ought to ignore such prescriptions, and "when election time comes, vote as you please, and the

American Eagle will take care of the Union." A journal in Little Rock rejoiced that disunionism seemed to be on the wane in that city and further asserted its belief that "the American Union stands on a firmer foundation than ever before. The Union of these States is cemented by a community of interest which will forever operate as a natural check to secession or dissolution. We may assure ourselves that the Union is not in danger."[21]

Such sublime confidence in the permanence of the American Union was remarkable in view of the turbulent disputes in Congress over slavery and secession and the general excitement throughout the South. With many such papers it was probably a case of "whistling past the graveyard." The Richmond *Dispatch,* for example, may have expressed hope, rather than conviction, when it announced on February 11: "We now regard the Union as indestructible—almost as much so as *matter* in the universe." Only two months later, the same paper was advocating secession in the event that a Republican was elected President.[22]

Fear that a bloody war would inevitably follow secession apparently was as strong a stimulant to editorial Unionism as love for the Stars and Stripes. This was especially true in the border states, where much of the fighting would take place should war break out. Many Unionist editors argued that "peaceable secession would prove an impossibility." They often professed belief that secession was legal, but denied that it was possible without bloodshed. "While we believe in the abstract right of secession, we believe a peaceable assertion of that right impracticable," confessed the Little Rock *True Democrat.* "Secession, if ever resorted to, will be a question more of *might* than *right*."[23]

A dissolution of the Union would not remove the causes of antagonism, others argued. On the contrary, by seceding the Southern states would be withdrawing the principal moderating influence from the national councils. Once

Southern conservatism was muted in the halls of Congress, there would be nothing standing in the way of the abolitionists. All protection of Southern property and interest would be lost, with the consequence that "the death knell of slavery would be sounded."[24]

Occasionally, a Unionist editor foresaw with startling clarity the bloody aftermath of secession. On January 6, 1860, a Virginia journal wrote:

It is impossible to exaggerate the horrors and sufferings which for years would follow a dissolution of the Union. For ourselves, we have no idea of such a thing as a peaceable dissolution. As we have said before, it would be war from the start, war to the knife and knife to the hilt. The widely extended border between the North and South would be a line of fire and blood. Every accessible bay and inlet of every river would be entered, and, ever and anon, large masses of men hurled upon the capitols and important points of Southern States. But the horrors of ordinary warfare would be far transcended by the barbarities of this cruel strife.

This came from a paper which a year later would strongly advocate secession. There apparently were other evils more horrible than the "barbarities" of "war to the knife and knife to the hilt."[25]

Few Southern newspapers, even of the Union, or Opposition, persuasion, were unconditionally committed to the Union's preservation in early 1860. Many editors were experiencing an "irrepressible conflict" of their own: torn between abhorrence of Northern abolitionism and devotion to the Union, they often followed a tortuous and ambiguous course. Most of them, while scoring disunionists, left a door open to the secessionist camp, just in case it proved impossible to maintain a Union of "equality." Thus, while denouncing "fire-eaters," the Lynchburg *Virginian* at the same time warned the North: "She [Virginia] will trust in God, and keep her powder dry. . . . When her rights are invaded beyond the power of redress, and the Constitution shall have been overturned in effect, she will then speak in tones that shall not be misunderstood." Another Virginia journal hedged: "We do not say that wrong is not to be righted and that intolerable oppression is not to be met with revolution *if necessary.*" Mississippi's Vicksburg *Whig* confessed: "Strong as is our attachment to the Union, we can readily imagine a state of public affairs which would at once convert the Vicksburg *Whig* into a resistance journal." The *Whig* explained that a Republican victory in 1860, followed by an effort to reduce the South "to a state of utter sectional degradation," would force that paper to contend for dissolution.[26]

Thus, a considerable portion of the Unionist press agreed with Southern-rights exponents that secession was a possibility. Unionist editors also believed that a dissolution of the Union was not justifiable on the grounds of previous Northern aggressions. The Clarksville (Texas) *Northern Standard* epitomized the attitude of many moderate Southern-rights Unionist papers when it declared: "We are not yet oppressed—perhaps the point at which resistance would be proper may never arrive. 'Sufficient to the day is the evil thereof.'" The most important words in this statement were "yet," "perhaps," and "may." Such qualifiers as these would enable the *Standard* one year later to come out for immediate secession, without being inconsistent.[27]

The question was, what would be a just cause for secession? Unionist and Southern-rights papers disagreed on the answer. Radical Southern-rights sheets agreed with the Alabama and Mississippi legislatures that the election of a Republican President in November would constitute an insult of such magnitude and a threat of such proportions that the South must secede.[28]

The prospect of Republican success in November provided the more extreme Southern-rights journals with an ideal issue. All of the bitterness instilled in Southerners by a generation of abolitionist agitation could now be directed at the latest and most successful political manifestation of the antislavery movement. Indeed, in the eyes of Southerners, the Republican party was the natural fruit of Northern sectionalism. Unlike the complicated tariff and territorial problems, this "alien institution" was a living organism which could be feared, hated, and, above all, resisted. Conveniently, the presidential election, which threatened to elevate a Republican to the nation's highest office, was months away; this enabled Southern-rights publicists to measure the Union by a single event in the future and to harden the minds of the people to the idea of disunion.

When Southern-rights journals equated Republicanism with abolitionism, they were technically misrepresenting the position of the Republican party, which did not advocate the eradication of slavery from the slave states, but only its proscription from the territories. Nevertheless, antisubmission sheets looked beyond the letter to the spirit. By citing statements of such leading Republicans as Joshua Giddings, William H. Seward, and Abraham Lincoln, they proved to their own satisfaction that the Republican party would never be satisfied until slavery was abolished in every part of the nation. The Jackson *Weekly Mississippian* expressed the conviction of many Southern-rights papers when it asserted:

There is no disguising the fact that the "irrepressible conflict" doctrine of the freesoil party means the total extinction of Southern institutions or it means nothing. This doctrine, dangerous, revolutionary and treasonable, was proclaimed by Abraham Lincoln of Illinois, briefly in these words: "I BELIEVE THIS GOVERNMENT CANNOT ENDURE PERMANENTLY HALF SLAVE AND HALF FREE." In other words, SLAVERY MUST BE ABOLISHED IN THE SLAVE STATES, OR THE GOVERNMENT AND THE UNION MUST BE OVERTHROWN. This is the doctrine of the Black Republican party, and it is the duty of the South to prepare resolutely to meet it—"peaceably if we can, forcibly if we must."[29]

The reasoning behind the doctrine of "resistance" was simple and logical. The Republican party regarded slavery as evil; that was why it opposed the extension of slavery into the territories. But would the Republicans be satisfied to forbid slavery in the territories only? Radical Southern-rights papers thought not. If the antislavery party did not yet seek openly to abolish slavery in the South, it was only because Northern public opinion was still too conservative to endorse such a policy.

Nevertheless, a hatred for the South's "peculiar institution" was growing stronger by the day. Once the Republicans gained a clear majority of the nation's voters, argued resistance editors, they were bound, as surely as sparks flew upward, to destroy the despised institution of chattel slavery, even in the states where it was sanctioned by the Constitution. "Submissionists" were fools for believing that slavery would continue to enjoy its constitutional protections under Republican rule, resistance journals insisted. "They tell us, *their* higher law is paramount to the Bible and the Constitution," a correspondent wrote in a fire-eating Mississippi paper: "What then has the South to expect from the majority that places such a man, with *such* principles in office." Since it would result in the abolition of slavery, "submission" would also lead to the South's destruction, for Southern-rights advocates believed that their society could not survive the eradication of its "peculiar institution." One country paper in Louisiana regretted to see "the bright political illusions of our youth pass," but declared: "With regard to [slavery] we recognize no arbiters, we admit no judges. African slavery is part of our political existence. In it, we 'move and have our being.' "[30]

According to the logic of states'-rights editors, it would be fatal for the South to follow the advice of those Southern Unionists who advocated waiting until the North had

committed some "overt act" against the South. Once installed in office a Republican President would fill all government posts with free-soilers and would place the full
power and prestige of the federal government in the service
of abolitionism. To wait until a Republican administration
committed an aggressive act would be to delay too long for
effective resistance. Such resistance journals as the Raleigh
North Carolina Standard argued that the election of a
Republican would be, in itself, virtually an "overt act" of
aggression:

Do hostile armies await overt acts? Is a declaration of war nothing
until arms are used on the field? Does a man who is told by his
adversary that he is to be assailed, wait until his adversary is upon
him, and has commenced to disarm and cast him to the earth?
Does a person who has taken arsenic by mistake, wait to see
whether arsenic will produce death? Does anyone doubt that cold
steel, well sharpened, will sever the jugular vein? *Must we wait
and become weaker, or act, and gather strength by preparation
on our own stern resolves?*[31]

Some of the more extreme fire-eating journals even
desired the nomination by the Republicans of Seward or
some other "abolitionist," so that all Southern people
could realize the desperate nature of the campaign. If such
a man were nominated and elected, they reasoned, it would
be easier to convince Southerners of the need to "resist"
his inauguration.[32]

Unionist papers, when they discussed the topic at all,
usually scorned the resistance journals' advocacy of secession in the event of the election of a Republican President.[33] They argued that secession on account of the simple,
constitutional election of any man by a majority of the
nation's voters would be illegal, even treasonous. They
further suspected that "resistance" was a political trick, or,
as the Hillsborough (North Carolina) *Recorder* put it,
"We regard this movement as 'all for Buncomb'—intended

merely for party effect before the Presidential election, with no resolute purpose of following it up afterwards."[34]

"Submissionist" papers, which in early 1860 were usually Opposition organs, ignored the pragmatic argument of "resistance" journals that waiting for an overt act would be fatal to the South. Instead, they took the legalistic view that the South had no right to secede, at least not until the new President had committed some specific aggression upon the South. In the words of the Columbus (Georgia) *Enquirer,* "The Constitution proscribes no man or party for his or their *opinions,* and . . . the South can only resist *acts* or *measures* of aggression."[35] To contend otherwise would be to impose intolerable conditions upon Northern voters. Indeed, if the South could refuse beforehand to accept its principal opponent, "then we say that the North might with equal plausibility pretend that the success of a Southern Democrat would warrant her withdrawal from the Union," asserted the Petersburg (Virginia) *Intelligencer.* Even the hated Seward must be accepted by Southerners, if elected in accordance with the Constitution.[36]

A Georgia journal summed up the attitude of most of the antiresistance press: "If the Republican party triumph, give them a trial, if DOUGLAS triumph, give him a trial, if the Constitutional Union candidate triumph, give him a trial, and in case of the triumph of either, if our common government is used as an engine of oppression and injustice, *then resist* to the last."[37]

Thus did the newspapers of the future Southern Confederacy approach the nominating conventions in the spring. A few already wanted secession. Like Texas's Matagorda *Gazette,* they believed that "the only terms upon which we can be friendly with the Northern States, is to give up the African—set him free." Therefore, "The South has but one remedy: To strike for her rights, her honor and her independence."[38] A few others could not or would not, under any circumstances, face the possibility of a dissolution of the Union. With the Washington (North Carolina) *Dispatch* they cried, "Let us still hold on to the Old Ship, and contend to the bitter end with fanaticism and sectionalism, maintaining our glorious Union and the Constitution."[39] Or they echoed the naïve faith of the San Antonio *Daily Herald,* that "whatever the decision of the people may be in next November, the whole country will cheerfully abide by the result, and all will be peaceful and prosperous thereafter."[40]

Most press opinion fell between these extremes. The principal disagreement between the Democratic and Opposition papers of the South was not over the possibility of an eventual dissolution of the Union, but over what constituted just cause for such a dissolution. Generally speaking, radical Southern-rights journals explicitly or implicitly contended that the Union could not survive the election of a Republican President. Nor were Unionist and moderate Southern-rights papers, on the whole, certain that it could do so, but they preferred to wait and see, rather than disrupt the nation over the "mere election" of a Republican and possibly plunge the country into bloody holocaust.

II

Douglas and Anti-Douglas Ruined Every Thing

IN early 1860 most Southern editors focused their attention on the national Democratic convention, which was to convene at Charleston on April 23. Little was said of the Republican conclave, to be held in Chicago in May: the "Black Republicans" had no organization in the South, and whoever their convention nominated would be unacceptable there. The Constitutional Union convention likewise attracted relatively little advance publicity, probably because it promised to be sedate and uncontroversial. The Democratic convention promised an abundance of fireworks, however; and though the party's editorial enemies professed little interest, the attention which they gave to the events at Charleston belied their feigned indifference and seemed an admission that they too realized that whatever happened at Charleston must profoundly affect the nation.

To be sure, much of the comment on the Democratic convention was typical of the kind of patter that had accompanied previous conventions. Papers buzzed with the usual speculation over possible nominees; rival platforms were debated; and much bad and good humor arose from the high prices which Charleston reportedly was going to charge for food and lodging. Expressing amusement at the plans of some delegates to escape the high rent rates by camping out in tents, one independent Virginia paper scoffed: "There are many octogenarians, men of olden times—in short, 'old fogies,' who would probably only regret that the politicians of all parties could not be banded together in one swamp, where 'Yellow Jack' could seize the whole of them."[1]

For all the usual excitement, there was a new, sinister element. By early 1860 a large segment of the Southern press had gone on record unequivocally as favoring secession, should the Republican party win the presidency. "If we win," said a typical radical Southern-rights paper, "the country is safe yet a little longer. If we lose, the South takes it to herself to *confederate for protection!*"[2]

Many Democratic papers believed that even a united party might have difficulty defeating a strong Republican candidate, and both Unionist Democratic and Southern-rights Democratic editors knew that victory would be extremely unlikely in the event of a division within the Democratic party. That is why so many Democratic journals urged that there be unity at Charleston. "That Convention will prove a most important one," observed a Mississippi newspaper, "for upon its action will rest in a great degree, not only the success of the Democratic party but the salvation of the Union itself."[3] The Wilmington (North Carolina) *Daily Journal* may have exaggerated a bit, but probably spoke the view of a majority of Southern Democratic newspapers, when it asserted:

The whole country looks to the Democratic party as the only party that can save this Union. Once that party divides, the Union is virtually gone. It is so viewed by our best men; and, although a dissolution may not take place immediately thereafter, it is just as sure to come as the rising of the sun on the morrow—

without unity of action in our ranks, a Black Republican President will be the inevitable consequence—there is no other alternative.[4]

Democratic papers of the South scorned as divisive the efforts of the Opposition to organize a new party. Such a move would only weaken the Democratic party, which alone could defeat the Republicans. According to Democratic editors, the Opposition's persistence in creating the Constitutional Union party was likely to endanger both the Constitution and the Union. "The only party in the South whose course tends practically to disunion is the Opposition," charged Texas's Austin *State Gazette*. The Fayetteville (Tennessee) *Lincoln Journal* declared: "There can be no question that the contest is between the Abolitionists and Democrats and that all efforts to rally a third party must be vain and fruitless, yet men persevere in their efforts to maintain a disolving [*sic*] organization with an adherence worthy of a better cause."[5]

Its lack of a platform and its multifarious composition subjected the nascent Constitutional Union party to much ridicule by Democratic editors. A Tennessee journal asserted that the new party "has offered no system of measures upon which it proposed to administer the government, but simply used whatever quackery it believed would deceive the people and put the Democracy out of power." The Fayetteville *North Carolinian* jeered: "What a wonderful party this proposed party must be. Let us call it by name once and we are done: Federalist—Federal Republican—Whig—Know Nothing—Free Soil Black Republican—Opposition—National American—National Union party—there now let us take a breath after pronouncing it."[6]

Their anxiety to unify the South around their party induced Democratic editors to stress the importance of all Democrats' going to Charleston in a genuinely conciliatory spirit. All should be willing to understand one another's points of view regarding both the platform and the candidates. "We would disclaim everything like sectionalism for the Charleston convention," averred the Dallas *Herald,* a radical Southern-rights paper, "for we shall all meet there as equals and as brothers, as Democrats and not as factionists." After all, reminded the *Herald,* any Democrat would be far preferable to any Republican as President.[7]

Only a few of the most radical Southern-rights papers opposed participation in the Charleston convention. In South Carolina, the scene of the only concerted newspaper opposition, a lively journalistic "war" broke out over the question whether the state should take part at all in the convention. The Charleston *Mercury* led the fight against the convention, declaring that since the Democratic party was hopelessly split on nearly every important issue, Southerners could no longer trust it to protect the South's interests. It would be far better for the South to withdraw from that party now and to prepare to defend itself, contended the *Mercury.* The Newberry *Conservatist* was the *Mercury*'s chief ally; it contended that the people of the state overwhelmingly opposed the convention, and it warned that the South must never place itself in a position of having to submit to majority rule.[8]

Moderate papers in South Carolina were unconvinced by the *Mercury*'s stand. They took the view of the vast majority of Southern-rights Democratic papers elsewhere that the Union itself hung in the balance at Charleston, and that since they still preferred the Union, they supported the convention. Moreover, they took vigorous exception to the assertions of the *Mercury* and the *Conservatist* that the "overwhelming voice" of South Carolina's people was against participation in the national convention. On the contrary, contended Colonel Arthur Simkins's Edgefield *Advertiser,* all indications showed that the people of the state solidly backed the convention. "As to the 'voice of

South Carolina,' the *Mercury* surely writes at random," said the *Advertiser,* which later became the nearest thing to a Douglas organ in the state.[9]

Neither were such extreme Southern-rights journals as the Spartanburg *Carolina Spartan* and the Newberry *Rising Sun* convinced by the *Mercury*'s arguments. The *Carolina Spartan* wrote: "It is astonishing to us that any paper should keep up an attack upon the convention or utter a word against the state being represented in it at this juncture." The *Spartan* further thought it ridiculous that South Carolina, by snubbing the convention, should imply superiority over her sister states, all of whom would participate; the display of such ill manners was a poor way to achieve Southern unity. The Newberry *Rising Sun,* while professing little interest in the convention, thought that South Carolina might as well attend it. No doubt, said the *Rising Sun,* the state would support any acceptable candidate, whether it had helped nominate him or not; therefore, "according to a vulgar maxim, 'one had as well eat the devil as drink his broth.' South Carolina had as well be represented there as to turn in, if she is not represented, and vote for the nominee, if he chances to be the right sort of man."[10]

Virtually all Southern Democratic papers wanted unity, but political brotherhood proved easier to preach than to practice, and even before the convention assembled there were signs of forthcoming disaster. Differences over candidates and platforms clearly forecast rough sailing for the Old Ship Democracy at Charleston.

Southern Democratic sheets early endorsed a wide variety of favorites for President. Jefferson Davis, R. M. T. Hunter, Andrew Johnson, John C. Breckinridge, Howell Cobb, and Stephen A. Douglas were just a few of those who had considerable support. Some journals simply refused to bind themselves to any particular candidate and, like the Atlanta *Daily Intelligencer,* thought that any "good Democrat" would do, "provided he is placed upon a sound platform, such as every *true* Democrat North or South can consistently stand upon."[11]

Conservative Northerners such as Daniel Dickinson and Joseph Lane qualified as "good Democrats" to many Southern Democratic editors, but, ominously, others expressed the belief that the next nominee of the party ought to be a Southerner. A Georgia paper, recollecting that the last two Presidents had been Northern men, contended that it was now the South's turn to fill the White House. Virginia's Richmond *Enquirer* thought it was high time that a Southerner be elected President: "If a Southern President cannot be elected in 1860, the day never will come when a son of the Southern States can be the Federal Executive, and a disgraceful ostracism exists upon the people of fifteen sovereign states."[12]

Stephen A. Douglas was easily the most controversial of the front-runners for the Democratic nomination. Just as Lincoln and Republican free-soilism embodied the Northern party threat to Southern institutions, Douglas and his popular-sovereignty doctrine represented the same menace within a single party. Radical Southern-rights Democratic papers were unwilling to "submit" to the election of a Republican President, because they thought it would mean the ultimate abolition of slavery. A large number of the same journals now predicted the identical result if Douglas should be elected.

Popular sovereignty—Douglas's theory that a territory of the United States could either legalize or proscribe slavery before it became a state—was thought by many radical Southern-rights editors to be quite as fatal to slavery as Republican free-soilism. In his famous debate with Lincoln at Freeport, Illinois, in 1858, Douglas had even asserted that a territory could effectively proscribe slavery simply by withholding protective legislation. Thus, Douglas had suggested the means by which a territory could legally obviate the recent *Dred Scott* decision of the Supreme Court, which, in effect, had declared slavery legal in the territories of the United States.[13]

If anything, radical Southern-rights editors regarded Douglas as even more dangerous than a Republican. They knew that the Little Giant would be acceptable as President to many of their colleagues who would never dream of submitting to a Republican. Thus, in the eyes of extreme Southern-rights editors, abolitionism in the guise of popular sovereignty was more apt to turn the Southern flank than abolitionism in the form of Republican free-soilism.

The fear of "abolitionism" sugar-coated as popular sovereignty explained the heavy barrage aimed at Douglas and his doctrine during the spring. The Columbus *Mississippi Democrat* and the Newberry (South Carolina) *Conservatist,* for example, argued that Douglas's popular sovereignty was at least as dangerous as the Wilmot Proviso.[14] The only difference that a Louisiana weekly could see between the Republicans and Douglas was "that the former would not let us into what they call their house, at all; while Mr. Douglas would invite us in, for the pleasure of afterwards kicking us out. By both are our blood-bought rights scorned and held at naught."[15] An Alabama paper clearly answered "no" to its rhetorical question: "Could a man so efficient in advocating the best Abolition measure ever passed by Congress [the Kansas-Nebraska Act] be a safe guardian of the rights of Southerners?" The Matagorda (Texas) *Gazette* predicted that if Douglas were elected, "the Supreme Court will be destroyed, the Fugitive Slave Law repealed, and everything smoothed for an attack upon slavery in the States."[16]

Many fire-eating journals accused the Little Giant of

treachery. The Spartanburg (South Carolina) *Carolina Spartan* called Douglas "a traitor to his party, traitor to his principles," and reasoned that "he must prove traitor to the South." The Little Giant was unreliable, warned a Florida newspaper: "That 'Arnold' in his name is too significant—too suggestive of intrigue, treachery and shame. We believe he is not an incorruptible politican. Give us anything in the world but a traitor." One Texas journal even regarded as traitorous anyone who supported Douglas.[17] The Opelika (Alabama) *Southern Era* branded Douglas "a hissing and a reproach to the Democratic party," and said one would have to go back to Old Testament days to find a punishment worthy of the senator's offense. Describing how Joshua had destroyed Ai, hanged its king, and deposited his body at the city's gates, the *Southern Era* concluded:

Such is the fate which—in a political sense—should be visited upon the giant Demagogue of Illinois. He deserves to perish upon the gibbet of Democratic condemnation, and his loathsome carcass to be cast at the gate of the Federal city, in order that demagogues and renegade partisans might view with horror the dreadful retribution which stern justice will, sooner or later, visit upon them.[18]

Some Democratic papers questioned whether the South ought to submit even to the election of Douglas, let alone that of a Republican.[19]

Douglas's Southern backers naturally defended their candidate on his most vulnerable point—his attitude toward slavery in the territories. Some editors pointed out that Southern leaders had agreed with Douglas's doctrine in the early 1850s. Moreover, they said, the whole issue was an abstraction. Slavery would not go where it was unprofitable, and these papers seemed convinced that the arid western territories would not prove congenial to the

South's peculiar institution. How foolish, then, for the South to risk the Union upon so impractical a point.[20]

The Little Giant clearly was the most "available" Democrat, his promoters argued. Among the leading aspirants for the nomination, only the senator from Illinois could carry the South and enough of the North to win in November. Douglas at the head of the ticket, asserted the Augusta (Georgia) *Daily Constitutionalist,* would give "Black Republicanism a back set that it would not rally from for years." But let the Democratic party nominate a less national candidate, upon an ambiguous platform, "and it is very certain that a Black Republican victory will sweep unbroken over the North." "Douglas," said a New Orleans paper, "could be elected, when probably any other candidate would be beaten. *Ergo* Douglas should be the choice of the convention, and will be unless Southern ultraists are bent upon discomfiture, and ultimate disunion."[21]

Douglas's advocates insisted that most Southerners would support their candidate, were it not for the "ultraist" editors, who continually agitated the Negro question. S. S. Fairfield, a schoolteacher-lawyer of Grenada, Mississippi, wrote Douglas that the press of Mississippi was "generally in the hands of young and inexperienced men controlled by the ruling dynasty. When a scheme is put on foot the [Jackson] *Mississippian* roars and all the little country papers yelp, the cross road and bar room politicians take it up and so it goes, and if any one opposes them they raise the cry of abolitionist and traitor, two words of awful import in this country."[22]

Although that part of the Southern Democratic press which explicitly promoted Douglas was in the minority, probably a majority in the preconvention period were willing to grant him at least grudging acceptance as the party's nominee. Many moderate Southern-rights Democratic journals which disliked the idea of Douglas's candidacy were willing to swallow their pride in order to maintain party unity and defeat the Republicans. Although they were uncertain how much damage might be done to Southern rights by popular sovereignty, these papers were positive that the Republican alternative would be worse. The Holly Springs (Mississippi) *Herald* typified the attitude of this element when it announced: "Stephen A. Douglas is by no means our choice, but if he is the nominee of the Charleston Democratic Convention, as much opposed to him as we may have been previous to that date, we will sustain his nomination."[23]

Opposition papers were another matter. The pleas of Democratic editors that the Opposition fold its political tents and move them to the Democratic camp had little effect. Journals of the Opposition continued to call Southerners to the support of their new party, which, they promised, would protect "the Constitution, the Union, and the laws." According to these papers, the projected Constitutional Union party represented the best hope for protecting the peace, now threatened by a corrupt Democratic party as well as by a sectional Republican party. Only in the care of the new party would the Union be safe and the government be returned to honest hands. "A third party is in our opinion a necessity, without which the government can never expect to be restored to its former purity," declared the Talladega *Alabama Reporter*.[24]

The Opposition press was virtually devoid of the strife over candidates and platforms which plagued the papers supporting the Democratic party. They argued little over particular candidates; John Bell of Tennessee early appeared to be acceptable to most. Nor were they concerned with rival platforms; their own was drawn in the broadest possible terms.

Since there was relative harmony in their own ranks, Opposition journals directed most of their fire against the Democrats. Opposition editors were particularly picqued by the contention of their enemies that only the Democrats could save the Union. The Clarksville (Tennessee) *Chronicle* accused the Democrats of using the same "pitch" in the election of 1856 and asserted the supposed danger to the Union "was a phantom conjured up by office-seeking fireeaters to frighten the timid and delude the weak." The Knoxville *Whig* was even more outspoken: Democratic sheets, it declared, clamored incessantly about the rights of the South, "as though no other section of our widely extended country, had any rights under the constitution. . . . If the Union is dissolved and the institutions of the country are overthrown, this vile, designing, corrupt and abominable Democracy are responsible for it." Noting that a Democratic paper envisioned disaster should the Democratic party divide, an Opposition paper in Virginia said: "We dispute that. The fate of this Union is not in the especial keeping of the Democratic or any other party."[25]

Opposition journals treated the approaching Charleston convention with contempt. The Knoxville *Whig,* in its usual crusty manner, confided its "candid opinion" that it was the President's duty to send "military chieftains" to Charleston and Chicago, and in certain contingencies likely to occur, to arrest the members of the Conventions, for treasonable designs." Commenting upon the date of the approaching Democratic convention, a Mississippi journal wrote: "This is certainly a day of great events. 'Tis said Shakespeare died, and Buchanan was born, and the Charleston Convention is to assemble, on the 23rd of April. When Shakespeare died the world lost one of the most wonderful men that lived in modern times. When

Buchanan was born, the world was not much improved in any respect."[26]

While in the preconvention period Southern Democratic journals were hopelessly mixed in their views on Douglas, Opposition papers almost invariably expressed strong disapproval of the senator from Illinois. For example, Georgia's Columbus *Enquirer* regarded Douglas "as the most objectionable and dangerous politician to whom the South ought to prefer *any other*." Another Georgia journal thought Douglas even more dangerous than Seward: "The end is to be the same in both cases— exclusion of slavery from all Territory of the United States." The Raleigh *Register* was amazed that Southern Democrats seemed willing to support "a man who lately 'pigged in the same stye' with Horace Greeley, the vilest, the dirtiest, the most mangy hog in the Abolition pen." There was little difference, said a Virginia paper, between Douglas and the "Black Republicans." The Richmond *Whig* believed that Douglas's doctrine of popular sovereignty was "worse then the Wilmot Proviso." And a country paper in Mississippi warned the Democrats that Mississippians would not support Douglas, "though he be endorsed by a hundred conventions."[27]

It seemed ironic that Opposition papers, which were diametrically opposed to Southern-rights Democratic organs on so many points, should agree with them that Douglas was anathema to the South. After the final division of the Democratic party in June, Opposition journals came to consider Douglas supporters as allies in the fight against Breckinridge and the secessionists; consequently, they then treated the Little Giant much more gently. But on the eve of the first Democratic convention Douglas still appeared to have the best chance for his party's nomination. A majority of Southern Democratic papers seemed at least willing to tolerate the senator from Illinois, though they clearly preferred some other candidate. As the potential nominee of a united Democratic party, Douglas was the logical target for Opposition editors, and they often attacked the senator quite as viciously as did extreme Southern Democratic journals.

The Democrats' choice of Charleston as the site for their most crucial convention of the century was extremely unfortunate. Undeniably, the city had great charm, particularly in the spring when its lush gardens were full of stunning pink and white azaleas and exuded the intoxicating fragrances of countless magnolia and camellia blossoms. But Charleston was not a "convention city." It lacked the facilities necessary to accommodate the crowd of delegates and visitors which descended upon the city for the convening of the troubled clan Democracy. Room and board was difficult to come by, especially for Northern delegates. Hotel space was so limited that Douglas men were forced to rent Hibernia Hall and convert it, temporarily, into a dormitory. Those who were lucky enough to find decent hotel or rooming house accommodations discovered, in many cases, that they had to pay the exceptionally high rate of five dollars a day for room and board. Unseasonably hot weather further distressed Northerners, whose apparel was too heavy for the near-100° heat. Southern "ultras" probably experienced little of the discomfort which so aggravated many Northern Democrats. They were used to the heat, and they had few problems with accommodations; polite Charleston society welcomed them to its hearths, its tables, and its bars.[28]

Charleston's political atmosphere, which Southern-rights advocates found as congenial as the city's geographical climate, added to the discomfiture of Douglas men. South Carolina had cradled and nurtured secessionism, and Charleston, its Queen City, had been the center of

Southern militancy for a generation. It was the home of Robert Barnwell Rhett's *Mercury,* whose sway over the radical Southern-rights press belied its tiny subscription list. The people of Charleston, many of whom would crowd into the galleries at the convention hall, could be counted upon to give ovations to those speakers who expressed Southern-rights sentiments but less happy responses to those who took a more national viewpoint.

The long-awaited Democratic convention met on April 23. Almost immediately, pro-Douglas and anti-Douglas factions locked horns in desperate battle, while the Southern press waited anxiously for reports, which often came days after the events. For those who still held out hope for the Union, the news was not good. By the middle of the fifth day, Murat Halstead, reporting the convention for the Cincinnati *Commercial,* had concluded: "It is ridiculous and absurd for this body of delegates to be pretending to try to agree on a platform when the whole country, themselves included, know well their disagreements are radical and absolute."[29] Light had no fellowship with darkness; neither was there any apparent basis for agreement between the advocates of popular sovereignty and the champions of protection; nevertheless, the protagonists played out their tragic drama. On April 30, after a week of feuding over platforms, the convention adopted the pro-Douglas platform. In the face of persistent Southern opposition to popular sovereignty, the Douglas forces finally offered to leave the question of territorial authority over slavery to the Supreme Court. Even this concession was insufficient to please Southern ultras, who demanded nothing less than a slave code for the territories. When Douglas's backers refused to agree to this demand, the delegations from Alabama, Mississippi, Louisiana, South Carolina, Florida, and Texas withdrew. These "seceders," as they were called by all factions, were then joined by majorities of the Georgia and Arkansas delegations. Unable to nominate a candidate, the rump recessed until June 18, when it reconvened in Baltimore, hoping to achieve more fruitful results.[30]

The pro-Lincoln Wheeling *Intelligencer* summed up what had happened at Charleston: "There was no prospect of reconciliation. The seceding States wanted Nigger protection. The Douglas men and the men from the North generally, would have been glad to have given it to them, but they dare not. And thus the quarrel stood between them. The South were defiant—the North immovable. Neither a platform or a man could be agreed on. . . . Never were men in such a hopeless strait. They didn't know what to do. Board was high, and we suspect liquor was running low." Opposition editors often reacted in a similarly light fashion to news of the Democratic cleavage. The Lynchburg *Virginian* poked fun at "the late Serio-Comic Entertainment at Charleston." "It was a mountain in labor and not even a mouse was brought forth," commented a North Carolina journal. Another paper in the same state discussed the demise of "the great, the tremendous, the all-powerful, the universal Democratic party" under the headline: "Satan's Kingdom's a Tumblin' Down!"[31]

The Democratic party was dead, alleged the Opposition papers, and some of them celebrated the event by printing mock funeral notices. After the Baltimore convention had failed to reunite the party in June, Parson Brownlow presented the following epitaph in his Knoxville *Whig:* "It is with a grateful heart we record the death of

ROTTEN DEMOCRACY

On Saturday the 23rd of June, 1860, after a protracted illness of *one month,* during which time its existence was only prolonged by the administration of powerful nostrums; it too [*sic*] sick at

Charleston—was removed to Baltimore for medical treatment—
and expired at midnight on the 23d instant. The disease which
was the immediate cause of dissolution, has not been clearly as-
certained—some of the Democratic Doctors who were present,
attributed it to gangrene of its huge Pouch and Bowels; more
generally known in the politic circles of Doggery keepers, as
ROT GUT—some supposed it died of a disease known as SECESSION
and DISUNION of soul and body—while others of large experience
assert that it died of a disease, which has prevailed as an epidemic
for years, called NEGROPHOBIA.[32]

The "death" of the Democratic party was especially
welcomed by the preponderance of Constitutional Union
journals, because they believed that their party now had
a chance to sweep the South and, perhaps, the nation. The
Vicksburg *Whig* predicted a veritable "stampede" to the
new party. The Fayetteville (North Carolina) *Observer*
imagined that "thousands will flock to their [Constitu-
tional Union] standard from both the other sectional and
divided and corrupt parties." To this end, Constitutional
Union papers frequently appealed to "conservative men"
to desert the riven party of their fathers and espouse the
cause of "the Constitutional, the Union, and the Laws."[33]

Constitutional Union journals argued that neither wing
of the Democratic party ought to command the support
of Southern men; if the Northern wing advocated free
soil, the Southern portion seemed headed toward disunion. These papers directed their most stinging criticism
at those Democrats who withdrew from the Charleston
convention. Many Unionist editors were convinced that
this was but the first step in a master plan for disunion.[34]
Nevertheless, some Constitutional Union papers sided
with the Charleston "seceders." The Rome (Georgia)
Weekly Courier, for example, sounded oddly like a secessionist paper as it sympathized with its Democratic opponents:

We cannot, and will not stand as idle and indifferent spectators and see noble and patriotic men fighting for *our* principles and our rights, beat down and trampled in the dust. As long as they fight faithfully, we will fight with them; and if they must fall we will fall by their side.[35]

This statement, and others like it, by editors of the Constitutional Union party served as a reminder that even though Southern Unionism was sincere, it nevertheless had its limits. A discerning observer might have concluded that the gulf separating Southern fire-eaters and Southern Unionists was not great after all.

Secessionist and extreme Southern-rights Democratic journals blamed the collapse of the Charleston convention upon the Douglas faction. Douglasites, they alleged, demonstrated by their intransigence at Charleston that they were determined either to rule the party or ruin it. "It seems strange to us," said the Carrollton *West Alabamian,* "that when the Northern Democrats found the South so united and determined against Douglas they still remained unwilling to make any concessions, and still refused to unite with us in presenting to the country some candidate whom both sections of the Union could have supported"[36]

Radical Southern-rights editors believed that Southern delegates had no alternative but to secede from the Charleston convention. A Texas paper wrote: "The Southern Delegations must have withdrawn or have returned to their people with the guilt of endorsing an odious heresy upon their heads, and of having acted contrary to the known will of their people." The False River (Louisiana) *Pointe Coupée Democrat* thought it "a matter of amazement" that any Southern delegate had remained in the convention, after the Northern majority had refused "the reasonable requirements of the Southern States." A deference to the Northern Democratic majority would have been quite as fatal to Southern interests as a future submission to a Republican majority, argued another Louisiana journal.[37]

Many Southern-rights Democratic newspapers were shocked and saddened by the dissolution of the party. Some thought that the disruption at Charleston meant the end of the national party. "It has gone; peace to its ashes!" mourned the Corsicana (Texas) *Navarro Express*. A South Carolina paper announced: "The Democratic party, heretofore the chief reliance against abolitionism, is destroyed." Others were more vindictive. "When shall we be again advised to go into a convention, which they control, to protect the rights of the South?" asked South Carolina's Newberry *Conservatist*. "We expect, as we sincerely hope, never!" The Savannah *Daily Morning News* expressed its belief that "the corrupt fungus has burst, and is only carried to Baltimore with its impurities to spread still wider the pestilence of its rottenness. We believe that the system of National Conventions is at an end."[38]

Fire-eating journals had warned all along that only the Democratic party could ensure the defeat of the Republicans in the fall. Many of them now were convinced that division in April had ensured defeat in November. Yet division and disunion were preferable to dishonor. If the South were to be denied her just territorial rights, then it would be better off out of the Union. The Tyler (Texas) *Reporter* asserted: "If these [rights] are to be persistently denied us, as has been done by Mr. Douglas and his followers, then the sooner we dissolve the partnership, the better for us." Defeat by the Republicans, with all its dire consequences, was better "than to succeed with such a man as Stephen A. Douglas and with such principals as he represents," declared a Mississippi paper. It was no longer simply a question of personality, said a bilingual Louisiana journal, *"c'était une question de vie et de mort."*[39]

Some secessionist papers once again were unequivocal in their advocacy of a Southern Confederacy. The Matagorda (Texas) *Gazette* declared that the government was at a virtual end and that, within six months, the South must govern itself. The Claiborne (Alabama) *Southern Champion* argued: "The South alone can protect the South. All national organizations are powerless for good. A Southern or Gulf Confederacy is our motto." The Newberry (South Carolina) *Rising Sun* declared: "The fact is, there never was a better time, and circumstances have never been dove-tailed in so well for the South to test the question whether she intends to go out of the Union or not." The dismemberment of the Union was now only a matter of time, predicted the Fernandina *East Floridian:* "And the South is as well prepared for that grave issue now, as she will be one or ten years hence."[40]

Generally speaking, extreme Southern-rights papers scorned participation in the Baltimore convention. They argued that the behavior of Northern Democrats at Charleston made it nearly impossible for Southern Democrats humbly to turn the other cheek and send delegates to Baltimore. Moreover, participation in the new convention would be folly. Nothing had changed, and unless the South were willing to "submit" to the will of the Northern majority, the convention at Baltimore must end, like that at Charleston, in failure.

Fire-eating newspapers therefore were appalled when Southern states prepared to send delegations to Baltimore. The Opelika (Alabama) *Southern Era,* for example, was amazed that Alabama would be represented: "Instead of standing up in the spirit of her wonted chivalry . . . she now abandons her own strong and elevated purposes,

and returns to the beggarly elements of compromise!"
A Georgia paper thought that even the invitation to the
South to participate in the convention at Baltimore indi-
cated "an utter disregard on the part of the free-soil ma-
jority . . . for the self-respect as well as the rights of the
Southern people."[41]

Most Democratic editorial opponents of the Baltimore
convention endorsed the Richmond convention, organized
by the Charleston "seceders" and scheduled to meet on
June 11.[42] No doubt many of these journals, the Charleston *Mercury* for example, already desired secession, but
others clearly hoped to avoid a disruption of the Union, if
possible. Many heatedly denied accusations by the supporters of Douglas and by the Opposition that supporters
of the Richmond convention had secession as their objective. "Let no man dare to call this a 'disunion movement.'
It is false in his teeth," wrote the Montgomery (Alabama)
Advertiser. The Savannah *Daily Morning News* echoed
this opinion and added: "Any one who either favors or opposes the Richmond Convention, because he imagines disunion is its object will find himself mistaken." Indeed, the
Spartanburg (South Carolina) *Carolina Spartan*, itself a
staunch Southern-rights paper, opposed Robert Barnwell
Rhett as a delegate to Richmond on the grounds that he
was a secessionist.[43]

Whatever their secret feelings about the Union, the
advocates of the Richmond convention believed it impera-
tive that the South yield no further on the question of
slavery in the territories. The scheduled "seceders'" convention at Richmond at least would demonstrate to
Northern Democrats the South's determination to maintain its "constitutional rights" in the territories, even if it
meant disrupting the party, even if it meant dismember-
ing the Union. In the view of its more moderate advocates,
this proposed convention ought to convince Northern

Democrats of the need to capitulate to the Southern point of view. Southern extremists, on the other hand, hoped that the Richmond convention would become the foundation upon which a Southern Confederacy could be built.

Pro-Douglas Southern papers angrily criticized the "seceders" for breaking up the convention at Charleston. They reiterated their belief that the question of popular sovereignty was but an abstraction. With the Greensboro *Alabama Beacon* they declared: "The question upon which it is now proposed to break up the Democratic party, is one of no present practical interest."[44]

Since they were convinced that nothing vital to Southern interests had been at stake at Charleston, many moderate Southern-rights papers suspected that secessionists had smashed the party in order that they might destroy the Union. "That the movement was one designed to lead to the disruption of the Democratic party and one whose tendency is calculated to lead to the dissolution of the Union itself, will scarcely admit of doubt," declared the Memphis *Daily Appeal*. As proof of the treasonous designs of the "seceders," Douglas papers often cited the famous "scarlet letter" which William L. Yancey had written in 1858 to James S. Slaughter of Georgia, in which the Alabama extremist had stated his intention to "fire the Southern heart" so that, at the proper moment, "we can precipitate the cotton States into a revolution."[45]

Unionist editors often reacted pessimistically to the breakup at Charleston. The New Orleans *Bee* warned that the secession from Charleston would have "the most baneful influence" on the party. The *Bee* accurately predicted that the rift begun at Charleston would widen at Baltimore and Richmond, and that the Democratic party would end up with two candidates. So disgusted was the Victoria *Texian Advocate* that it suggested, half seriously, that the Southern states be sold to Mexico for "claquos or tortillas."[46]

Most Douglas supporters took a more optimistic view than either the *Bee* or the *Texian Advocate*. The reason for their optimism was a belief that public opinion in the South would rebuke the seceders and reject overwhelmingly the design of the fire-eaters, who had engineered the disruption of the Democratic party. The Greensboro *Alabama Beacon* wrote: "That the course of the disruptionists will meet with very little favor from the masses, we confidently predict." The Van Buren (Arkansas) *Press* asked: "Is Arkansas for Disunion? To this question we answer emphatically, NO. . . . The people, the honest freemen of the State do not entertain the question for a moment." The Harrisonburg (Virginia) *Rockingham Register and Advertiser* thought it well for the country and "for the trembling heart of human freedom, everywhere, that these gentlemen seceders do not represent the sentiments of the people of the States from which they came as delegates." The Edgefield (South Carolina) *Advertiser,* a "quasi-Douglas" supporter, remarked: "We have seldom known a political movement to command so little enthusiasm as the one inaugurated at Charleston by the seceding Delegations."[47] Such papers were confident that the people would support the Baltimore convention, which they now saw as the only hope for the party and for the Union.[48]

Other moderate Southern-rights journals shared the desire of pro-Douglas papers to save the national Democratic party, since they too believed that the Union depended upon it. For this reason they strongly discountenanced the Richmond convention and advocated Southern participation at Baltimore.[49] Although some moderate Southern-rights papers now took a dim view of the Democratic prospects in November, many of them professed a belief that all would yet be well with the party. "We are not disturbed by the events at Charleston, for we anticipate future good to the party from what appears to be present evil," said the

Norfolk (Virginia) *Southern Argus.* The Greenville *South Alabamian* thought that the Democracy had simply "purged itself." Another Alabama paper believed that Southerners might now be able to dictate both the platform and the candidates to the convention.[50] Others thought that the adjournment to Baltimore would benefit the delegates by giving them time to cool down and ascertain the views of their constituents. As one Georgia paper put it: "The lapse of a few weeks will afford all parties time for reflection and subsidence—time to find out the 'home feeling,' which troubled Horseshoe Ned so much."[51]

When they were disposed to fix the blame for the debacle at Charleston, moderate Southern-rights journals often censured both sides. For example, a Florida paper deplored "the vaulting ambition and restless tempers of some of our leading men in both sections of the Union." " 'Douglas and anti-Douglas' ruined every thing," fumed the Atlanta *Daily Intelligencer.* The Wilmington (North Carolina) *Daily Journal* asserted that the crisis had been produced by "hotheaded Southern men and the uncompromising spirit of the Douglas delegates."[52]

Nevertheless, if they sometimes blamed Southern Hotspurs for their precipitous secession at Charleston, moderate Southern-rights journals often resembled fire-eating papers in their indictment of Douglas. Georgia's Milledgeville *Federal Union* warned that not a "baker's dozen" of Georgia Democrats would subscribe to the Douglas platform, and it alleged that it was Douglas alone who "has been the cause of all this strife and confusion; and all of this danger to the Union, and the Country." The Clarksville (Texas) *Northern Standard* called Douglas "the embodiment of humbuggery and abolitionism" and charged that the disruption of the convention had resulted from the determination of his backers to force his platform upon it. An Arkansas journal asserted: "Douglas and his odious squatter sovereignty doctrines have produced [the split], and until he is out of the way, there will be neither peace or harmony in our ranks."[53]

The disruption of the Democratic party had its greatest impact upon those moderate Southern-rights papers that had been willing, before the convention, to accept Douglas, even though they had found him unpalatable. The Fayetteville *North Carolinian,* which earlier had defended Douglas, now declared: "We are opposed to Mr. Douglas, to his view, to his theory and his sentiments—in fact to the man." The Atlanta *Daily Intelligencer,* which began to sound increasingly anti-Douglas and jingoistic, advocated participation in the Baltimore convention but noted forebodingly: "If then the rights of the South could not be secured by the Baltimore convention, the South might calculate the value of the union . . . and govern themselves accordingly."[54]

With few exceptions, after the final breakup of the Democratic party at Baltimore, moderate Southern-rights papers supported the candidacy of John C. Breckinridge. The shift in opinion of such a large segment of the press would help to ensure that Breckinridge would carry much of the South. Moreover, this growing radicalism in the Southern press was symptomatic of an increasing extremism in the Southern people at the beginning of the presidential campaign of 1860.

III

We Are Anxious to Holler for Somebody

WHILE Southern Democratic editors argued over the responsibility for their party's disruption at Charleston, the Republican party convened in Chicago to nominate the man who many now believed would be the next occupant of the White House. An estimated 25,000 to 30,000 delegates and visitors swarmed into the Windy City, although not nearly that many could expect to find seats in the convention hall—called the Wigwam—whose galleries could accommodate only about 7,500. The exuberance at Chicago contrasted greatly with the gloom that had pervaded the Democratic ranks at Charleston. Hotel lobbies and the Wigwam seethed with an excitement not unlike that which a prizefighter must feel when the championship is in the balance and the referee is counting over his battered opponent. The prevailing belief of the delegates was that a combination of the right nominee and a shrewd platform would ensure a Republican victory in November, regardless of whom the Democrats might nominate.[1]

But the opponent, though down, was not yet counted out. Whether the schism wrought at Charleston would prove fatal to the Democratic party's chances in November would depend in large measure upon what the Republicans did at Chicago. Unity was essential. In order to win, the Republicans had to agree upon a platform that would serve a broad spectrum of economic, sectional, and ethnic interests. This they achieved by offering a tariff to manufacturers, homesteads to farmers, a Pacific railroad to the West, and the protection of their citizenship rights to the alien-born. The platform writers also needed to sound the right moral note on slavery, but, in the process, they must not offend the racial prejudices harbored by many potential Republican voters. Thus, while they opposed any further introduction of slavery into the territories and reaffirmed, in a general way, the egalitarian principles of the Declaration of Independence, the Republicans not only failed to mention civil rights for Negroes in their platform, but even pointedly declared that the states should be left free to manage their own domestic institutions as they saw fit.[2]

To capitalize upon the opening provided them by the Democrats at Charleston, the Republicans also had to select a standard-bearer who would suggest moderation on the key issues and who therefore would appeal to the broad center of the Northern electorate. Choosing a candidate was even more difficult than writing a platform, not because there was a dearth of aspirants, but because most of the party's leading presidential timber had serious liabilities. For example, Missouri's Edward Bates, while he had the support of Horace Greeley, was tainted with Know-Nothingism and, consequently, was anathema to German-American voters. Salmon P. Chase of Ohio was known as an antislavery zealot, and the mention of his name caused the more racially conservative Republicans to frown. Abraham Lincoln was the favorite son of his home state of Illinois and a "comer," nationally, but he did not yet appear to have the broad support necessary to win the nomination. The most prominent Republican was William H. Seward of New

York. Unfortunately, Seward suffered from his talent for making controversial phrases that stuck in the public mind; his remark that there was a "higher law" than the Constitution had led some to believe that he condoned abolitionism, and his statement that there was an "irrepressible conflict" between the sections sounded like warmongering to others. Seward nevertheless led the early balloting, but he lacked enough votes to be nominated and was unable to gain significantly in the subsequent voting. Lincoln, who was in second place on the first two ballots, gained strength as Seward began to fade, and the supporters of the other candidates, sensing a band wagon for the Illinois lawyer, flocked to his banner. On the third ballot Lincoln won the nomination, to the immense delight of the partisan gallery.[3]

The Republicans' nomination of Lincoln in preference to Seward, Chase, Bates, and others surprised the Southern press. Even the Republican Wheeling *Daily Intelligencer,* whose editor was a delegate to the Chicago convention, admitted that it "had not the most remote idea" that Lincoln would be the nominee.[4] For months Southern editors had looked upon Seward as the probable Republican choice; consequently, they had most often singled him out when attacking Republican leaders. They now quickly shifted their fire to Lincoln.

Many Southern editors knew relatively little about Lincoln. A Virginia editor wrote: "The history of Mr. Lincoln is somewhat obscure. He has never done anything to raise him above the sphere of a rollicking cross road politician in Illinois until he was brought forward to contest the seat of United States Senator with Mr. Douglas." "The nomination of Lincoln and Hamlin, by the Chicago Convention, has created some surprise in this quarter," said the New Orleans *Picayune.* "They were so little prominent that the political biographers have not thought it proper to send us in advance, any extended memoir of their lives in aid of the journalists."[5] Some editors consulted Lanman's *Dictionary of the United States Congress* for background material on Lincoln, and almost all papers depended heavily upon exchanges for information about the new leader of the Republican party.[6]

Some Southern journals found Lincoln's character and background amusing. Not only was the Republican an honest man, declared the Wilmington (North Carolina) *Daily Journal*, but he must also be "somewhat religious," since his wife was a member of the Presbyterian church, "and Abe himself never says anything nearer swearing than an emphatic 'damn him!' launched against the object of his wrath."[7] An Arkansas paper summed up a campaign biography of Lincoln published shortly after the Chicago convention:

Old Abe is born. He suffers from teething and a bad "nuss." He deserts said "nuss," and with a spirit astonishing in an infant, leaves his home with an ax on his shoulder for Illinois. While yet at a tender age, he becomes midshipman on a flatboat, and distinguishes himself. He deserts the service, flings his commission to the wind, again shoulders his ax and commences his career as a "rail-mauler." . . . He is just building into manhood. An extraordinary convulsion of nature casts him into the state legislature. A still more extraordinary convulsion lands him in Congress, where he denounces the Mexican war, opposes the American soldiers, and *got his mileage*. He goes home and is driven into obscurity by an indignant constituency. He is picked out to run at the head of the Abolition machine for President, and anxiously awaits the results.[8]

A few Southern editors thought Lincoln's nomination a weak one. The San Antonio *Ledger and Texan* called Lincoln "a bold, vulgar, unscrupulous abolitionist, without any experience in administrative affairs. We do not regard him as a very formidable candidate." North Carolina's Newbern *Weekly Progress* thought Lincoln "coarse, vulgar and uneducated, and what success he has attained in life is more attributable to his *brass* and muscle than to mental or moral endowments." A Virginia paper asserted that neither Lincoln nor Hamlin had "the ability, experience, or fitness for the office to which they aspire."[9]

But many other Southern newspapers considered Lincoln a strong adversary. The New Orleans *Delta* warned its readers that Lincoln was a formidable candidate. Its neighbor, the *Bee*, agreed and declared the Republican nomination to be a "master stroke." The Charleston *Courier*'s New York correspondent wrote: "Lincoln is a strong man. The best thing I know about him is that he was born in Kentucky." A paper in Georgia called Lincoln a "strong" and "rough" candidate. And a North Carolina journal thought that the Republican standard-bearers composed perhaps "the strongest ticket that could have been nominated at Chicago."[10]

Only a small number of Southern papers thought Lincoln more moderate than Seward on the slavery question, and even these said that Republican moderation—indicated in the choice of candidates and in the Chicago platform—was more apparent than real. The Paulding (Mississippi) *Eastern Clarion* dismissed the nomination of Lincoln, whom it judged more moderate than Seward, as only a "dodge," by which the Republican party hoped to gain votes. The New Orleans *Bee* conceded that the Republicans had put up a moderate candidate and a surprisingly conservative platform, but it warned that this had been done deceitfully. Once the Republicans were victorious, the *Bee* said, they would forsake the Chicago platform for a policy more in line with abolitionist principles.[11]

Most Southern papers regarded Lincoln as more dangerous than Seward. Such journals sometimes quoted Lincoln's "House Divided" speech of 1858, in which he had stated his belief that the nation could not continue half-slave and half-free but must become entirely one or the other. For many Southern editors this was simply Seward's "irrepressible conflict" doctrine stated another way. Some journals now reported that, contrary to wide belief, it actually was Lincoln, and not Seward, who had originated the theory that there was an irrepressible conflict between the North and the South that ultimately might have to be resolved by force. Indeed, in the view of one North Carolina paper, Seward was "secretly in favor of the Union," while Lincoln was representative of "the strictest and most unrelenting fanaticism."[12]

Southern papers further argued that Lincoln's relative lack of experience and formal education would tend to make him less restrained and less wise than Seward in the handling of sectional differences. Lincoln, asserted the Wilmington (North Carolina) *Daily Journal,* had "all the ultraism of Seward without his sense, education or administrative talent." Similarly, the Milledgeville (Georgia) *Federal Union* declared Seward safer for the country than Lincoln, because Seward at least was "a man of good sense, but there is no telling what such men as Lincoln and Hamblin [*sic*] would do if they had power."[13]

The Southern press often depicted Lincoln as an ogre, ready to pounce upon the South and to destroy her cherished institutions at the first opportunity. Southern-rights journals, in particular, took the view of the Clarksville (Texas) *Northern Standard* that Lincoln opposed "everything that savors of a Southern breath." For many, the possible election of Lincoln conjured up a nightmare. None perhaps painted a more vivid picture of the horrors that must accompany a Republican administration than the Corsicana (Texas) *Navarro Express:*

As soon as Lincoln is installed into office . . . he will wave his black plume Southward. With the army and navy, and the fanatical North, he will invade us. He will issue his ukase, enfranchising the negroes, and arming them; he will confiscate property, and commend us to the mercy of torch and steel. Of this we are not left to doubt.[14]

Rumors that the Republican ticket itself was not without Negro blood lent credibility to predictions that a Republican administration would threaten slavery. Southern editors frequently accepted uncritically Robert Barnwell Rhett's false allegation that Lincoln's running mate was a mulatto. Some expressed horror that they were now to be subjected to "Negro rule." An Alabama paper typified the scurrilous attacks made upon the Republican vice-presidential candidate when it declared: "A free nigger to preside in the United States Senate! How would Southern Senators like that? The humiliation and disgrace of the thing would certainly be something, but the smell would be awful." Hamlin was a very appropriate choice, said a Memphis paper, "for, in all the acquirements of mind, manners, morals, form, features, complexion, woolly hair and all, he comes nearer being a negro than any one we have ever seen who claimed to be a white man—Fred Douglas [sic] not excepted." In a similar vein, the Newberry (South Carolina) *Rising Sun* said: "Think of it—*a nigger* in principle, elected President, and a mullatto [sic], for Hamlin is said to be one, sitting as Vice President and presiding in the Senate. What Southern man could submit to sit under the shadow of such a creature. It would be disgraceful in the extreme."[15]

Not surprisingly, many Southen-rights journals warned that they would advocate secession, should Lincoln win the presidency.[16] Their reaction probably would have been the same regardless of whom the Republicans nominated, for, as a North Carolina paper observed: "Lincoln embodies a *system* with an avowed object, that object being the ultimate extermination of slavery."[17] Any other standard-bearer would also have personified abolitionism to Southern-rights editors.

The Southern press was almost unanimous in its disapproval of Lincoln, but the Constitutional Union party's nominee, John Bell of Tennessee, aroused more controversy. The Constitutional Unionists convened in Baltimore a week before the Republican convention met in Chicago. Compared with the Charleston and Chicago spectacles, theirs was a bland affair. To Murat Halstead, who so recently had witnessed the tumult at Charleston, the Constitutional Union convention had too much unanimity to be interesting. "Everybody is eminently respectable, intensely virtuous, devotedly patriotic, and fully resolved to save the country. They propose to accomplish that political salvation so devoutly to be wished by ignoring all the rugged issues of the day." One amusing incident occurred when the Texas delegation arrived late on the first day of the convention and pretentiously made its way to seats at the front of the hall. Its leader, A. B. Norton, editor of the Austin *Southern Intelligencer,* caught even the jaded Halstead's attention with his homespun clothing, his large buckhorn-handled cane, and his beard "a half yard long." Apparently feeling the need to satisfy a general curiosity concerning Norton's unusually long growth of whiskers, a Texas delegate explained to the convention that the editor had once vowed that he would not shave until Henry Clay had been elected President. This explanation naturally inspired "tremendous applause" among the delegates, many of whom were old Whigs and former supporters of Clay.[18]

On the second day of the convention the delegates easily agreed upon a platform that completely ignored the slavery issue. They resolved: "That it is both the part of patriotism and of duty to recognize no political principles, other than

THE CONSTITUTION OF THE COUNTRY,
THE UNION OF THE STATES, AND
THE ENFORCEMENT OF THE LAWS."[19]

Next, the convention turned to the task of nominating a candidate. John Bell led the balloting from the beginning, although Sam Houston, nominated by his friend A. B. Norton, showed considerable early strength. Other candidates, such as John J. Crittenden, Edward Everett, William A. Graham, and William C. Rives, had only a smattering of support. On the second ballot a Bell band wagon developed, and the Tennessean swept on to victory. The addition of Everett's name as the vice-presidential nominee completed the ticket.[20]

Constitutional Union papers generally greeted the news of the Bell-Everett nominations with unqualified approbation. "What two more glorious living names does the history of our nation show?" asked the Augusta (Georgia) *Chronicle and Sentinel*. A North Carolina paper exulted: "This is a glorious ticket, which cannot fail to excite the utmost enthusiasm throughout this broad land." Parson Brownlow's Knoxville *Whig* predicted that these nominations would "every where inspire confidence, and elicit unbounded enthusiasm."[21]

Constitutional Union editors especially hoped that their ticket would excite enthusiasm among disgruntled Southern Democrats, for they recognized that without Democratic support John Bell could not assume his exalted role as a savior of the Union. Bell papers reasoned that a factionalized Democratic party had no chance of defeating the Republicans; only by rallying to the support of the Constitutional Union candidate could Southerners defeat Lincoln. "Why should not the Democrats of the Union unite upon Bell and Everett?" asked the Parkersburg (Virginia) *Gazette:* "The contest in this presidential election is between Bell and Lincoln—between the National

Union party and the Black Republicans. That is as clear
as it is that two and two make four." To reject the Constitutional Union ticket, argued a Tennessee journal,
would be "to strengthen the Republicans and court disunion. Let sensible Democrats think well before they act,
for upon them rests a heavy responsibility."[22]

In the pursuit of Democratic votes, Constitutional
Union journals often pictured Bell and Everett as national
candidates who were above the base partisanship so bla-
tantly exemplified by the leading Democratic politicians
of the country. The Salisbury (North Carolina) *Carolina
Watchman* struck this note when it wrote that Bell and
Everett "are offered to the country as patriots—in the true
sense—rising above party, owing allegiance to no party."
The Little Rock *Arkansas State Gazette* was confident that
the masses of Democrats would support the national candidate, Bell, rather than "follow the leaders of the party who
appear to have been smitten with madness and blindness
worse than that with which Sampson [*sic*] was afflicted,
when he pulled down the pillars of the temple and lost his
own life that his enemies might perish with him."[23]

The Camden (Arkansas) *Ouachita Herald* ran the following "Union Song" in its quest for Democratic voters:

> Loud the Union Bell is ringing
>   Pampered Locos funeral knell;
> Gladness to all hearts is bringing,
>   Who still love the Union well.
>
> Now on the eve of the election,
>   By three rival parties torn,
> Let us throw aside all section,
>   By our love of Union borne.
>
> Let the hope of victory keep us
>   Ever steady to our trust;
> And the Union men will greet us,
>   For our cause is true and just—

> Till at length, by ever adding
> Numbers to our Union band:
> To the White House we'll escort them,
> Bell and Everett hand in hand.[24]

Generally speaking, Constitutional Union papers that had favored candidates other than Bell before the nomination gracefully acceded to the will of the Baltimore majority.[25] A few spurned the party's choice of candidates; for example, the Benton (Alabama) *Weekly Herald,* which called itself an organ of the "State Rights Opposition," flatly refused to endorse Bell and Everett. While the *Herald* insisted that it did not contemplate baptism "in the Democratic pool," it later supported the Southern-rights Democratic candidate. In a like manner the Montgomery (Alabama) *Weekly Mail* refused to endorse the Constitutional Union ticket. Although the *Mail* admitted that some of its subscribers were displeased by its action, it nevertheless endorsed both the candidate and the platform of the Southern-rights Democrats, while stressing that it was not thereby aligning itself with the Democratic party.[26]

Occasionally, a Democratic journal endorsed Bell and Everett. One such paper in Louisiana annouced its support for the Constitutional Union ticket, because it saw no "earthly chance for a reconciliation between the two wings of the Democratic party" and because it was disillusioned with party leaders "from whom we had reason to expect better things."[27] But most Southern Democratic papers were scornful of Bell, whose negative votes in the senate on the Kansas–Nebraska Act and the Lecompton Constitution had made suspect his loyalty to the South, at least in the eyes of Southern-rights Democrats. "Bell," said the Athens (Georgia) *Southern Banner,* "although a Southern man, is not sound upon the paramount question of the day. He is not more than one remove from a free-soiler."[28] Others were contemptuous of the failure of the Constitutional

Union party to face up to the issues and insisted that, as a consequence, it could expect little support in the South.[29]

Still other Southern Democratic editors dealt with the Constitutional Union ticket in a cavalier manner. The Leesburg (Virginia) *Democratic Mirror* said that Bell and Everett were both gentlemen, "though there is nothing in the record of either specially calculated to win upon the popular heart—and their chances of success, small, decidedly." The Memphis *Daily Appeal,* noting the choice of the "venerable gentlemen" by the "Old Gentlemens' Party," asserted that Bell and Everett had in the past stood on many different platforms; therefore, they could not now be taken too seriously.[30]

No candidate, not even Lincoln, was the target of more devastating satire from the Democratic press than was Bell. Although only in his early sixties, he was often pictured as virtually senile. The New Orleans *Daily Delta* wrote:

John Bell is a quaint, homely, sleepy old gentleman, of sterling honesty and good heart, of enormous continuity of speech and tenuity of thought. If a half dozen such men could be scattered through every community, there would be a great decline in the sale of other kinds of anodynes. His power in this respect is so great that we believe he would supply that great desideratum in medical practise of calming and composing the victims of delirium tremens.

Writing in the same vein, a Texas journal called Bell "a fossilized relic of a remote period. . . . These antiquarian gropers [the Constitutional Union delegates] have impiously disentombed this honored mummy from the tomb of the Pharoahs, and have set him up in public places again to be gazed at with more wonder than he ever inspired during his palmiest days."[31]

In mid-June, even as the Southern press debated the nominees of the Republican and Constitutional Union parties, the Democrats reassembled at Baltimore. The "seceding" wing, composed of the Charleston bolters, met first at Richmond and, over the objections of some of the more extreme fire-eating journals, recessed its proceedings until the outcome of the Baltimore convention could be known.[32]

Most of the bolters then proceeded to Baltimore, where they sought recognition as the bona fide delegates from their states. They had a strong claim, since the Charleston convention had not adjourned but had merely recessed until it reconvened at Baltimore. In the interim between Charleston and Baltimore, however, delegations loyal to Douglas had been chosen in several of the states. These Douglas delegations now clashed with the seceding delegations for recognition as their states' true representatives. The Douglas-dominated convention recognized the new, pro-Douglas delegations from Alabama and Louisiana but attempted to mollify the renegades and reunite the party by dividing the convention votes of Arkansas and Georgia between Douglas and seceder delegations, and by admitting the bolting delegations from Texas, Mississippi, and Delaware. This attempt at compromise failed to satisfy the anti-Douglas forces, and the Southern-rights delegates withdrew to Market Hall and nominated John C. Breckinridge of Kentucky for President and Joseph Lane of Oregon for Vice President. The rump meanwhile chose Douglas as its presidential candidate and Senator Benjamin Fitzpatrick of Alabama as his running mate. When Fitzpatrick declined the nomination his place was given to Alexander H. Stephens of Georgia.[33]

Southern newspapers had fully aired both Douglas's virtues and faults in the months preceding the disintegration of the Democratic party. They now added little that was new. Once again the Little Giant's critics of the fourth estate chorused their opinion that the senator and his program were unacceptable to the South. The Fernandina *East Floridian* said that Douglas's nomination was "entirely sectional in its character" and was "quite as objectionable as that of Lincoln at Chicago." Douglas's election, warned an extreme Southern-rights paper in Alabama, must inevitably signal the dissolution of the Union.[34]

Douglas's advocates, on the other hand, insisted that all Southern Democrats ought to support their candidate, because he had been regularly nominated by the party and because as a national figure he stood a far better chance of defeating Lincoln than did Breckinridge, who, they said, was nothing more than a sectional candidate dominated by fire-eaters. Moreover, Douglas editors insisted that, contrary to the allegations of his enemies, the Illinois senator was, and had always been, a friend of the South. Georgia's Augusta *Daily Constitutionalist* called Douglas "the man who has fought a hundred successful battles for the South, and not one against her." Indeed, declared the *Constitutionalist,* Douglas was "the real author of the Compromise of 1850, and the first man in the North who dared raise his voice for the fugitive slave law."[35]

Some papers which espoused Breckinridge and Lane did so reluctantly, not because they disliked the ticket, but because they opposed splitting the party.[36] Nevertheless, most Breckinridge papers played down the significance of the final division at Baltimore and greeted their candidates' nominations with unreserved enthusiasm. Perhaps none went to greater lengths in extolling Breckinridge's virtues than the Florence (Alabama) *Gazette,* which wrote: "The gifted, the eloquent, the incorrupt, the patriotic, the gallant John C. Breckinridge, is our chosen leader. His soul is as unsullied, his ambition as pure and chaste as the heart and soul of a virgin, and his patriotism is as lofty as the stars that glitter over his humble home in Kentucky."[37]

Anticipating the accusations of Bell and Douglas papers that Breckinridge was a tool of secessionists, Breckinridge journals argued that the Kentucky vice president and his Oregon running mate constituted an eminently national, conservative Unionist ticket. It was a ticket, said the Wilmington (North Carolina) *Daily Herald,* around which "all truly national men can safely rally for the preservation of the Union and the integrity of the Constitution." The Savannah *Daily Morning News* hailed Breckinridge and Lane as "sound, able, national men; the nominees, not of a 'sectional organization' . . . but of the only truly national party existing in the country." The election of Breckinridge, said an Alabama paper, would secure "the lasting perpetuation of the Union, with all its glories, and all its inestimable privileges and blessings."[38]

As his advocates had anticipated, Breckinridge's critics often stressed the sectional nature of his candidacy. They pointed out that regardless of how strong Breckinridge was among Southern-rights men, he could hardly expect to carry a single Northern state. The Vicksburg *Whig* thus assessed the chances of the Breckinridge-Lane ticket: "The fact is, it cannot be elected—it don't deserve to be elected, and what is more, it won't be elected."[39] As the campaign wore on, Bell and Douglas papers increasingly associated Breckinridge with the secessionism of his more extreme backers.

In the weeks following the conclusion of the national conventions, Southern newspapers fell more or less naturally into the camp of one or the other of the candidates. Virtually all secessionist and radical Southern-rights journals, as well as many moderate Southern-rights papers, gravitated to the Breckinridge column. Other moderate Southern-rights journals and some Unionist sheets with Democratic antecedents went to Douglas. Opposition news-

papers, most of which were Unionist journals, usually
endorsed Bell.

For various reasons some papers ostensibly were independent but actually favored a particular candidate in
their editorial columns and in the choice of materials
which they reprinted from other papers. The New Orleans
Daily Delta, for example, praised Breckinridge's nomination and clearly favored him throughout the campaign but
never endorsed him because it said that it was not a "party
paper." The New Orleans *Daily Picayune* likewise never
formally endorsed Bell, in spite of its strong Unionism.
The New Orleans *Bee,* although it often defended Douglas, never formally endorsed him; while it explicitly opposed Breckinridge, the *Bee* wrote that either Bell or
Douglas was acceptable.[40] The Prattville (Alabama) *Autauga Citizen* and Edgefield (South Carolina) *Advertiser,*
both Douglas papers in Breckinridge country, dodged what
might have been ruinous decisions by declaring that either
Breckinridge or Douglas would do.[41] Many South Carolina
newspapers, though often regarded as pro-Breckinridge,
scarcely discussed the campaign at all and did not even
bother raising the names of Breckinridge and Lane to
their mastheads, apparently because they had already
given up hope of preserving the Union.[42]

Occasionally a paper adopted a position of genuine
neutrality, but this was unusual except among religious
and literary journals. Political partisanship was the *raison
d'être* of most Southern newspapers. Only by serving as an
"organ" for a particular political faction could many
papers gain the wherewithal to pay the expenses of publication.[43] Partisan editors enjoyed the give and take of
political battle and often expressed disdain for neutral
journals. "You may talk as you please about neutral papers—the thing is an absurdity," declared a North Caro-

lina journal. "The editor who has not mind enough to have a political creed is unfit for his position, for surely mind, intellect and firmness are necessary in the conduct of his paper. If then he has these qualifications, he will most certainly be established in some political faith or other." Parson William G. Brownlow of the Knoxville *Whig* refused to place neutral newspapers on his exchange list. "When we take a paper in hand, and read its motto 'neutral in Politics and Religion,'" wrote the Parson, "we dash it to the ground, with hate and contempt."[44]

The need to mirror public opinion in the choice of a candidate sometimes caused editors to equivocate painfully in deciding whom to support. One Democratic paper articulated the dilemma of such editors when it said: "We are decidedly at a loss to know what will be the result of all this 'mix,' and we are in a greater loss as to how to holler; we are anxious to holler for somebody, but are afraid to, for you know we might wake up the wrong passenger—that is we might get on the wrong side—and then we would be in a circumstance."[45]

Often papers were forced by public opinion to change candidates in mid-campaign. For example, popular pressure led the Bolivar (Tennessee) *Democrat* and the Greensboro *Alabama Beacon* to forsake Douglas for Breckinridge. "After mature deliberation," wrote the *Beacon*, "we have determined to *take down the Douglas flag*. In deciding upon this course, we have been influenced mainly by the following considerations: Political newspapers, as a general rule, are the exponents of the opinions of those who sustain them. But as most of the subscribers to the Beacon—five-sixths, at least, if not a greater proportion— are opposed to Douglas, in advocating his claims to the Presidency, the Beacon is the exponent of the Opinions of but a very small proportion of those who sustain it." The editor confessed that he still would vote for the Little

Giant in November, but business was business and he thus rationalized his desertion of Douglas during the campaign: "Our advocacy of Douglas' election, while it would continue to embarrass us, could do him no possible good—as he stands not the slightest chance of getting the vote of Alabama. Nor could any service that we could render him change the result."[46]

William Woods Holden of the Raleigh *North Carolina Standard,* sometimes called the "Talleyrand of North Carolina politics" because he shifted positions so often, lamely endorsed Breckinridge in July, even though he had consistently defended Douglas and had attacked the fire-eaters after the disruption of the Charleston convention. Since Holden was pledged to support the candidate of the Democratic majority in North Carolina, he had no choice but to endorse Breckinridge. Nevertheless, the complicated proviso which he attached to his endorsement of the Southern-rights candidate indicated the reluctance with which he had made his decision:

We shall support this ticket for President and Vice President on these conditions: That the Electors will vote for the strongest man, Breckinridge or Douglas, as the case may be, against Lincoln. That is, if the vote of this State will elect either of them over Lincoln, or will put either of them in the House, it is to be cast accordingly. But if the vote will elect neither, nor put either of them in the House, the Electors to vote as they please.[47]

Editors who found it too difficult to transfer their loyalties to the candidate preferred by their subscribers sometimes lost their papers. On July 11 the Clarksville (Tennessee) *Jeffersonian* reported that the editor of the Chattanooga *Advertiser,* who was a Douglas man, had been forced to sell his journal. "Not wishing to publish a Douglas paper with the present prospect for that gentleman in Tennessee, he sells out and retires." In a similar case, editor J. G. Carrigan of the Shelbyville (Tennessee)

True Union preferred Douglas to Breckinridge. "But," as the Nashville *Republican Banner* put it, "the Yanceyites made him believe they were the biggest crowd, and so he vacated the chair." Carrigan himself explained his action at a Democratic meeting:

Mr. Chairman:—Repeated have been the solicitations of the Breckinridge and Lane party on yesterday and today, for me to resign the editorial position of the *True Union*, inasmuch as I cannot conscientiously advocate the claims of their candidates for the Presidency, to a gentleman who can and will, contending at the same time that the organ should reflect the will of the majority of the party in this county.

I am candid enough to-day to say that the tide of enthusiasm is for Mr. Breckinridge and Mr. Lane, and those to whom I look for support being among you, it would incur a pecuniary embarrassment on me to pursue a course opposit [*sic*] your desires and wishes. . . . I trust God that I am honest in my opinions, and as I cannot approve the ticket now before the convention, I therefore resign my position as editor of that paper.

The pro-Douglas editor of the Fayetteville (Tennessee) *Lincoln Journal*, reporting the case of the *True Union*, confessed that he might also be forced by local pressure to give way, "but like Carrigan we shall die game."[48] Southern-rights Democrats had no monopoly on such pressure tactics as those used against Carrigan. The staunchly pro-Breckinridge editors of the Hayneville (Alabama) *Watchman* were forced to lease their paper to the Constitutional Union party for the campaign for lack of support. One of the *Watchman*'s resigning editors, I. A. Pruitt, bitterly complained in his valedictory that the people were not strongly enough for Southern rights.[49] There was much switching of colors among newspapers during the summer and fall; it seems clear that the pressure of public opinion was most often responsible for the changes.

Very rarely an editor appeared to ignore his own financial well-being to endorse the candidate he preferred. The Montgomery (Alabama) *Mail,* an anti-Democratic but Southern-rights Opposition paper, formally endorsed Breckinridge and Lane on July 6, "at whatever risk of pecuniary loss it may involve." But it is quite likely that the fire-eating *Mail* picked up as many subscribers as it lost by its stand. Another Alabama Opposition journal, announcing that "duty" required it to support Breckinridge instead of Bell, noted that although it had alienated some of its readers the Breckinridge party had come to its support.[50]

Sometimes editorial staffs disagreed over whom to support for President. When such divisions occurred, the senior partner, or partners, naturally prevailed, often leaving the dissenting editor no choice but to dispose of his interest in the paper and vacate his chair. One such case involved Leonard Trousdale, an editor and part-owner of the Memphis *Daily Appeal.* Trousdale announced on July 19 that he had sold his interest in the *Appeal* to one of his former partners, Benjamin F. Dill. Explaining his action, Trousdale said that he had "for several weeks" disagreed with the *Appeal*'s editorial course, and he added: "While my colleagues, who now control the policy of the paper, yield their support to Judge DOUGLAS, who has ever been their favorite, I feel it incumbent on me to raise a hearty and decided voice in favor of Kentucky's gifted young statesman, JOHN C. BRECKINRIDGE, who, it is well known to many, I have heretofore designated as my first choice as the nominee of the Democratic party for the presidency."[51] N. A. Taylor of the San Antonio *Ledger and Texan* found himself in a similar dilemma, except that he favored Douglas instead of Breckinridge, the senior editor's choice. The *Ledger and Texan* delayed making an endorsement for several weeks because of the difference of opinion between the editors. When finally the senior editor overruled Taylor and raised Breckinridge's name to the paper's masthead, the junior editor clearly was unhappy. But in spite of the "disgust" that he felt at being "connected with those who have brought the country to the verge of ruin," he concurred in the decision to support the Southern-rights candidate in the interest of "harmony." Nevertheless, Taylor left the *Ledger and Texan* a few weeks later, because his steadfast refusal to criticize Douglas had angered a large number of the paper's subscribers.[52]

As the campaign wore on, more and more Southern newspapers committed themselves to one candidate or another. In early 1860 there were about 700 political newspapers in the eleven future Confederate states alone. Virginia led with 117; Alabama had 89, Georgia 75, Mississippi 70. There were 60 political journals in North Carolina, 68 in Louisiana, and 71 in the frontier state of Texas. Because of the rise of "campaign papers"—partisan journals intended to last only until the election—the number of newspapers increased dramatically during the summer. For example, Arkansas had 37 papers of all types in the spring; by September it reportedly had about 60. And Florida, where 20 political newspapers were published in early 1860, counted 25 by November.[53]

Breckinridge dominated the Southern political press in the campaign of 1860. A clear majority of papers in Florida, Alabama, Texas, Arkansas, South Carolina, and Georgia endorsed the Kentuckian. He also captured more papers in Virginia, Louisiana, North Carolina, and Mississippi than his closest competitor, Bell.[54]

Outside of South Carolina, where he had no friendly papers, Bell had fairly well-distributed newspaper support; nevertheless, Breckinridge's journals substantially outnumbered his papers in every Southern state except perhaps

Tennessee, and even there Breckinridge appears to have had virtually as many papers as favorite son Bell. Even in such areas of pronounced Unionist strength as Northern Alabama, Western Virginia, and Eastern Tennessee, Breckinridge appears either to have matched or exceeded the Tennessean in newspaper endorsements.

Douglas placed a weak third in the race for newspaper support. In no state did the Illinois senator come close to achieving a majority or even a plurality of newspaper endorsements; and in Florida, Texas, North Carolina, Arkansas, and South Carolina his press was almost non-existent. Professor Roy F. Nichols exaggerated when he wrote: "South of the Washington *States and Union* there was of course no editorial echo [for Douglas]." But the echo was indeed a faint one.[55]

As the race progressed, Douglas lost newspaper support. In late August the number of his journals in Arkansas reportedly had shrunk from seven to three. In late July, Douglas newspapers in Tennessee were said to be down to three, with the defection to Breckinridge of the Bolivar *Democrat*. The Newbern (North Carolina) *Daily Progress* admitted on July 3 that thus far it was the only paper in the state "that had said a good word for Douglas," and apparently the situation had not improved by late August, when the Wilmington *Daily Journal* observed that there was not at that time a Douglas paper in the state. Even in Virginia, where the Little Giant had a fairly sizable representation of newspapers, there were weaknesses. The Fairmont *True Virginian* pointed out that of the fifteen electoral districts in Virginia, only four had Douglas newspapers that had been published before his nomination. The rest were campaign papers. The Richmond *Enquirer* alone had more influence in the state "than all the Douglas papers and orators combined," asserted the pro-Breckinridge *True Virginian*. In August the San Antonio *Ledger and Texan* prefaced a report that the Lavaca *Gulf Keys* was supporting Douglas with Thomas Moore's lines:

> 'Tis the last rose of summer left blooming alone;
> All its lovely companions are faded and gone.

But the *Ledger and Texan* erred in even ascribing that Texas paper to Douglas, since it too supported Breckinridge.[56]

Since the press generally mirrored the views of the reading public, its overwhelming endorsement of one candidate clearly presaged the election's outcome. In each of the future Confederate states, with the single exception of Virginia, the candidate who received the most newspaper endorsements won the state's electoral votes, and in the Old Dominion he lost by only 358 votes.

Southern editors knew the importance of building strong newspaper support for their candidates, and they frequently exaggerated the number of journals endorsing their favorite. Occasionally, however, an anti-Breckinridge paper admitted that the Southern-rights candidate had outdistanced Bell and Douglas in the race for press support. On August 7 the pro-Douglas Homer (Louisiana) *Iliad* wrote: "So far as we have been able to learn, a majority of newspapers of the South are for Breckinridge and Lane." The *Iliad* assailed Southern editors for lacking the backbone to resist the popular will. "They find it easier to succumb to a local prejudice, void alike of principle and common sense, than to combat error with the sword of truth. Gentlemen—if such you may be called—our contempt for you is unfathomable. You are traitors to your country, to truth, and to God."[57]

Breckinridge's hegemony over Southern newspapers would help him carry most of the Southern states in November. Perhaps even more important, the large number

of Breckinridge papers throughout the South would provide Southern-rightists with an excellent network of organs
presenting the secessionist point of view during the post-
election crisis. Conversely, the comparative weakness of
the Constitutional Union press would seriously cripple the
Unionists in the propaganda war over secession following
Lincoln's election.

IV

The Devil Quotes Scripture

PERHAPS no presidential campaign in American history has been accompanied by a more ferocious newspaper war between adherents of the principal candidates than that in the South in 1860. The strong partisanship which normally marked elections in the ante bellum South was heightened by the emergence of three parties, each of which was convinced that it alone could defeat the despised "Black Republican" Lincoln.

During this period of unprecedented stress, Southern journalism exemplified, as never before, the truth of Robert S. Cotterill's statement: "Every Southern political editorial contained the ingredients of a duel; many of them were potential invitations to homicide."[1] Numerous acts of violence involving editors were reported. The most sensational incident occurred when George and William Hardwick of the pro-Breckinridge Lynchburg *Republican* confronted Joseph and Robert Button of the pro-Bell Lynchburg *Virginian* on the streets of Lynchburg. According to one account, all four started shooting "as if by common consent," and when the smoke had cleared, the

Button brothers lay mortally wounded. Possibly the most amusing incident occurred between William L. Yancey's son and J. J. Seibels, editor of the pro-Douglas Montgomery (Alabama) *Confederation;* each principal claimed to have severely chastised the other in a duel involving a cane and an umbrella. Although such editorial violence was the rule rather than the exception in the South, the added tension created by the emotional presidential campaign of 1860 must have contributed to the frequent conflicts in which newspapermen were involved.[2]

After the hue and cry over Charleston and Baltimore died away, the Breckinridge press paid less attention to Douglas and his doctrine of popular sovereignty. The Little Giant's failure to generate much support in the South was probably the main reason for the slackening of the Breckinridge press's assault against him.

Some of the more radical Southern-rights journals continued to snipe sporadically at Douglas and his supporters. Usually they reiterated the earlier assertions: Douglas was little if any better than Lincoln, since the Illinois senator's interpretation of popular sovereignty was but "a short cut to all the ends of Black Republicanism."[3] Moreover, they still blamed Douglas for dividing the party through his insistence upon popular sovereignty and his determination to head the Democratic ticket. One bit of doggerel that made the rounds of such papers stressed the radical Southern-rights view that Douglas had split the party:

> Quoth Abe to Steve, "I cannot fail,
>   I'm bound to fill *that* station;
> Long, long ago, I split the rail
>   To fence this mighty nation."
> "Of what *you've* split don't talk to me,"
>   Quoth Steve with chuckle hearty;
> "I've split old Jackson's hickory tree,
>   The Democratic party." [4]

Douglas provided the Southern-rights press with new ammunition when he decided in August to campaign personally in the South. Apparently convinced that his chances of
winning the presidency were nil, and fearing that certain
fire-eaters in the South were preparing a *coup d'état* in the
event of Lincoln's election, the Little Giant toured the
border states of Virginia, Maryland, and North Carolina
in late August and early September in an attempt to shore
up Unionist resistance to secession pressures. Later, after
Republican victories in Northern local elections seemed to
confirm his earlier suspicions of an impending Lincoln
victory, he visited the deep South in an unsuccessful effort
to stem the secession flood in the Gulf states. Douglas continued on his fruitless mission in the cotton states until
after Lincoln's election. News of the Republican's victory
reached the exhausted Illinois senator as he sat in the
office of his friend, John Forsyth, editor of the Mobile
Register.[5]

Douglas's Southern trips, the first such junkets by an
American presidential candidate, met with criticism in
several papers. Ante bellum presidential aspirants were
supposed to refrain from stump politics; such activities
were regarded as unseemly for one seeking the highest
office in the land. Thus Lincoln and Bell made no speeches
on their own behalf, and Breckinridge made only one, and
that in his home state of Kentucky. The contrast between
Douglas and his rivals, therefore, was all the more notice-
able. A South Carolina journal's pious denunciation of the
senator for breaking campaign precedent would seem curious indeed to the ubiquitous candidates of the twentieth
century:

We have fallen on evil times when the high office of President can
be sought by arts of electioneering. Alas for our country! Douglas
not content with interpolating the most fatal political heresies

into our government, trails the imperial purple of the confederacy through the mire of party strife. Shame! Shame![6]

Most Breckinridge papers were more concerned about what Douglas said, however, than they were about his breaking campaign tradition. On August 25 at Norfolk, Virginia, he declared the South would have no right to secede upon the mere election of Lincoln as President and that he would support a federal policy of coercion if any Southern state should attempt to leave the Union on that account. A few days later, at Raleigh, Douglas left no room for doubt concerning his view of secessionists. "I would hang every man higher than Haman who would attempt to resist by force the execution of any provision of the Constitution which our fathers made and bequeathed to us."[7]

Radical Southern-rights and secessionist editors reacted angrily to Douglas's Union pronouncements. They questioned his real motives for journeying into the South, since he could hardly expect to carry any of the states that he visited. Why then had he made the trip, instead of remaining in the North, hammering away in Pennsylvania, Ohio, Indiana, and other states where he might have a chance of defeating the Black Republican candidate? The reason, they said, was that Douglas had decided that he could not win, and since he preferred Lincoln to Breckinridge, he had left the North at the critical stage of the campaign in order to make the Republican victory more certain. He had come south, they further charged, to destroy the radical Southern-rights party and, thereby, to strengthen his hand for 1864. "Will you, can you support a man who is willing that Lincoln should be elected if thereby he may be promoted?" asked the Raleigh *Democratic Press.* "Will you? Can you?"[8]

As the campaign wore on, and despite the flurry of anti-Douglas journalism set off by the senator's southern excursions, John Bell replaced the Little Giant as the leading target of most Breckinridge papers. This shift was a logical development, since the Constitutional Unionist posed the only real threat to Breckinridge in the South. Moreover, Bell's press, which included perhaps 200 well-distributed newspapers, maintained a constant, strident assault upon Breckinridge and his party. Understandably, Southern-rights journals replied in kind. When one Breckinridge organ in Alabama noticed in late July that some Southern-rights journals were still "firing away at Douglas," it said: "This is a great waste of the raw material. Douglas is thoroughly defunct in Alabama—a dead cock in the pit. . . . But old Madam Bell, under the manipulations of her senile admirers, is having some signs of life galvanized into her decrepit carcass, and may, if well nursed, be able to strike up a dog trot by November."[9]

Breckinridge organs variously accused Bell of corruption, of opposing the Mexican War, of anti-Catholicism, and of abolitionism. Southern-rights sheets in areas containing large numbers of immigrants emphasized Bell's Know-Nothing background. If Bell were elected, the Richmond *Enquirer* predicted, "Know-Nothingism will rule the United States, and Roman Catholics and foreign-born citizens will either be beaten and murdered, as in 1856, or else deprived of the right of voting and holding office; and thus be reduced to the level of the degraded negro!" Louisiana's Opelousas *Courier* wondered if Bell's alleged anti-Catholicism would "prove sweet in the nostrils of St. Landry's loyal citizens." A New Orleans journal reminded Catholics that Bell was "the sworn enemy of that liberty of conscience and of the political rights which the Constitution gives you, and will conspire against you to deprive you of the rights, privileges and immunities of citizenship."[10]

Most Breckinridge papers concentrated principally upon

Bell's slavery record. Going back to old speeches made by him in the 1840s and -50s they lifted from context phrases which made him appear a veritable Black Republican. He was criticized for voting against the tabling of abolitionist petitions in the House, for voting in the senate against the pro-slavery Lecompton Constitution for Kansas, for favoring the Republican-backed Homestead Bill, and for declaring in 1850 that he would not mind seeing slavery abolished in the District of Columbia.[11]

Not the least of Bell's weaknesses in the eyes of the Southern-rights press was his running mate, Edward Everett. If the Breckinridge papers often depicted Bell as a senile old man whose past words and deeds made him doubtful on the slavery question, they asserted bluntly that the second man on the Constitutional Union ticket was a bona fide abolitionist. One Georgia newspaper charged that Everett was "against the South on the slavery question. . . . He is a millstone around Bell's neck, and would sink a much purer and greater politician than John Bell." The Montgomery (Alabama) *Weekly Mail,* itself formerly an Opposition journal, was scandalized at Everett's alleged belief that the Negro was capable of intellectual equality with the white man: *"Whitemen of Alabama!* are you ready for the doctrine of *negro equality,* as advocated by Edward Everett? Do you believe in sending your sons and your daughters—aye, your *daughters!*— to school with negroes and in asserting that the negro is their intellectual equal?"[12]

In view of the indictments which they brought against Bell and Everett, it was hardly surprising that Breckinridge newspapers often equated the Constitutional Union ticket with that of the Republican party. The Murfreesboro (Tennessee) *News* thought Bell worthy of a place in Lincoln's cabinet; a country paper in Mississippi declared that all who supported Bell would be virtually supporting Lincoln. Bell, asserted Florida's St. Augustine *Examiner,* was co-operating with the Republicans "in an insane attempt to equalize the African slave with the white man." If the South should support the Bell-Everett ticket, warned a Breckinridge advocate in Alabama, "she will thus, not only warm the viper to her bosom, but warm it after she has felt the power of its deadly fangs!"[13]

Bell journals faithfully defended their candidate from the assertions of the Southern-rightists. Their reading of Bell's record indicated that his was a Southern as well as a national record. Bell himself was a large slaveholder, they pointed out; consequently, there could be no question that he would protect slave interests. "Would a sane man burn his own barn, or destroy his own property?" asked the Tuskegee (Alabama) *Republican.*[14] There developed a fatuous controversy between Bell and Breckinridge publicists over which candidate really was a slaveholder. Bell's Negroes, said his critics, legally belonged to his wife; thus the Constitutional Unionist must be regarded as "unsafe" for the South's "peculiar institution." Bell editors, on the other hand, charged Beckinridge with using white laborers on his Kentucky farm and asked whether such a man could be trusted to protect slavery.[15]

Until the final division of the Democratic party in June, Bell papers had been at least as critical of Douglas and popular sovereignty as they had been of Yancey and secessionism. By July, Constitutional Union journals all over the South were concentrating their attacks almost exclusively upon the Breckinridge party. Not only did Bell papers cease their criticism of the Little Giant, they even began praising him editorially, printing his speeches, and publishing letters favorable to his candidacy. One Texas newspaper even added Douglas's name to that of Bell at its masthead.[16]

The changing attitude of Bell organs toward Douglas

was duly noted by the Breckinridge press. In midsummer the Natchez *Mississippi Free Trader* wrote: "The Opposition papers in the South have discovered peculiar excellence in Mr. Douglas, which, so long as they thought he, instead of Mr. Breckinridge, would be the regular Democratic nominee, they were wholly unable to see." The Matagorda (Texas) *Gazette*'s editor declared that he often took up a Bell and Everett paper, "and were it not for the names of the candidates at its masthead, we should take it for a genuine Douglas organ. The squatter sovereignty candidate is called all the good, sweet and pretty names that the language affords." Breckinridge organs often accused Douglas and Bell forces of a dark conspiracy against their candidate.[17]

Bell and Douglas papers scarcely denied the new rapport between them. Nevertheless, the rather sudden attachment clearly was more a marriage of convenience than of love. The Bell and Douglas factions shared two principal objectives: stop Breckinridge and save the Union. Both parties also nursed slim hopes of winning the election, but clearly neither could win unless Breckinridge was stopped in the South. In any case, both Bell and Douglas journals generally opposed secession should Lincoln win the election. The pro-Douglas New Orleans *Bee* cited the preservation of the Union as the reason for the new warmth between supporters of Bell and Douglas:

In the first place they agree in devotion to the Union. They are openly, avowedly and everywhere opposed to Disunionism in all its forms. North, South, East and West the Bell men and Douglas men advocate the supremacy of the Constitution and the perpetuity of the Union. They do not threaten to overturn the one, or to dismember the other in case the Black Republican candidate should be elected.[18]

According to several historians, most Southerners who voted for Breckinridge were not voting for secession;

therefore, disunion was not really an issue in the election of 1860.[19] Southern Unionist newspapers were convinced otherwise and did their best during the campaign to attach the onus of disunionism to the Breckinridge party. Repeatedly they accused the Southern-rights Democrats of plotting to overthrow the Union. Indeed, they often relied upon the issue of secession to the exclusion of almost all other campaign material.

Douglas and Bell organs usually avoided Breckinridge himself. It was his supporters whom they found most culpable and most vulnerable. They often quoted such fire-eaters as Lawrence M. Keitt, James L. Orr, Robert Barnwell Rhett, Robert Toombs, and William L. Yancey to demonstrate the secessionism of many of Breckinridge's leading supporters. The Breckinridge advocate most often scored was William L. Yancey, whose "scarlet letter" to James S. Slaughter in 1858 had appeared to call for a secessionist conspiracy of Southern fire-eaters.[20] The Unionist press once again seized upon that missive as the most damning evidence of a plot to precipitate the South into revolution. Without doubt the Slaughter letter was more frequently printed during the campaign than was any other document. Some Unionist journals ran it daily as a reminder of Yancey's treason.[21]

The Nashville *Patriot,* on July 11, published the most elaborate attack against Yancey and his fire-eating cohorts. This multi-columned exposé was copied by Unionist papers all over the South and also circulated in pamphlet form.[22] Basically, the *Patriot* and other anti-Breckinridge papers accused Yancey and his fellow "conspirators" of plotting several steps in order finally to achieve a disruption of the Union. First, they had planned to split the Democratic party; this they had accomplished by the secessions from Charleston and Baltimore. Next, the "seceders" had nominated their own candidate in order to so weaken the party's regular nominee, Douglas, that he would have no chance to defeat Lincoln. Meanwhile, asserted the Unionist press, Breckinridge papers were to preach secession in the event of Lincoln's election, an event which Southern-rights politicians were working assiduously to achieve. In such manner would Southerners be prepared for "precipitation out of the Union."[23]

If Bell and Douglas papers found the leaders of the "disunion conspiracy" guilty of treason, they found the rank and file of the Southern-rights party to be willing followers. An Arkansas paper asserted that nine tenths of Breckinridge's supporters in that state hoped for a Lincoln victory and secession. Breckinridge's backers in Georgia were out-and-out for disunion, declared a pro-Bell editor in that state. And the New Orleans *Bee* wrote: "Point out through the entire extent of the land an individual who is anxious to witness a dissolution of the Union and we will show you a supporter of John C. Breckinridge."[24]

Unionist editors seldom accused Breckinridge himself of disunionism; they were satisfied to find him guilty by association. Until Breckinridge repudiated such men as Yancey, Orr, and Rhett, argued the Alexandria (Louisiana) *Constitutional,* he was guilty of treason: "All the eloquence of a Cicero will not aid his cause, nay! the blood of a thousand bullocks will not suffice to wipe out the indictment. Guilty! Guilty!!" One pro-Bell paper in Virginia admitted that Breckinridge was no disunionist, but added: "And yet there can be no question that he has suffered himself to be used by the enemies of the Constitution and the Union." A Mississippi journal observed: "Light has no fellowship with darkness. If Mr. Breckinridge is loyal, why is he the leader of the disaffected and disloyal?" Perhaps the most laconic indictment of the Kentuckian appeared in the San Antonio *Alamo Express:*

"Mr. Breckinridge claims that he isn't a disunionist. An animal not willing to pass for a pig shouldn't stay in the stye."[25]

Many Breckinridge newspapers gave the Unionist press ample grounds for its accusations. Mississippi papers ceased publishing much from the speeches of Jefferson Davis when he became cautious and guarded in his remarks on the issue of secession in the event of Lincoln's election. Meanwhile, Ethelbert C. Barksdale of the Jackson *Mississippian* proudly announced that ninety-nine of every hundred Breckinridge supporters advocated secession, should Lincoln win. By July even the most conservative of South Carolina's journals backed secession in the event of a Lincoln victory. Moreover, the Charleston *Mercury* openly boasted of its part in creating the division within the Democratic party. Other Breckinridge papers of the lower South often frankly admitted a preference for Lincoln over Bell and Douglas. For example, the Woodville (Mississippi) *Republican* asserted: "The election of Breckinridge will save the South and the Union; the election of Lincoln may save the South; but the election of Bell or Douglas will surrender the South to the fanaticism of the North."[26]

Still other Breckinridge papers of the lower South seemed to desire disunion regardless of the election's outcome. Even as the Claiborne (Alabama) *Southern Champion* endorsed Breckinridge, it wrote: "Give us that Gulf Confederacy. It is the only hope for the South." In a like manner another country paper in the same state announced its support of Breckinridge and added: "We have unwaveringly contended for the last ten years that it would be better (for all concerned) to make two or more distinct governments of all the territory comprising the United States of America—and that such will be done, there can be no sort of doubt." The Houma (Louisiana)

Ceres said: "Although a Disunionist, we feel compelled to support Breckinridge and Lane, as they are the only men representing a party true to the South."[27] Most Southern-rights papers, however, were embarrassed by such candid professions of secessionism and sought to discredit the Unionist efforts to identify their movement with disunion. The South might be jealous of her rights, but she also still regarded Andrew Jackson as a hero for suppressing sectionalism in South Carolina in 1832–33. To be too closely associated with disunionism might still mean political disaster in most areas of the South in the fall of 1860.

Breckinridge himself, who had planned an inactive campaign, was forced to make a speech in his own defense.[28] His press, particularly in the upper South, ardently defended him from the Unionist assault. For example, Tennessee's Jonesborough *Union* denied the charge of disunionism against Breckinridge and Lane and added: "A more disgraceful and reckless calumny was never uttered. We will not characterize the assertion as it should be, for decency forbids it." Another Breckinridge advocate in the same state called the Unionist allegations "most ridiculous"; a Virginia journal thought them "absurd, false and slanderous"; and to a Louisiana Southern-rights paper they were "degrading." Even the radically Southern-rights Newberry (South Carolina) *Rising Sun* said of Breckinridge and Lane: "Two stronger simon-pure, fixed *Union* men never breathed the breath of life. No particle of disunion about them. They are Union all over, body and soul."[29]

Defending Yancey was more difficult, and some Breckinridge organs frankly admitted the presence in the Breckinridge ranks of some secessionist soldiers. But a few bad troops did not spoil the whole army, they argued. "What if a hundred disunionists were in favor of the ticket?" asked the Plaquemine (Louisiana) *Gazette and Sentinel:*

"If the fountain head of the great party itself is pure, free from the accursed taint of disunion (which we hope has a barren soil in the land,) it is all and enough for the patriot to know." Others denied that Yancey was an outright secessionist. Declaring that the Alabama fire-eater was great enough to be compared with Thomas Jefferson, a Virginia paper further wrote: "Like other great men, he is very much slandered." After all, an Alabama journal pointed out, Yancey's famous letter to Slaughter had called for secession, "only at the next aggression."[30]

Breckinridge newspapers were not above throwing the charge of disunion back into the faces of Bell editors. They recalled a speech Bell had made in the Senate during the territorial crisis of 1850, in which he had said: "If our future career is to be one of eternal discord, of angry crimination and recrimination, give me rather separation with all its consequences." Many Breckinridge editors printed the condemnatory sentence and professed to be scandalized by the Unionist's "extremism." The Florence (Alabama) *Gazette* demanded: "Tell us, kind friends of the Union, is John Bell a Disunionist? In our opinion, he has gone farther than any living politician." "Let the Bell Clappers ring the changes on Bell's disunionism," wrote a Georgia paper.[31]

So strongly did the Breckinridge papers protest their loyalty to the Union that some Unionist journals took sardonic notice of this new emphasis by the Southern-rights press. The Wheeling *Daily Intelligencer* thought it interesting that each of the two Democratic parties now solemnly declared itself to be more "national" than the other and, in a later editorial, added: "It is really cheering to know that the Union is not to be 'incontinently smashed' by our Southern friends in the event of Lincoln's election. They are growing more merciful. A few months ago the nomination of a Republican candidate was enough to throw them into spasms of secession eloquence." An independent Virginia paper observed: "All the political parties now in the field are unanimous and vehement in their protestations of devotion to the Union, from which we conclude that the Union is popular."[32]

But secession was far from being a dead issue. Indeed the theory and practice of secession were much more thoroughly debated during the campaign than in the preconvention period. Unionist papers now frequently denied the legality of secession and accused its exponents of treason. The hallowed names of Washington, Jefferson, Clay, Webster, and especially Jackson often were invoked to demonstrate the scorn which the great leaders of the past had held for secession. The San Antonio *Alamo Express* asked: "Is it truly so that what Washington and Madison, Jefferson and Jackson, called TREASON, and the people then called TREASON, is now looked upon as a *harmless* enterprise and peaceful remedies?"[33] Southern-rights journals naturally bristled at such tactics. The pro-Breckinridge Montgomery (Alabama) *Weekly Advertiser* wrote: "Whenever the opposition to the Democracy desire to pull wool over the eyes of honest people, to lull them into quiet while they would rob them—they invoke Jackson, Jefferson, Madison, and other great lights, and quote them to bolster up and cover their sneaking designs—just as the abolitionists quote the same men, and just, too, as the devil quotes scripture. . . . Too many rings of the coon's tail are left exposed in this matter to cajole any old Jackson Democrat. Neither of these great men ever counselled their countrymen to submit to be robbed of their rights and property for the sake of the Union or for any other purpose; and it is deplorable that there are men in the present day who dare desecrate their memories by imputing to them such cowardly sentiments."[34]

Not only was secession illegal, argued Unionist editors,

it was also highly impractical. War must surely follow any attempt to secede. Had not the great Daniel Webster demonstrated in his famous seventh of March speech in 1850 the impossibility of "peaceable secession?"[35] Unionist papers often painted bleak and terrible pictures of a seceded and besieged South. "Our beautiful cotton and other fields would soon be converted into soldiers' camps and flooded with human blood," said the Shreveport (Louisiana) *South-Western*. The result of secession, warned another Louisiana paper, would be, "not dissolution, but a war of extermination the very prospect of which sends a thrill of horror through every patriotic heart." A North Carolina journal wrote: "We cannot believe that they [North Carolina's citizens] are willing to see their hearthstones desolate, their now smiling fields harrowed by cannon balls, and manured with human blood and bones, and worse than all, their wives and daughters subjected to butchery, or a yet more wretched fate, at the hands of a brutal and licentious soldiery." To the Richmond *Central Presbyterian* the most horrible aspect of the predicted civil war was not the carnage, but "the corrupting habits contracted in the camp," which at war's end would "scatter seeds of vice and crime through the whole length and breadth of the land. . . . The grim slaughter of a hundred battle fields would be more endurable than one moral death which war, especially civil war, engenders."[36]

Antisecession papers further condemned a dissolution of the Union on economic grounds. They predicted that the South's secession would signal the destruction of the cotton, sugar, land, and slave markets in the South. "Suffer it [the Union] to be rent asunder, and you are lost, lost forever!" admonished the Wadesborough *North Carolina Argus:* "Your hopes—your prospects—your prosperity— your houses and lands—your bank stock and your bank notes, *what will they be worth?*" A Virginia paper warned:

"Let the schemes of the Disunionists be carried out, and the rich lands along the Potomac, which now teem with abundance and are valued at from fifty to sixty dollars an acre, would not bring as many cents. Negroes, which are now worth one thousand dollars a head, in six months would not be worth the taxes now paid upon them."[37]

Even excessive talk about disunion might prove ruinous, said the opponents of secession. The Montgomery (Alabama) *Confederation* warned secessionists: "Just go ahead with your shouts and huzzas for disunion and revolution one month longer, and then you will have something to complain of. You haven't seen anything yet. Just let the impression get out, and be pretty generally believed, that the Union is going to be dissolved, and we will see whether you can sell cotton, or anything else, at any price at all."[38]

Many Unionist papers of the Upper South also accused Southern-rightists of plotting to reopen the African slave trade, a step which would ruin the border states' lucrative slave market in the cotton states.[39]

It was more difficult for Breckinridge editors to defend secession than it was for Unionist editors to denounce it. Southern-rights Democratic journals were forced into the seemingly contradictory position of justifying the doctrine of secession and, at the same time, of protesting their party's innocence of any disunionist taint. The efforts of Southern-rights editors to reconcile their antisecessionist professions with their belief that the South must leave the Union in the event of Lincoln's election inspired a good deal of illogical exposition. One Arkansas supporter of Breckinridge sounded like a Bell journal when it declared: "Secession is an unpopular phrase and tenet. It is an odious doctrine, in the narrow and ultra sense of the term. . . . It is so odious because hated by a vast majority of citizens from the absolute injury, not to say destruction, it would bring upon a community." Then, in mid-editorial,

the paper began to sound more like the orthodox Southern-rights journal it was: "But the right of revolution,
under oppression or where a solemn National compact is
repeatedly and boldly infracted, or its guarantees are per-
petually and manifestly jeopardized, is essential to freedom. Such a separation of the South from the North could
not be called secession." A remarkable concluding sentence demonstrated the need for Southern-rights papers,
at least in the Upper South, to dissociate themselves from
ultra-secessionists such as Yancey and Rhett: "Revolutions
in government are no trifles; they are *never* to be *precipitated.*"[40] Most Southern-rights journals neatly and logically resolved their apparent ambivalence toward the doctrine of secession by arguing that the Union could be saved
only by those who were willing to risk its dissolution under
certain circumstances.

Few Southern-rights editors professed to believe in secession without further provocation, but almost all contended
that the South could secede if its rights were violated. In
the view of Breckinridge editors, only a Union in which
there was mutual respect and perfect equality among the
states was worth preserving. States-rights Democratic papers thus justified and threatened secession, they said, not
because they loved the Union less, but because they loved
it more than did the "Union-savers." Only if the South
stood firmly on its "rights" would the North come to its
senses and mend its ways before disunion became inevitable. Those who manfully sounded the secession alarm,
therefore, were the true friends of the Union as well as
of the South. Conversely, those who cried: "The Union at
any price!" were, in reality, the enemies of both the Union
and the South.[41]

But suppose the firm policy advocated by the Breckinridge party did result in a dissolution of the Union? Then
the sin would fall upon the North and not the South,

argued Southern-rights newspapers. "Will it be our fault?" asked a Virginia paper: "Is it a *crime* to contend for our rights, against a political party . . . which says we shall not have them? In a Union based upon the equality of the States, is that equality to be destroyed without a struggle?" The Jackson *Weekly Mississippian* wrote: "It does not seem to occur to the aggressors, that if there is any disunion, in consequence of the aggressions, that *they are the disunionists*. Disunion, which follows a perverted Union, is the work of the pervertors. He who violates a contract is the true author of a dissolution of the contract made, in consequence of his violation."[42]

Southern-rights journals also contradicted the Unionist contention that secession would bring economic disaster. Just the opposite was true, they said. For too long the South had labored under the incubus of an exploitative Northern tariff; a separation now would usher in a period of unprecedented prosperity. The Charleston *Mercury* wrote that the South, "in control of her own commerce and destinies, will bound forward in a career of prosperity and power, unsurpassed in the history of the world." The North, on the other hand, would be plunged into depression. Manufacturing, commercial, and shipping interests in the North all would be destroyed if the South should secede, predicted the Fernandina *East Floridian:* "The South in the meantime would suffer nothing." A Georgia paper estimated that the South had contributed $231,500,000 to the support of "Northern enmity towards the South . . . . Peaceable secession will be the salvation and the glorification of the South." The same paper further believed that New Yorkers must be made "to reflect upon the consequences to them, to see the grass growing on Broadway, and the Fifth Avenue palaces tottering in decay, as will inevitably be the case should the South secede."[43]

Breckinridge supporters denied that war would inevitably follow secession. Southern-rights sheets deplored the horrible pictures of civil war painted by Unionist editors. For example, the Corsicana (Texas) *Navarro Express* scoffed at those who imagined secession to be fraught with "hobgoblins": "Secession, if approached and examined thoroughly, will be found not to be that terrible Gorgon which the submission journals imagine or attempt to make others believe." The Charleston *Mercury* minimized the threat of war by demonstrating the North's economic dependence upon the South: "Peace therefore, will be the policy—the *necessity* of the North with the South, in case the Union is dissolved."[44]

Southern editors from June to September gave little space to Lincoln and his party. They were too involved in Southern campaign battles, in which Lincoln figured only as a bogeyman to be resisted, not as a politician to be defeated. "Mr. Lincoln having no party in our State, we have not thought it proper to spend much of our ammunition upon him," explained the pro-Breckinridge Atlanta *Daily Intelligencer.*[45]

Newspaper editorials dealing with the program of the Republican party were as rare during the summer as articles on the party's leading personalities. Southerners who wished to examine the Republican platform probably did not consult papers of their own section, since few of them published it.[46] There was only an occasional article reiterating the view that the Republican party planned to abolish slavery as soon as it could gain control of the government.[47] All Southerners concurred in a negative opinion on Lincoln's party, said the Nashville *Republican Banner,* a Bell paper:

We have not, therefore, in this canvass, devoted much of our space to an exposition of the position and purposes of the Republican party, preferring rather to leave that duty to our gallant

Northern Union men, who have the enemy in their midst, while we meanwhile turn our attention to the sectional spirit which infests the Southern states, and which, under the lead of such restless and dangerous spirits as Yancey, Keitt, Rhett, Spratt, and their fellow-disunionists, threatens, equally with Republicanism North, to prove a wedge to split the Union in twain.[48]

Virtually the only Republicans able to divert the attention of Southern editors from their bitter internecine political war were Senators Charles Sumner and William H. Seward. On June 4 Sumner made in the Senate one of the venomous attacks upon slavery and slaveholders for which he was famous. The Massachusetts senator had only partially recovered from the vicious beating which he had received at the hands of Preston Brooks on the Senate floor nearly four years before. That celebrated incident had been in response to Sumner's scathing indictment of the South, entitled "The Crime Against Kansas." Still weakened, but undeterred, by that near-fatal chastisement, Sumner now stood once more to point the finger of condemnation at the South. The title of Sumner's oration, "The Barbarism of Slavery," was indicative of its contents. Slavery, he said, far from being the cornerstone of a superior civilization, as its advocates claimed, was a cursed institution that brutalized both master and slave. "Barbarous in origin; barbarous in the instruments it employs; barbarous in consequences; barbarous in spirit; barbarous wherever it shows itself, Slavery must breed Barbarians."[49]

Southerners in Washington were outraged. For days after the speech they greeted each other by asking whether Sumner had "got it yet." So intense was the Southern reaction to Sumner's speech that the senator's friends feared for his life—so much so that they took steps to protect him, surrounding him, day and night, with armed guards.[50] Elsewhere, throughout the South, Southern newspapers of all parties were scandalized by Sumner's speech.

The conservative New Orleans *Daily Picayune* called the speech "the most furiously bitter and malignant tirade against slavery and slaveholding . . . which has ever been uttered in this country by a man above the standard of Fred Douglass or Garrison." One North Carolina paper scarcely could find enough words to describe the tirade: "Charles Sumner's recent speech is a curiosity that has no parallel, at least on our Senatorial record. Pedantry, egotism, fatuitious [*sic,*] hypothesis, malice, rhapsody and verbosity stripe and emblazon it with disgusting conspicuousness." Said a Georgia paper: "All the punishment Sumner deserves is a cowhiding from the hands of a big buck nigger."[51] Seward made several antislavery speeches during a late-summer tour of the Midwest; however, since his speeches were less vicious than Sumner's oration, they provoked a somewhat milder reaction.[52]

Not surprisingly, radical Southern-rights journals sometimes cited the speeches of Sumner and Seward as illustrative of the reason why the South could not remain in the Union if the Republicans should win the election. The Austin (Texas) *State Gazette* articulated the views of such papers on October 13, when it wrote of Sumner: "With such a bloated and corrupt carcass at the North, can there be a Union of the South? Never! Never!"[53] Well might the *State Gazette* fulminate. It had only recently played a significant role in convincing much of the South that Sumner's party was guilty of aiding and abetting what appeared to be the worst American slave insurrection since 1831, when Southampton County, Virginia, had felt the avenging hand of Nat Turner.

V

By the Light of
the Texas Flames

SOUTHERN newspapers neglected Republican activities in the North, but they more than compensated for the oversight by disclosing allegations of a vast, insidious abolitionist plot to burn many towns in Texas and to murder their citizens. No other issue during this emotion-charged campaign so completely caught the fearful imaginations of Southern editors as the "Texas Troubles." Breaking as they did just before the climax of the campaign, the sometimes irrational, usually exaggerated, and always vivid stories of the alleged abolitionist scheme probably did more than any other issue to steel the minds of many Southerners against the acceptance of a Republican President.[1]

The sensational reports grew out of costly fires which occurred almost simultaneously on July 8 in Dallas, Denton, and Pilot Point. In each of these towns the fires began mysteriously on a hot Sunday afternoon. Since most of the residents of the ill-fated communities had taken refuge in their homes from the 106°–110° heat, the fires were not discovered until it was too late to prevent extensive damage. A lengthy drouth had made the predominantly wooden structures tinder-dry, and a strong southwesterly wind fanned the flames, adding to the extent of the destruction in all three towns. An estimated $400,000 damage was done in Dallas alone. Denton reportedly suffered $80,000 damage.[2]

Although the fires occurred on the same afternoon and not more than forty miles apart, there was no immediate effort to blame the conflagration upon arsonists; newspapers attributed them to a combination of carelessness and the exceedingly dry, hot summer. Nevertheless, the potential was great for a slave-insurrection panic. Throughout the decade of the 1850s, Texas had been extremely susceptible to rumors of slave revolts. Only the previous year, citizens of Dallas had beaten and expelled two Northern Methodist ministers, William Blunt and Solomon McKinney, for allegedly preaching insurrection to slaves. It was hardly surprising that, soon after the fire, little knots of men gathered on street corners, "grim-faced, and speaking in hushed tones," amid the still smoldering ruins of Dallas. Many years later, Judge Nat M. Burford recalled: "They were desperate. They gathered in groups and they were sure that nothing was said in the presence of anybody who was not known to be with them."[3]

Cyrill Miller, a farmer who lived near Dallas, apparently supplied the "evidence" for which the suspicious Dallasites were looking. Miller lost his barn to fire a few days after Dallas had burned. Suspecting his slaves of setting fire to his property, he reportedly forced a confession from a small Negro boy by threatening to kill him if he refused to reveal the identity of the conspirators and warning him that if he died lying, "the devil would get him sure." The young Negro's confession led to the interrogation of other blacks, and there unfolded an incredible story of abolitionist-planned arson, murder, and rapine. By mid-July, the rest of the Southern people began to hear, via their newspapers, the horrifying details of the Dallas "plot."[4]

The chief publicist of the "plot" was Charles R. Pryor,

pro-Breckinridge editor of the Dallas *Herald*. Undaunted by the destruction of his own press and office, Pryor spread the alarm in a series of letters to other editors of a similar political persuasion. On July 12 Pryor wrote a frightful account to another Breckinridge advocate, John Marshall, editor of the Austin *State Gazette*. For reasons which Pryor did not bother to reveal, the whites had come to suspect certain Negroes of deliberately setting the Dallas fire. The suspected blacks had been arrested.

"and in the course of the examination the particulars of the plot were elicited. . . . It was determined by certain Abolition preachers, who were expelled from the country last year [Blunt and McKinney], to devastate, with fire and assassination, the whole of Northern Texas, and when it was reduced to a helpless condition, a general revolt of the slaves, aided by the white men of the North in our midst, was to come off on the day of election in August. . . .

The stores throughout the country containing powder and lead were to be burned, with the grain, and thus reduce [*sic*] this portion of the country to helplessness. When this was accomplished, assistance was expected from the Indians and Abolitionists.[5]

Pryor followed this alarming missive with one to another Breckinridge supporter, L. C. De Lisle of the Bonham *Era*. In this second letter, Pryor gave further details of the plot. The conspirators allegedly planned no less than the devastation of "this entire portion of Northern Texas, extending even to the Red River counties. . . . The whole plan is systematically conceived, and most ingeniously contrived. It makes the blood run cold to hear the details." The culprits were well organized: "Their sphere of operations is districted and sub-districted, giving to each division a close supervision by one energetic white man who controls the negroes as his subordinates." Calling the conspiracy "a regular invasion, and a real war," Pryor urged the editor of the *Era* to sound the tocsin in the Red River counties of North Texas:

You and all Bonham are in as much danger as we are. Be on your guard, and make these facts known by issuing extras to be sent in every direction. All business has ceased, and the country is terribly excited.

> In haste,
> yours, truly,
> Charles R. Pryor[6]

Pryor sent a third letter to E. H. Cushing, editor of the Houston *Telegraph* and another Breckinridge stalwart. This third version of the conspiracy was similar to the other two, but it added some new, even more sinister, details. Many prominent white citizens had been singled out for assassination and would be shot "whenever they made their escape [*sic*] from their burning homes." Poison was to be added to wells, presumably to take care of those who escaped death at the hands of the incendiaries. Negro participation now was alleged to be even more general than had been thought. "Negroes never before suspected are implicated," wrote Pryor, "and the insurrectionary movement is wide spread to an extent truly alarming." Pryor's letter to Cushing also added news of a sort that always struck the most sensitive racial nerves of white Southerners. Insurrectionary blacks not only would murder the white men and old white females, but young white maidens they would distribute among themselves for the satisfaction of their bestial appetites. "They had even gone so far as to designate their choice [*sic*], and certain ladies had already been selected as the victims of these misguided monsters."[7]

Other Breckinridge papers in Texas and throughout the South unquestioningly accepted the allegations made in Pryor's letters. One Texas editor added the following postscript to a lengthy story which had unequivocally attributed the Dallas fire to spontaneous combustion: "It is now believed Abolition emissaries [*sic*] were the incendiaries." A number of other fires occurred in such Texas communities as Ladonia, Honey Grove, Belknap, and Henderson, making it easier for Texans to believe Pryor's allegations of a widespread plot. The blaze at Henderson, which occurred on August 5, was the most spectacular, and the most costly, of the later fires. The entire business section of the town was destroyed, and damage was estimated to be $200,000.[8] The number of Texas towns allegedly victimized by Negro firebrands increased almost daily. At least two dozen towns were said to be included in the abolitionist scheme to commit arson.[9]

The Texas "conspiracy" apparently was contagious. In August and September the press alleged that similar, if less extensive, plots existed throughout the South. Abolitionists reportedly had planned murder, fire, and rapine for many communities—most notably in Virginia, Georgia, Alabama, Mississippi, and Arkansas.[10] The many hangings and whippings that occurred during the summer of 1860 make it clear that in the aftermath of the Texas fires the South experienced one of the greatest witch hunts in American history. The press, which gave screaming headlines to each new rumor, played the key role in spreading fear. Editors all over the South reprinted Pryor's shocking account of the Dallas plot and reminded their readers that, unless the strictest vigilance was observed, Texas's sad plight might become their own as well. Papers defended Judge Lynch as the best means of dealing with "abolitionist emissaries," who allegedly had infiltrated virtually every community in the South.

Meanwhile, hysteria swept Texas. On the eve of the state elections, which were to be held on August 6, many people sat up all night with guns in their hands, determined to sell their lives dearly when the expected insurrection began. On a farm near Marshall, a woman heard a firearm discharge in the distance. Apparently thinking that she was about to be seized by Negroes and abolitionists and unable to appeal to her husband who was in town voting, she fled into the woods. A search party finally located her the next day, miles from home, and "in a wretched condition." Another report stated that fear had made a number of Texas women and children "almost confirmed maniacs."[11]

Communities from the Red River to the Gulf of Mexico formed vigilance committees to ferret out and punish guilty Negroes and their white co-conspirators. Southerners had often utilized such committees before. Many apparently believed that the ordinary legal processes were too slow and too restrictive to deal effectively with slave-tamperers and incendiaries. Vigilance committees, on the other hand, were unhampered by due process of law; therefore, they could act expeditiously, often on the flimsiest of evidence, to quash any real or imagined threat. There may have been another reason for the reversion to vigilante law during the panic of 1860. Negro testimony, which was virtually the only evidence of an abolitionist conspiracy, could not be used against white men in a court of law.[12] Thus in the eyes of many whites it was necessary to set aside, temporarily at least, the usual process of law enforcement. With few exceptions, sheriffs and judges acquiesced in the usurpation of their powers by vigilance committees.

The vigilance committees were large, usually numbering from fifty to one-hundred men. They quickly established night patrols to protect their communities from Negro and abolitionist firebrands. In the town of Rusk, for example, seventy-six men stood vigil, and the Rusk *Enquirer* reported that "no man can walk fifty steps during the night without being hailed by one of those vigilant sentinels." The Tyler *Reporter* attributed Tyler's escape from incendiarism to the constant vigilance of the town's citizens. "Over one hundred citizens are on patrol duty every night. Every man who is met by one of them is hailed, and if he fails or refuses to answer, his life would not be worth a straw." Even newsmen apparently were expected to serve on the night patrol in Tyler. At the height of the excitement the *Reporter* observed that every man on its staff had been on duty for four consecutive nights, "and we are all completely worn out, and if this excitement still continues to exist, we must stop our regular issues, and furnish the news in the form of extras, for it is impossible for us to watch all night and work all day. We shall keep up, however, as long as possible."[13]

The suspicions of vigilance committees often fastened upon white men of Northern origins, particularly upon those who had recently come south. An unidentified correspondent to the New York *Daily Tribune* reported that all Northern men were now considered "unsafe for reliance on that 'tender vital question to the South' [i.e., slavery]." Vigilance committees closely questioned and scrutinized every stranger, and if a Northern accent was detected "he is at once suspected of being a possible Abolitionist emissary." Individuals who were unfortunate enough to have been born and bred on the "wrong" side of the Mason-Dixon Line often were considered guilty of abolitionism until they had proven their innocence. One Texas journal asserted that abolitionists were about in various disguises and warned: "Northern men of recent emigration, of all classes, trades, and profession must, in justice to ourselves, be watched, until they have proven themselves reliable. Dangerous times demand and justify this course." A committee in Ellis County passed a resolution stating that all persons who had come from free states would be suspected of abolitionism, unless they could produce "satisfactory evidence" that they held no antislavery opinions. And a citizen of Fort Worth wrote that it was "the universal sentiment of this community," that "it is better for us to hang ninety-nine innocent (suspicious) men than to let one guilty one pass, for the guilty one endangers the peace of society, and every man coming from a northern State should live above suspicion."[14]

Traveling in Texas was particularly hazardous during August and September. Vigilance committeemen in Dallas carefully searched the wagons of Northern immigrants passing through their town; however, they never found evidence to indicate that any of the newcomers were abolitionists. One resident of Rusk later recalled that patrols in that town carefully scrutinized the credentials of each passing stranger. "The poor pedlar [sic], especially, was in imminent danger of being mobbed at any time on mere suspicion."[15] A Virginia paper wisely commented: "It strikes us Texas would be a very unwholesome State just now for emigrants."[16]

Even native Southerners had to take care when traveling, lest they, too, be accused of abolitionist activities. The New Orleans *Picayune* told of a respected New Orleans slaveholder who, while on a business trip to Texas, barely escaped a crazed lynch mob, which believed him to be an abolitionist. In Clarksville, vigilantes seized one J. M. Peers, an itinerant worker, and accused him of burning Henderson. After being jailed, beaten, robbed, and threatened several times with death by hanging, Peers was released and made his way to Marshall, where, ironically, he was well known as a proslavery zealot, who recently had engaged in routing "abolitionists" from East Texas. Noting that Peers was a subscriber to such fire-eating journals as the Richmond *Enquirer,* the Galveston *News,* the New Orleans *Delta,* "and several other journals of similar politics," the Marshall *Texas Republican* observed: "If he is sound upon anything we should suppose it was the 'nigger question.'" One man, writing from Marshall to his father in Houston, said that he expected to have difficulty on an impending business trip to Red River County. "Every man that travels through this country is taken up and examined, and if he does not give a good account of himself, he is strung up to the nearest tree. I have to get a passport from here to Red River, and then, I expect to have a hard time getting through, for a man's word is nothing in these critical times."[17]

Newspapers frequently urged the committees to impose the death penalty upon abolitionists. The Corsicana *Navarro Express,* for example, called lynching "an excellent plan to rid our country of such characters, and the only sure one. Let us put it into practice." Even religious papers sometimes betrayed a blood lust when speaking of alleged insurrectionaries. The *Texas Baptist* credited God for its escape "from the murderous hands of our enemies" but apparently believed that the Divine Arm needed human supplementation: "We would not encourage the taking of human life, or the shedding of man's blood, when it can be avoided but if any of these demons are caught in our country they will be shot like wolves or hung like dogs, just as they ought to be."[18]

Vigilance committees had little need of such encouragement. Many alleged white abolitionists and Negroes expiated their "crimes" on the gallows. Three blacks were hanged in Dallas for setting the fire in that city. Two white men, who were accused of inciting Negro violence in Tarrant County, were hanged at Fort Worth. A white man and a Negro woman were lynched at Henderson, after a vigilance committee adjudged them guilty of setting fire to that city. Two white preachers died on the gallows in Grimes County for alleged abolitionist activities. And so it went throughout North Central and East Texas.[19]

Although first-hand reports confirm about thirty "executions," the total number of deaths that resulted from the panic is unknown; vigilance committees failed to leave records of trials and executions. Moreover, the vigilante guardians of the public safety often worked in secrecy, ostensibly because they deemed it essential that the "abolitionist plotters" not discover the details of their deliberations. At the height of the panic in North Central Texas a citizen of Ellis County reported: "No one but those immediately interested know who compose the committees, nor where or when they meet, or what they are doing." Thus, while a number of executions were highly publicized, many others occurred at least half secretly, in the more traditional mode of Southern lynchings. According to the Belton *Democrat,* North Texas vigilantes had "quietly hung" several "abolitionists" so that other suspects would not become alarmed and flee before the "appropriate committees" could take them into custody. The Galveston *Civilian and Gazette* cited reports of executions that had been carried out secretly, "by men disguised and unknown to either the parties punished or the people at large." An almost casual announcement in the Weatherford *White Man* exemplified the work of the phantom vigilantes: "ANOTHER MAN HUNG— A man was found at Hannah's Tank, on Big Creek in McClellan county, on Sunday, last—supposed to be an abolitionist."[20]

It may be that most of the deaths resulting from the Texas Terror went almost entirely unpublicized. For example, there were persistent rumors that two preachers were hanged, two Negroes burned to death, and another fatally whipped, at Dallas. And, although the newspapers reported only two white men hanged at Fort Worth, Colonel Nathaniel Terry, in a letter to a friend at Rusk, asserted that seven white men had been hanged already and added, "and I expect before it is over not less than fifty Negroes will be hung." As early as August 12, a correspondent of the New York *Day Book,* identified only as "W.R.D.W.," wrote: "But unfortunately up to this time Judge Lynch has had the honor to preside only in ten cases of whites, (Northern

Lincolnites) and about sixty-five of negroes, all of whom were hung or burnt, as to the degree of their implication in the rebellion or burning." Even allowing for possible exaggerations in these reports, it seems likely that at least fifty men, black and white, lost their lives between July and October in consequence of the worst Southern slave panic since the Nat Turner insurrection.[21]

Not all suspects were killed. Vigilance committees evicted many suspicious whites from the state.[22] Some of the exiles only narrowly escaped with their lives. At Caddo, in Milam County, a white man named Cawly, who was accused by certain Negroes of attempting to incite them to insurrection, was hailed before the local vigilance committee. "Some," said the Cameron *Sentinel,* "were in favor of hanging, others banishing. The rope was placed around his neck and all was ready for a swing, when those opposed to this method of disposing of him prevailed, and he was released with the positive order to immediately leave the country."[23] Another Texas journal reported that an abolitionist suspect was arrested at Quitman, "and his life would have paid the forfeit, had not his wife's tears and supplications prevented it."[24]

Small wonder that many fled the state to escape the scrutiny of the vigilance committees. By late September three-hundred wagons carrying "suspected incendiaries" were reportedly rolling northward in the vicinity of the Red River.[25] The deep suspicion with which many Texans regarded all Northerners placed many Yankees in precarious positions in the Lone Star State. A Northern businessman, writing to the New York *Tribune* from "somewhere near the sea coast in Texas," probably typified the frustration felt by many residents whose antecedents were north of the Mason-Dixon Line: "No matter how well disposed or quiet an Eastern man here may be, he is continually questioned and annoyed, and distrusted. So a residence here in Texas is at this time exceedingly unpleasant, and were it not for the delay incident to disposing of my goods, I should depart hence without delay at once."[26]

Some editors refused to be stampeded into panic by the sensational reporting of their colleagues. It was beyond doubt that there had been several disastrous fires in northern Texas, but the Texas press itself soon made it clear that the fires were not nearly so numerous as first reported. One Southern-rights editor, Thomas J. Crooks of the Paris *Press,* categorically denied published reports that there had been fires or plots in Paris. Another Breckinridge supporter, R. W. Loughery of the Marshall *Texas Republican,* assured the world that Marshall had not yet fallen to an incendiary's torch, as had been reported. The independent Mount Pleasant *Union* refuted yet another widely circulated rumor that abolitionists had burned Mt. Vernon and Daingerfield in Titus County.[27]

Even the sight of smoke was enough in some instances to inspire rumors that a whole town had burned. For example, burning trash in back of the court house in Brenham led to published reports that abolitionists had tried to destroy the town.[28] Widely published reports that incendiaries had attempted to reduce Austin to cinders proved baseless, as did many other accounts of arson.[29] Noting that the editor of the Weatherford *News* had expressed surprise upon reading in one of his exchanges that the town of Weatherford had burned, another Texas journalist commented: "Rumor has burned almost every town in Texas this season."[30]

Nor was it clear that such fires as indisputably had occurred were the work of arsonists. A report that abolitionists had set the costly fire at Fort Belknap proved false, when it was shown that the blaze had started accidentally in one of the government buildings.[31] The fires which damaged stores in the North Texas communities of Ladonia, Honey

Grove, and Milford were incontrovertibly laid to the spontaneous combustion of the new and highly volatile phosphorous matches.[32] A resident of Ellis County, which experienced one of the greatest abolitionist scares in the state, later recalled how the local citizenry learned that spontaneous combustion was the probable cause of the local fires: "It was thought the fires were the work of incendiaries, as in most instances no cause could be traced whereby the buildings could have taken fire from accidental causes, but finally matches in old Uncle Billy Oldham's store in Waxahachie took fire whilst lying on a shelf, right under the sight of the clerks and proprietor, in broad daylight. The cat was out of the bag; the explanation of all the mysterious and alarming conflagrations was plain spontaneous ignition."[33] The committee which investigated the origins of the Denton fire apparently made a similar discovery. C. A. Williams, a resident of Denton at the time of the fire, later recalled that suspicions of abolitionist incendiarism were dispelled after it became known that other fires, which had occurred in the vicinity of Denton at about the same time, had been caused by spontaneous combustion. According to Williams, "the day was an oppressively hot one and there is no doubt in my mind but what the fires were all caused from the matches exploding by reason of the hot weather."[39]

R. F. Tannehill, secretary of the vigilance committee in Athens, reported to the Palestine *Trinity Advocate* that the committee's investigation into allegations of a widespread abolitionist-Negro conspiracy had shown to the committee's satisfaction that no plot existed. Indeed, Negro slaves of the area seemed to be at least as frightened as whites by the stories of abolitionist activity. Two vials which the committee confiscated from Negroes and which assertedly contained deadly poison proved upon examination to contain whiskey and snake root, in one case, and paregoric in the other. "The Vigilance Committee of Athens dissolved itself just as soon as they could," concluded Tannehill, "and the excitement so far as the fear of 'niggers' is concerned has all died away."[35]

There is even reason to believe that the Dallas fire, which gave rise to the panic, began innocently. Thirty-two years after the holocaust, a Dallas reporter sought out several citizens who had resided in the small Trinity River town at the time of the fire and asked them for their recollections. One of those interviewed had served on the vigilance committee which had condemned three Negroes to death. The man at first refused to be interviewed, saying that "this was a bit of Southern history that was not good." But he finally consented to talk and gave his opinion that the Northern Methodist preachers who had been accused of instigating the alleged insurrection were not guilty. "In fact," he said, "there was no insurrection. People became frightened and almost panic stricken." The former vigilante then gave his own version of what had occurred:

When the town was burned it was a hot day—so hot that matches ignited from the heat of the sun. Wallace Peak had just finished a new two-story frame building and in the upper story that day a number of men were lounging and smoking. Piled up near the building was a lot of boxes filled with shavings, and I think a cigar stump or a match was thrown into one of the boxes, and from that the fire started about 2 o'clock in the afternoon. Several fires had occurred; there was a great deal of excitement about the apprehended negro uprising; somebody had to hang and the three negroes went.[36]

In view of the mounting evidence indicating that no plot existed, some Texas journals argued that the Texas "abolitionists" were nothing more than phantoms conjured up by the fertile imaginations of frightened men. "That most of the accounts we have received from the Northern part of the State are falsehoods and sensation tales, is too evident to every well informed man to need contradiction," wrote

the independent La Grange *True Issue*. The pro-Breckinridge Paris *Press* agreed and further declared: "We have
heard so many reports of 'attempted insurrections,' 'well
poisoning,' 'diabolical plans of abolitionists' & c, within
the past few weeks, the majority of which when fully investigated turn out to be totally false, that we are tempted
to disbelieve all reports of this kind." The same paper may
have touched on one reason for the recent proliferation of
"plot" stories when it added: "A thousand rumors are in
circulation every day and the public taste seems to demand
something horrible."[37]

Many Unionists saw more sinister forces behind the panic
than a public demand for the macabre. Governor Sam
Houston, rising from a sickbed to address a mass Union
meeting in Austin, deplored the pernicious effects that the
panic had wrought in the state. Houston dismissed as false
the stories of an abolitionist scheme to destroy Texas and
charged that those responsible for the stories were themselves nonslaveholders, who had deliberately spread false
rumors for political effect.[38] A. B. Norton, editor of the
Austin *Southern Intelligencer,* and leader of the Opposition
press in Texas, agreed with the governor. Norton charged
that Democratic editors, by fabricating and spreading
stories of an abolitionist conspiracy, had sought to inflame
the emotions of the electorate so that the more radical
Southern-rights candidates would win the state elections in
August.[39] Other partisans of the Opposition made the same
allegation. The wife of E. M. Pease, a leading Texas Unionist, wrote to her sister: "There was a little excitement
got up by the newspapers before the election for political
effect—but the stories of fires and murder are all exaggerated."[40] Many anti-Breckinridge newspapers throughout
the South agreed with this assessment of the "Texas
Troubles," and a few reacted with mock alarm to the strident accounts in radical Southern-rights papers. For ex-

ample, the Hayneville (Alabama) *Watchman* parodied the lurid headlines of its fiery competitor, the Montgomery *Mail:*

> Blood, Thunder, Destruction!!
> DESTRUCTION, THUNDER, BLOOD!!
> Blood, Destruction, Thunder!!
> Houses Burnt, Niggers Abolished,
> Things in Confusion!!

"For this startling news we are indebted to that unequalled paper the Montgomery *Mail,* which has made the collection of abolition news a *specialty,* and has it by telegraph very frequently days in advance of its transpiring."[41]

Other conservative papers took a less humorous view of the sensational treatment given to the conspiracy stories by the Breckinridge press. They believed that the "abolitionist plot" in Texas was really a ruse, hatched by the fire-eating press as a means both of swinging undecided Southern voters to Breckinridge and of preparing Southerners for resistance should Lincoln be elected. Wrote the Richmond *Whig*: "We have no doubt that the Breckinridge Disunionists would readily aid the impression that invaders and insurrectionists abound in the Southern States. Their object is to increase the enmity between the sections, in order to bring about a dissolution of the Union." The Newbern (North Carolina) *Weekly Progress* expected such sensational revelations to be "all the rage now until after the election. We wish it was over." The Raymond (Mississippi) *Hinds County Gazette* asserted that all "intelligent citizens" regarded the plot stories "as the groundless fears of very timid people, or the fabrics manufactured for political consumption."[42]

The efforts of some Bell editors to turn what purported to be an abolitionist plot to burn Texas towns into a fire-eater's scheme to intimidate Southern moderates drew a torrent of ridicule from Breckinridge papers. Some Southern-rights editors even questioned the Southern loyalty of those who criticized the brave publicists of so dastardly a conspiracy. The Athens (Georgia) *Southern Banner* suggested that any editor who suppressed the Texas stories "deserves the closest scrutiny himself." The Houston *Telegraph,* one of the most active publicists of Charles Pryor's original allegations, professed to be scandalized by the efforts of the Austin *Southern Intelligencer* and "some other papers of that class" to depict the plot as a Democratic hoax aimed at causing the defeat of Unionism. The *Telegraph* left no doubt as to its answer to the question: "We now ask: Are these men sound on the slavery question?" A committee of citizens in Fort Worth apparently agreed with the *Telegraph*'s opinion of Norton's paper, for it resolved: "That we look upon the course of the Austin Intelligencer, and other papers and persons who attribute the late fires to accident, and who assert that the hue and cry about Abolition incendiarism has been raised for political effect, as insulting to the intelligence of Texas, and as justly subjecting the editor of the Austin Intelligencer, or any other papers or persons guilty of the like offense, to be placed at once on the list of persons whose future course is to be carefully watched by the proper committee."[43]

The quarrel between Norton and John Marshall, the Democratic editor of the *State Gazette,* became so acrimonious that they took steps to resolve their differences on the field of honor. Since dueling was illegal in Texas, the two adversaries set out, separately, for the Indian Territory, some three-hundred miles north of Austin. One laconic resident of Travis county wrote to a brother: "Politics run pretty high with us. Our Editors have gone of [*sic*] to try to kill each other I suppose. . . . Some reflections of Marshalls upon the private character of Nortons is the cause—immediate of the troubles and politics the cause—remote."[44] News of the impending duel went ahead of the feuding editors, however, and when they reached Sherman, in North Texas, they were arrested on the grounds that it was not only illegal to fight a duel in Texas, but it was also against the law to challenge an adversary to such an encounter. The two antagonists were soon released, though not together, and both returned to Austin, their mutual hatred unrequited. There later arose a dispute over allegations by Norton that Marshall had returned to Austin, rather than slip across the Red River and face Norton, who, assertedly, had been willing to proceed with the duel. Marshall hotly denied these insinuations of cowardice. The amused Galveston *Civilian and Gazette,* reporting the fiasco, said that perhaps the two antagonists would henceforth subscribe to the old adage that "the pen is mightier than the sword."[45]

Although some Southern Opposition journals refused, like the *Southern Intelligencer,* to accept the allegations of an abolitionist plot in Texas, many other Unionist newspapers throughout the South accepted the accounts which appeared in Breckinridge journals. The Raleigh *Register* wrote: "The proof of a wide-spread plot in Texas to incite the negroes to insurrection is daily accumulating." A Bell paper in Virginia deplored the recurrence of incidents such as those reported in Texas and asked: "How long if these things continue, will the strain upon the Union bonds continue, before they are broken." Brownlow's Knoxville *Whig* accepted the reports of conflagrations in Texas and commended the towns for forming vigilance committees. Other conservative journals, such as the New Orleans *Daily Picayune* and Montgomery (Alabama) *Weekly Post,* believed the stories to be exaggerated but seemed to feel that where there was so much reportorial smoke there must be at least a little abolitionist fire.[46] The gullibility of even much of the Opposition press, which had heard similarly frightful stories during other elections, demonstrated how

deep were the racial fears which underlay the South's opposition to the Republican party and which made "abolitionist" one of the most terrible words in the Southern
lexicon.

Skeptics charged that Breckinridge supporters had fabri-
cated the plot stories in order to elect radical Democrats to
office and to weaken Unionism in the South; however, the
charge of deliberate fraud cannot be proved. Clearly, there
was a good deal of evidence to indicate that spontaneous
combustion, not incendiaries, ignited the fires of July 8.
Not only did Southern-rights editors frequently ignore such
evidence, they often printed the most irresponsible rumors
of conspiracy without bothering to check the reliability of
their sources. Nevertheless, irresponsibility was a hallmark
of the ante bellum Southern press, and the failure of many
editors to confirm the alleged facts of the rumored abolitionist conspiracy does not prove fraud. The Southern mind
had often shown that it was capable of great credulity where
stories of racial insurrection were concerned, and Pryor and
his colleagues may well have believed the stories which
vigilance committees extorted from frightened Negroes.

Yet even if the radical Southern-rights editors were innocent of charges that they had invented the plot rumors, it
is clear that the general panic which they created by their
emotional reporting of the "conspiracy" served their political purposes perfectly. Indeed it is safe to say that if there
was a conspiracy involved in the "Texas Troubles" it was a
tacit one among members of the radical Southern-rights
press to help elect Breckinridge, and, failing that, to prepare the South for secession.

Fire-eating editors often cited the alleged plot as evidence
that the South must support Breckinridge and that it must
not submit to Lincoln's election. Only Breckinridge, they
asserted, could deliver the South from Dallas's fiery agony.
To the New Orleans *Delta,* the Texas "conspiracy" was

"the logical and inevitable consequence of Black Republican teachings." "If," continued the *Delta*, "Southern States are invaded, Southern property destroyed, Southern towns delivered over to the merciless torch of the incendiary, while the government is still administered by a party friendly to the South, what are we to expect in case an avowedly hostile party, a party whose teachings have stimulated these outrages, a party which avowedly aspires to subjugate the South—what are we to expect in case such a party should gain control of the Federal Administration?" If Breckinridge and Lane should fail to be elected, warned the Fayetteville *Arkansian,* "We believe from the bottom of our souls, that events will immediately take place so dark and terrible that the imagination now refuses to picture them." An Alabama paper asserted: "This [the series of fires in Texas] is the beginning of Black Republican operations in the South! This is *practical Lincolnism!* This is what we must 'acquiesce in,' if we 'acquiesce in' Black Republican government. If Lincoln is elected, let the people see, by the light of the Texas flames, that we shall be forced to fight or go out." Clearly, such journals made no distinction between Republicanism and abolitionism. The editor of the Galveston (Texas) *Christian Advocate* wrote that he could understand how, before the Texas fires, a man might have been duped into joining the Republican party, "but now, how a man can teach abolition doctrines, or support the Black Republican party, and not be a villain, our casuistry does not enable us to determine. Such a man is, logically, an incendiary and murderer, whatever he may be in purpose."[47]

It is impossible to exaggerate the role of the Southern press in fanning the hot-weather flames of the Texas prairie into a roaring inferno of terror that swept the whole South. Pryor's letters to the *State Gazette,* the *Era,* and the *Telegraph* were read and believed by thousands of people throughout the region. Radical Southern-rights editors elaborated upon these fearful reports from Texas and suggested, none too subtly, that this was but the beginning of the horrors Southerners must suffer if they accepted Lincoln as their President. Fire-eating politicians such as Wise of Virginia, Wigfall of Texas, Yancey of Alabama, and others of their ilk chorused their opinion that Lincoln, once ensconced in office, would send abolitionists scurrying into the South to complete the work begun by Brown in Virginia and continued by his cohorts in Texas.

From June to October—or for three-fourths of the presidential campaign—the Southern press had occupied itself primarily with bitter, personal feuds, in which the adherents of Bell and Douglas usually sided against Breckinridge. An outsider reading Southern newspapers might have thought that one or all three of these candidates, but not Lincoln, posed the greatest threat to the South, so vicious were the recriminations. Alleged incendiarism in Texas, followed by abolitionist scares in other states, served to refocus the attention of the Southern press upon Lincoln, and to set the stage for the last month of the campaign, when the dominant question would become: "Would the South submit to Lincoln's election?"

VI

Prejudice Has Usurped
The Place of Reason

DEVELOPMENTS besides Texas incendiarism added urgency in the fall to the newspaper debate over Lincoln's acceptability to the South. Until late in the campaign most Southern papers had definite hopes of defeating Lincoln. Indeed, throughout the summer almost every Southern paper seemed convinced that its candidate alone could defeat the "Black Republican." Some were almost arrogant in asserting their man's claims to the White House. A few were even willing to back their predictions of victory with money. Georgia's Albany *Patriot,* for example, offered to bet $10,-000 that Breckinridge would be the next President, "provided no Providential cause should prevent." The Little Rock *Arkansas State Gazette,* showing somewhat less confidence than the *Patriot,* was willing to wager $100 "that Mr. Bell beats Mr. Breckinridge in the popular vote of each slave-holding State—all of the slave-holding States to be taken together if the bet be made."[1]

By their extravagant optimism, newspapers everywhere so distorted the actual course of the campaign that it was difficult to know which candidate was actually ahead. Commenting upon the conflicting political claims made by the press, the New Orleans *Picayune* wrote:

As might be expected, a strong desire prevails in every section of the Union, to learn the character of public sentiment elsewhere, and the journals of the day are carefully sought to obtain the desired information. But it is scarcely possible for an honest seeker for facts to arrive at any satisfactory conclusions. The advocates of Bell and Everett assert that the country is full of enthusiasm for those representatives of the conservative Union men of the land; the favorers of Douglas assure you that his candidacy is received with an enthusiasm only fitly represented by a fire in the prairies; the admirers of Breckinridge confidently claim the certain support of a large majority of the electoral votes of the nation; while the Black Republicans are absolutely certain that the rail-splitter, Lincoln, will ride upon the wave of popular favor triumphantly into the White House. Every nomination is said to be enthusiastically received everywhere, and every candidate is going to carry every thing.

The *Picayune* could only conclude: "From this confusion of facts and assertions it is impossible to deduce anything reliable in regard to the actual prospects of the canvass."[2]

One reason for the optimism of Southern editors was the effort of Lincoln's opponents in several key Northern states to fuse electoral tickets in order to defeat the Republican candidate. Should Lincoln lose Pennsylvania and New York, the election would go to the House of Representatives, which then would choose as President one of the top three candidates. The House would vote by states, each state casting one vote, and, according to the fusionists, the Republicans would lack two votes having enough to elect Lincoln.[3]

Many Southern papers of all parties seemed genuinely to believe that fusion would be achieved in the critical Northern states. Northern conservatives, they said, would rise up *en masse,* vote the united ticket, and thereby deal the Black Republican monster a death blow. One pro-Bell editor from Georgia, vacationing in Vermont, reported that there was an excellent chance that conservative men in the North would join hands "in one solid phalanx" to "overcome these hordes of fanatics." A conservative New Orleans journal voiced the optimism of many Unionist papers in the South when it opined that the critical state of New York had "a mighty conservative power in that body of citizens who have never bowed the knee to Baal. If the South but shows its determination to stand by the Union, it may be believed New York will stand there too."[4]

Almost all Bell papers advocated fusion, but the bitter legacy of Charleston and Baltimore led many Douglas and Breckinridge journals to oppose any kind of unification, even if the alternative were Lincoln's election. In a cutting denunciation of such a proposal, a pro-Douglas journal in Alabama wrote: "Let us *forever* stand aloof, at least in a state of armed neutrality, from such an intolerant and proscriptive set of Jacobin conspirators." A pro-Breckinridge paper in South Carolina, on the other hand, opposed fusion in the fear that it might result in Douglas's election, which would prove as disastrous to the South as that of Lincoln: "It [fusion] should be viewed by the South with distrust. . . . If Constitutional provisions, Congressional enactments, and a *sense of duty, fail to secure her rights, fusions cannot.*"[5] This feeling of acrimony among factions of the Democratic party apparently extended into the North, for efforts to achieve fusion met with small success.[6]

Though partisanship prevented a perfect coalition of the anti-Republican factions in the North, Southern newspapers persisted in believing that a basically conservative Northern people would vote against Lincoln on November 6. Even this dream vanished when, in October, the state elections in Ohio, Indiana, Pennsylvania, and New York went strongly Republican. "The result of the recent elections in Pennsylvania, Ohio and Indiana, which went with a whoop for the Black Republicans, renders the election of Lincoln and Hamlin almost certain," said the Hayneville (Alabama) *Chronicle*. The Dallas *Herald* considered the Northern state elections "the keynote" of the presidential election and warned: "The first wail of sorrow echoes from that land and seems to breathe a prophetic warning of the great disaster that hangs over us." A Georgia paper wrote: "We are loud to admit that nearly all our Southern exchanges have the entire body of starch taken out of them by the Pennsylvania election." The Albany *Patriot* hastily withdrew its earlier offer to wager $10,000 on Breckinridge.[7]

Viewing the Northern state elections as a certain portent of Republican victory, secessionist papers intensified their warnings that Southerners must soon decide between submission and resistance. Yancey's Montgomery (Alabama) *Advertiser* predicted:

Within one month from this time the South will be called upon to choose between submission to the rule of a party whose avowed purpose is the abolition, not the restriction, of slavery, and a glorious career of uninterrupted prosperity as a separate nationality. We are not permitted to doubt what that choice will be. From every point in our bright and sunny South come the notes of preparation for the great event. We are defeated in the Union, but out of it we are still masters of the world. There will be no bloody conflict now.[8]

Even after the Northern elections some Bell papers still professed hope of defeating Lincoln. "We have a little hope yet left for our cause," said a Georgia paper. And a Tennessee journal speculated: "While Pennsylvania may choose to have a Republican government, it is another thing to choose for herself and force upon the South a Republican President."[9] But such optimism seemed forced and unconvincing. Many other Unionist newspapers frankly admitted that Lincoln's election was virtually assured by the Republican sweep in the Northern elections. As late as October 15 the

San Antonio *Alamo Express* had assessed Lincoln's chances as becoming "small by degrees and beautifully less. . . . In fact, we have good reason to congratulate the country upon the defeat of Abraham Lincoln." One week later, the same paper confessed glumly that returns received from the North augured certain victory for Lincoln. A Georgia paper undoubtedly voiced the apprehensions of many conservative journals in the South when it wrote: "There is a thick gloom overspreading all this land. While the thick cloud hovers over us, there is not a tremor in the air—there is the silence which bodes the storm's fall."[10]

Convinced of the inevitability of Lincoln's election, Southern editors turned from abstract arguments over secession to the immediate question: Should the South secede upon Lincoln's mere election, or should it wait for some "overt act of aggression?" Until the latter part of the campaign most Breckinridge journals avoided making any explicit endorsement of secession in the event of Lincoln's election.[11] There were apparently two reasons for this. Throughout the summer Breckinridge papers generally sought to create an image of Unionism for their party in order to counter the charges of disunionism so often made against them by Bell and Douglas journals. Moreover, until early fall Southern-rights editors remained hopeful of defeating Lincoln, and the question of secession did not seem pressing. In October the realization of an almost certain Republican victory led to an increased radicalism in the Breckinridge press. As late as August 14, according to the moderate Macon *Daily Telegraph,* there were but two newspapers in Georgia pledged unconditionally to disunion in the event of Lincoln's election. On October 25 the same journal reported that it was the only Breckinridge paper in the state still opposed to secession, if Lincoln should win. Ominously, secessionist opinions gained respectability as the election approached. The Knoxville *Register* reported: "Disunionism has been robbed of its hideous mien, and is now philosophically regarded as a safe retreat from greater evils."[12]

Breckinridge papers of the lower South were especially aggressive in declaring for secession in the event of a Republican victory on November 6. Some went so far as to call for a dissolution of the Union regardless of the outcome of the election. Such a journal was the Columbus (Georgia) *Corner Stone,* whose editor wrote: "Yes, we are in favor of going out whether he [Lincoln] is elected or not, no matter who is. To us the election of Lincoln would afford no additional reasons. We have had reason to satisfy us for thirty years—we have been for that length of time satisfied that there was at the north a strong and growing determination to use the power of the Government for our destruction, and for that reason we have desired a dissolution of the Union."[13] An extreme Southern-rights paper in South Carolina implied a similar view when it said that Lincoln's defeat, even by Breckinridge, would at best give the South only a four-year respite from Northern oppression, "but at the end of that time, the same battle will be to fight again, and we had best settle it now." Such declarations as these unquestionably inspired Unionist newspapers to press with new vigor their old charge that Breckinridge supporters desired disunion. The pro-Bell Columbus (Georgia) *Enquirer,* for example, alleged that the *Corner Stone's* partiality to Breckinridge "proves that it knows which party is most likely to aid it in bringing about its heart's desire—the object for which its editor has striven 'for thirty years.' "[14]

Most Breckinridge journals continued to profess a desire to maintain the Union, but only if Lincoln were defeated. "We do not desire disunion," declared the radical Montgomery (Alabama) *Mail;* "We deprecate it—although we hold it as far preferable to submission to Lincoln." Another Southern-rights paper in the same state warned: "Whether there be secession, revolution, or what not, one thing is certain—*Lincoln never can be President of the Southern States.*" A Georgia paper of like persuasion predicted a "Pandora's Box" of evils for the South if it should submit to Lincoln's election.[15]

"Submission" was out of the question, radical Southern-rights and secessionist newspapers reasserted, because Lincoln and his party hated slavery and must therefore do all within their power to abolish it. A leading Democratic organ in Louisiana quoted the Chicago *Press,* which it called "the home organ of Mr. Lincoln," to the effect that the eventual aim of the Republican party was the emancipation of all slaves. Many radical Southern-rights papers further predicted that the Republicans, should they acquire dominance of the national government, would go beyond emancipation and implement a policy of racial equality. This would mean that Negroes would attain political rights, a possibility which Southern whites found abhorrent. The Richmond *Enquirer* expressed the revulsion of many journals when it said:

Lincoln will be the next President of the United States—Lincoln, who openly avows eternal hatred to the institution of slavery in the South—Lincoln who seeks to overwhelm the people of the South by placing the negro on an equality with the free white voters at the polls—Lincoln, whose supporters tell us that "the negroes are more numerous than the Germans, or Irish either, and would have more power in the elections than either"—Lincoln, whose bosom friends and advocates seem willing to sink the proud Anglo-Saxon and other European races into one common level with the lowest races of mankind.[16]

Nevertheless, the prospect of Negro enfranchisement, repulsive as it was, became as nothing when compared to the greater horror of widespread miscegenation, which, many Southern editors prophesied, would be the consequence of submission to Lincoln. One of the most strident Jeremiahs warning the South against amalgamation was the Montgomery (Alabama) *Mail*. After the Northern elections in October had demonstrated the probability of Lincoln's election, the *Mail* poured out its paranoid apprehensions in an editorial, the hysterical tone of which can be revealed only by a lengthy quotation:

The recent elections, resulting in the success of Lincoln candidates, show that the North believes in the doctrine of negro equality. That is the expressed doctrine of their leader, Lincoln. Here in the South, we believe that the white man is better than the negro; and the poorest white man in Alabama would cut the throat of his daughter, before he would marry her to a negro, if he were as rich as Croesus. Horace Greeley, Senator Seward and such representatives of Northern sentiment, would be proud to have buck negroes for their sons-in-law. Hamlin, who is on the ticket with Lincoln, is a free negro, and boasts of his African blood.

We may well, then, be united at the South—we white men of the South. If the North chooses to mulattoize itself, that is all right, though we do not believe that communities of mulattoes can long exist on this continent. Let the North, however, be the home of the mixed race; and let the South be the home of the *white man*, proud of his race, and proud of his race's superiority!

Amalgamation at the South, as well as the North, is the programme and hope of Seward and Greeley. Their aim is to free the negroes and force amalgamation between them and the children of the poor men of the South. The rich will be able to keep out of the way of the contamination. But the poor white men of the South will not consent to the Seward plan: They will fight to the death, first. We do not know what it is that makes the Southern white man so superior in his instincts, to the Seward class; but it is certain that amalgamation is viewed with horror here. Greeley and Seward and Lincoln may practice it, in their own families, and may recommend it to the whole country; but the white race of the South will never submit. There is no doom that they would not prefer.

But, with the South united—aye, with a single cotton State, to lead the way to independence—all the amalgamationists in the world cannot compel us to submit to their odious and hideous programme. . . . If Lincoln and his free nigger outrider are elected, we must not submit. We must leave the North with its vile free-negroism, to shift for itself. . . . Southern men are *white men* and intend to *continue* such![17]

Pro-Breckinridge editors of the upper South often were as extreme in opposing submission to Lincoln's election as were their colleagues of the lower South, although they were not so unanimous in that opinion. Should Lincoln be elected, said the Clarke County (Virginia) *Journal,* "our mind is clear that we must revolutionize. Our people will be too disspirited, demoralized and degraded to submit to the rule of a foreign people." "Will the South obtain peace by cowardly submission to Black Republicanism?" asked another Virginia advocate of Breckinridge. Yet another paper of the Old Dominion asserted: "To submit to the sectional yoke and the doctrines avowed and purposes declared, is simply impossible. No one will think of it for a moment." The Lynchburg *Republican* of the same state agreed: "The moment the lightning flash shall convey the intelligence of the election of Lincoln, [we] will unfurl to the breeze the flag of Disunion."[18]

Many Southern-rights newspapers that had remained cautious for most of the campaigns on what course they would advocate in the event of Lincoln's election became noticeably bolder as the election approached. For example, on September 15 the St. Augustine (Florida) *Examiner* professed not to fear a dissolution of the Union in the event of a Republican victory in November, but one month later it wrote that, should Lincoln win, "we shall advocate with all the force God has given us the IMMEDIATE FORMATION OF A SEPARATE CONFEDERACY OF THE COTTON STATES. If that be Secession or Treason make the most of it." In a like manner a Georgia paper, while it disliked the idea of a Republican President, believed in October that disunion was not neces-

sarily the proper solution: "With an anti-abolition majority
in both houses of the next Congress—as may be the case—
the South *may* feel herself justified in fighting this battle
over again at the ballot box, and *in the Union* four years
hence." But just before the election the same newspaper
warned that a victorious Republican party would "build
up an abolition party in the Southern States, who will distribute arms and strychnine among the slaves with which
to murder their masters. It will encourage abolition 'nigger'
stealers to steal your property, and by repealing the fugitive
slave law, leave you without the slightest redress."[19]

Some moderate Southern-rights papers equivocated painfully between their love for the Union and their abhorrence
of "Black Republicanism." Such papers usually approached
the question of secession with deliberate ambiguity. For example, The Fayetteville *Arkansian* wrote: "The simple
election of Lincoln is and can be no cause for a dissolution
of the Union; it is only the principles upon which he is
elected being made living and active deeds, and therefore
fatal, which can disrupt the Union." The editor of Texas's
Clarksville *Northern Standard* confessed his own disposition
"to put afar off the issue of disunion; yet it is evident that
the election of Lincoln would precipitate difficulty, the end
of which no man can foresee."[20] A small minority of Breckinridge papers announced unequivocally their desire to ad-
here to the Union even if Lincoln were elected. Without
some violation of the Constitution by the Republicans, asserted the Marietta (Georgia) *Southern Statesman,* there
could be no possible basis for secession: "So far we have not
the slightest grounds to justify us before the world in resist-
ing his administration." A country paper in North Carolina
believed that the South had a legal right to secede but
thought that it would be "unwise and imprudent to exercise
the right without a cause of greater magnitude than the
mere election of Lincoln to the Presidency." Still other

moderate Breckinridge papers implied that they would support secession should Lincoln triumph but refused to make any formal announcement to that effect before the election. The Macon (Georgia) *Daily Telegraph,* for example, viewed secession as "a deplorable alternative against something worse," but added: "It will be time enough for the *Telegraph* to develope [*sic*] its policy when the occasion arises and this we shall try to do calmly and reasonably."[21]

Bell and Douglas newspapers, like Breckinridge journals, took a grave view of Lincoln's prospective elevation to the presidency. The Little Rock *Arkansas State Gazette* echoed the feeling of many Unionist papers: "The Country is in danger. The Black Republicans have nominated Lincoln for the Presidency. His election will be a sectional triumph which, if it does not dissolve the Union, will weaken its bonds." Another Bell advocate in Georgia wrote: "All parties, except of course the Black Republicans, regard Lincoln's election as the direst calamity that could befall the country, and the inevitable prelude to the destruction of the Union, at an earlier or later day. The aims and designs of the Black Republican party are such that if carried out in the administration of the government, would reduce the South to a condition of most degrading inequality."[22]

In understanding the gravity with which Unionist editors regarded the prospective election of Lincoln, it is important to understand that many of them secretly shared the racial fears which Breckinridge papers expressed so openly. The pro-Union editor of a conservative, independent Texas paper revealed the extent to which the demon "Race" could haunt the Southern psyche by relating a remarkable dream to his readers. Several months before the election of Lincoln the editor dreamed that "a Northern fanatic" had become President, "and Southern men were rushing home to the Sunny South, bare-headed and in their shirt-sleeves, shouting war! war! war!" There followed a terrible scene of the embattled sections, in which the gory sights and clashing sounds of battle were "thickly interspersed with black and yellow negroes, who had hoes, brickbats, fence rails, blun-der-busses, pepper-boxes, and dog-knives in their hands, looking very mad." Reduced in his dream to his last bullet, the editor experienced a suitably heroic salvation when Sam Houston himself rode to the rescue, killing many Ne-groes and driving the remainder into the Colorado river. Editors having such dreams could hardly feel comfortable when they contemplated the prospective election of a man whom most Southerners regarded as a "Northern fanatic." There were not enough Sam Houstons to go around.[23]

Nevertheless, antisecessionist journals of all parties and candidates rejected disunion on account of the mere election of Lincoln. Said the pro-Bell Wadesborough *North Carolina Argus:* "If Lincoln is elected—the Union must be preserved —*in any event* the Union must be saved." The pro-Douglas Raleigh *National Democrat* wrote: "Lincoln's elec-tion would be calamitous, yet in our opinion, a dissolution of this Union at the present time would be a calamity the parallel of which can not be found in the history of na-tions."[24] Not only was secession likely to prove disastrous, but it was also impractical. A number of Unionist newspa-pers argued that disunion would be economically damaging to Southern interests, that it would sacrifice the South's interest in the territories, and that, far from ending viola-tions of the Fugitive Slave Act, it would make such viola-tions more numerous and more flagrant.[25]

Unionist papers sometimes minimized the danger that a Republican victory was supposed to present to the South. Others contended that Lincoln might even become an ac-ceptable President. Still others doubted that Lincoln could do worse than his Democratic predecessor; they reminded Southerners that high tariffs and nonenforcements of the Fugitive Slave Act were characteristics of the Buchanan administration.[26] The presidency, some observed, tended to make a man more catholic in his outlook; perhaps Lincoln, as national leader, would rise above the narrow sectionalism which he had exemplified as party leader. The Greensboro (North Carolina) *Times* wrote: "We . . . believe that man will not be easily found, who having Constitutionally reached the exalted position of President of the United States, will suffer his name to go down in history as a perjured man, be the principles of the party that elected him, what they may."[27]

Relatively few Southern editors trusted in the ennobling powers of the presidency. Many, however, viewed the constitutional checks and balances as the South's principal protection from Republican aggression. After all, they pointed out, an American President was hardly a king. He was subject to and limited by Congress and the Supreme Court, both of which were yet dominated by Democrats. Said the Hayneville (Alabama) *Watchman:* "Suppose Lincoln should carry all the Northern States and be elected. What then? We will have the Senate and perhaps the House. . . . We will still have the Supreme Court, and thus he will be powerless for evil if elected."[28]

Some Unionist editors promised to oppose secession even if a Republican administration should manage to circumvent the constitutional checks and violate Southern rights; they would advocate "resistance within the Union" in such an eventuality. Such papers agreed with the New Orleans *Bee:* "If the North should be lunatic enough to commit overt acts of aggression, and to drive the South to desperation, she means to fight antislavery and its zealots, if needs be, but always in the Union." Just how such "resistance in the Union" was to be carried out was never explained.[29]

But most Southern Unionist papers had long placed limits upon their Unionism. Should a Black Republican administration commit any "overt act" against the South, they said, then without hesitation they would join the fire-eaters in armed resistance. The pro-Bell Alexandria (Louisiana) *Constitutional* warned: "When Lincoln commits some overt act, which will destroy all party acerbiety [*sic*] in the South, then will the people of all parties rise *en masse* and rebel against the tyrant and the Union party then will be proud to be called REBELS!!!" Even Parson Brownlow, the staunchest of Southern Unionist editors, promised at one point to support secession should Lincoln commit aggression against the South, but the Parson later changed his mind.[30]

The Unionist journals' insistence upon waiting for an "overt act" by the Republicans filled the more radical Breckinridge editors with scorn. In their view, Lincoln's election, whether accomplished constitutionally or not, was itself an overt act of aggression, because the "Black Republican" candidate was pledged to carry out a program involving the violation of the South's constitutional rights. "Have we not a right to presume that Lincoln, if elected, will do all that he says he will do, if in his power?" asked the Anderson (South Carolina) *Intelligencer*. To wait until the Republicans had within their grasp all of the power of the federal government would be to invite disaster. Alabama's Florence *Gazette* wrote:

Will the people of the south act while they hold in their hands the means of successful resistance? or will they wait until both the spirit and the power to resist are gone? We know not. But this we do know, that the truly wise, brave man meets his enemy at the doorsill, falls, if he falls at all, *there;* and does not crouch, like a spaniel by the hearthstone, and wait until all his weapons are taken from him one by one, and he is bound hand and foot in the very presence of his wife and children.

If secession were contemplated, asked another Alabama journal, "would it not be better to [secede] immediately after the result of the election is known, while Buchanan and his Cabinet who are friendly to the South have the reins in their hands, than to wait till Lincoln and his Wide-Awakes get possession of the purse and the sword?"[31]

Radical Southern-rights editors grew increasingly impatient with those papers that advocated "submission." The New Orleans *Delta* called a neighboring paper's determination to advocate the Union "under every conceivable circumstance," "certainly the most astounding and revolting declaration ever made by a Southern journal." It was the *Delta*'s view that such "submissionist" propaganda did only mischief by convincing Northerners "that the South can not be kicked out of the Union." A Georgia paper criticized Unionist newspapers in general and warned: "The day is not far distant when it will be dangerous to avow and promulgate the doctrines, in any Southern State, that are now put forward unblushingly by Editors of the Presses we have referred to. If our judgement led us to a correct opinion on the subject—a drumhead trial and ten feet of hemp will be their reward, and that before very long." In a like manner, a Mississippi journal wrote darkly of "hundreds" of abolitionists, "whose business here it is to *prepare our people for the rule of Lincoln*"; therefore, Southerners who were told that Lincoln could be tolerated as President should suspect their informants of holding abolitionist opinions. An Alabama editor of like mind exulted in the growing radicalism of the South: "The blood of the South is becoming hot. The day is not three weeks off, when the 'agents' and 'pioneers' will have to be very, very cautious."[32]

Already, before the election, pressures mounted on editors whom the Breckinridge press considered unsound on Southern rights. John Hardy, editor of the pro-Douglas Selma *Alabama State Sentinel,* told of efforts by secessionists to drive him out of business because of his criticisms of their activities. His opponents first tried to buy him out. Failing to meet Hardy's selling price of $10,000, the Breckinridge party attempted to ruin him by spreading the false rumor that he had been "bought" with money by the Douglas faction. When this tactic failed, Hardy's enemies allegedly procured the names of the *Sentinel's* subscribers from post offices and then hired agents who attempted, unsuccessfully, to persuade the paper's readers to drop their subscriptions. Next, William L. Yancey brought a libel suit against editor Hardy in Tuskegee, Macon County, which, Hardy alleged, was a "remote county—a county where it was entirely inconvenient for me to attend," chosen purposely "so as to annoy and harrass me as much as possible." Finally, said Hardy, the persistent secessionists had gotten up a public meeting to prejudice the local populace against him. The beleaguered editor appealed to his friends to stand by him.[33]

Similar pressures were brought to bear against other Unionist editors. At the height of the abolitionist scare in Texas, two alleged abolitionists, named Bewley and Crawford, were hanged in Fort Worth. Shortly afterward, a grand jury in neighboring Parker County recommended that A. B. Norton, Unionist owner and corresponding editor of the Fort Worth *Chief*, be given a similar treatment. Norton took the hint and in September 1860 sold his paper to a secessionist. He later wrote that "the hostility of the people growing out of Secession views, compelled the *Chief's* discontinuance after the hanging of Rev. Anthony Buley [*sic*] and [William] Crawford." One pro-Bell editor in Florida, J. N. Bowen of the Lake City *Independent Press,* blew out his brains with a pistol on October 19. Although no reason was given for the suicide, Bowen may have been depressed by the torrent of ridicule which he had received from the Breckinridge press.[34]

Radical Southern-rights sheets sometimes even saw "abolitionist" doctrines in fellow fire-eating editors. The Atlanta *Intelligencer,* for example, said that the Reverend Samuel Boykin, editor of a paper called the *Christian Index,* ought to be hanged for publishing a letter from a Northerner who criticized talk of disunion. The moderate Southern-rights Macon *Daily Telegraph*, in criticizing the *Intelligencer*, pointed out that Boykin was himself a "fire-eater" and added that such threats were "not caluclated to conciliate and harmonize public opinion for any useful purpose whatever. The *Intelligencer* should, at least, be sparing in the use of his [sic] halters among slaveholders, natives of the State and Southern Rights men."[35]

If Southern editors kept a wary eye out for heresy among their own, they were doubly vigilant in their efforts to exclude Northern Republican journals from the South. They were aided in their self-assigned inquisitorial duties by postmasters, many of whom carefully examined papers arriving from the North. The Bellville (Texas) *Countryman*, for example, published the letter of an observant rural postmaster who wrote: "It is no trivial matter to find, in the post office, a paper published by Black Republicans, and bearing upon its first page the names of Abraham Lincoln and Hannibal Hamlin. Such a paper I find in the office at this place, published at St. Louis, Missouri, in the Bohemian language, with no less than three agents in Austin county and one in Colorado." He then listed the names and addresses of the three agents, as well as the name and place of residence of one of the subscribers. Fortunately, the "agents" in question were able to convince a vigilance committee that they had given their support to the new publication without knowing that it was a Republican organ. With Texas postmasters showing such zeal in rooting out "abolitionist" papers it is easy to understand why several people in that state asked the pro-Republican New York *Tribune* to remove their names from its subscription list.[36]

Greeley's *Tribune*, the largest, most influential, and one of the most anti-Southern of all the Republican journals, was the favorite newspaper target of Southern-rightists. Perhaps the most sensational case involving the *Tribune* was that of a newspaper agent, Henry A. Marsh, of St. Louis. Marsh established news depots in Camden, Arkansas, and Memphis and made the mistake of accepting an order at Camden for fifty copies of the *Tribune*. The package arrived from New York while he was in Memphis on business. When the local vigilance committee heard of the arrival of Greeley's paper, it dispatched men to Memphis to seize Marsh. At Memphis the culprit was taken bodily off the steamer *John Walsh*, over the protests of the vessel's captain, and was returned to Arkansas. At Camden he was arraigned before the vigilance committee, which determined to its satisfaction that he was an abolitionist and sentenced him to hang. Small wonder that its subscription list for the Southern states was so small, snorted the *Tribune,* when "the penalty of buying it is death by strangulation."[37]

Breckinridge newspapers reacted defiantly to suggestions that the federal government might prevent the secession of the South by coercion. At Norfolk, on August 25, Douglas had denied the right of the South to secede in the event of Lincoln's constitutional election. Should the South attempt secession upon Lincoln's election, Douglas had said, the government ought to prevent it, by force if necessary. The Breckinridge press reacted caustically to Douglas's "Norfolk Doctrine." For example, the Jackson *Mississippian* accused the Little Giant of "treason." A Georgia paper called the senator's approval of coercion "odious," and asked how any Southern man could support such doctrines. A South Carolina paper wrote: "The Southern people would be great fools to let such talk as this deter them from asserting and protecting their rights. They must be lost not only to reason but to all courage to be so easily frightened into submission."[38]

Before the election, Bell and Douglas newspapers seemed somewhat divided on the question of coercion. The pro-Douglas New Orleans *Bee* solidly endorsed the Norfolk speech and declared: "Should the brawling extremists of South Carolina attempt an overt act of revolution, they would be speedily put down, either by the overwhelming power of an adverse public opinion, or by stronger and more efficacious means, if requisite." One who joined his state in secession was a traitor, warned a Bell paper in North Carolina, "and is liable to the penalty of such an offender, provided the Government has power sufficient to enforce it." Secession and a Southern Confederacy were out of the question, argued the pro-Bell Shreveport (Louisiana) *South-Western:* "The federal government has a power that can easily put down all rebellion on the Atlantic and Gulf of Mexico—the navy. And we feel assured that the democracy nor any other party could complain if that force was employed for the suppression of rebellion."[39]

Many Douglas papers were embarrassed by their candidate's pronouncement on coercion and sought to soften his remarks by further explanations. The Memphis *Daily Appeal* pointed out that Douglas also had promised to resist Lincoln, should he play the tyrant: "Who dares assert, in the face of this fact, with the least show of sincerity, that his [Douglas's] position can be tortured into favoring the coercion of a sovereign State that secedes from this Union on account of violated faith and unconstitutional oppression?" After all, wrote the Montgomery (Alabama) *Confederation,* Douglas had not said how far he would go in supporting an attempt of the Federal government "to coerce a sovereign State, which had seceded."[40]

Significantly, many Unionist editors recognized the probability of their being dragged into the vortex of rebellion against their wills if Lincoln were elected. This realization must have contributed to the equivocations which many defenders of the Union evinced. For example, the New Orleans *Bee* scornfully explained the fallacy of the fire-eaters' contention that there was a "right" of secession, but, at the same time, it emphasized its belief that "revoluion" was perfectly respectable, legally. An Arkansas journal damned Northern fanaticism in the same issue that it dismissed as ridiculous the idea that "peaceable secession" was possible. And, in North Carolina, a self-proclaimed "old fogy conservative" journal, which prided itself on its ability "to see things in their true light," said: "We are opposed to division under any pretext whatever; yet we are for *our rights* and we must have them."[41]

Unionist editors might denounce secession on principle and even approve of federal coercion, but they still were Southern men by geography and breeding. They knew that when the chips were down they must go with their states. Thus some were placed in the curious position of supporting Douglas's pronouncement on coercion, and, at the same time, serving notice that they would resist such coercion. Georgia's Augusta *Daily Constitutionalist* defended Douglas's remarks on coercion, yet promised to stand by the South, "RIGHT OR WRONG." Another Douglas paper in North Carolina believed that its state had "no right to withdraw," yet if she did so, "we should go with her, *right or wrong*, because all that we have and all that we hold most dear is here; and our native State having our heart's purest affections and affording to us all the protection we require claims our allegiance."[42]

Two months before the election a new editor of an independent Texas journal sorrowfully observed that "prejudice has usurped the place of reason," and said that it would be hard for any editor to follow "the peaceful walks of literature, and remain untouched by the prevailing epidemic."[43] As the election approached, it was even more difficult than ever to resist the pull of secession. A tide of excitement which was almost impossible to resist was sweeping the South. By the end of October it was difficult to find in the great preponderance of Southern newspapers a cool examination of the issues or a fair evaluation of the candidates. Emotionalism, like a great magnet, drew editors farther and farther from the path of common sense and reason, into a morass of fear and hate from which any exit—even secession —might seem a desirable alternative.

VII

He Who Dallies
Is a Dastard

On November 6 the dreaded event occurred: Lincoln was elected President of the United States. The recipient of only thirty-nine percent of the popular vote, Lincoln nevertheless triumphed because he carried the critical large states of the North by solid margins. His electoral vote total was 173, twenty-one more than he needed to be elected. Although a large number of Southern editors had predicted the outcome after the state elections in October, the actual event seems to have stunned many of them. Some could scarcely believe the news; they had prepared their minds for the evil day, but not their emotions. "The idea of Lincoln's election has been frequently talked about it is true," wrote a Georgia paper, "but it has always seemed to be at vague distance with its hideous deformities, and has rather existed as a creature of the imagination than as one that could possibly have a realization in the practical working of our Government."[1]

Perhaps because they were shocked by the news of Lincoln's election, many editors reacted cautiously at first. To the question "What should the South do?" a Texas editor could answer only: "That is a grave question more easily asked than answered." "What course Louisiana has to take," said a paper in that state, "we do not presume to indicate or foreshadow." A Virginia journal stated: "Lincoln is the President elect. We make no predictions and indulge in no expressions of fear as to the consequences." Said the Montgomery (Alabama) *Weekly Confederation:* "As our readers may have observed, we have as yet refrained from taking any decided position on the present alarming posture of national affairs. Nor shall we be in haste to do so. The questions of what shall be done and how it shall be done, are of grave and deeply momentous import, affecting intimately, for weal or for woe, the peace and prosperity of every citizen in the Commonwealth." Citizens should remain calm, "neither singing hosannas to the Union or unnecessarily rushing into hasty and precipitate movement." Many other papers simply called for calm, wisdom, and patriotism without indicating whether the people ought to be calmly, wisely, and patriotically for the Union or for secession.[2]

Some vacillated, but the great majority of Southern-rights journals of the lower South showed little hesitation in endorsing secession. The election of Lincoln by a sectional vote, in utter disregard for the South's feelings, was the final insult, they declared. If the South accepted the "Black Republican," secessionist papers warned, he would exclude slavery first from the territories and later from the South itself. Not only would the slaves be freed, they would be made socially equal with the whites. Negroes would even rule white men, for Lincoln most certainly would appoint them to office in the South. Abolitionist activities such as the recent incendiarism in Texas would be resumed, predicted the fire-eaters, encouraged by a Republicanized federal government. A North Carolina paper warned: "We proclaim it now, *and mark us if it is true—if we submit now to Lincoln's election, before his term of office expires, your home will be visited by one of the most fearful and horrible butcheries that has cursed the face of the globe.*"[3] Lending immediacy to such warnings were stories of new abolitionist plots. On December 11 the Montgomery (Alabama) *Mail* reported a planned uprising, which allegedly was to take place during the Christmas holidays. "We are now whipping our negroes," said the report, "taking them as they come." Not surprisingly, the lash evoked a number of dramatic confessions. "We hear some startling facts. They have even gone far enough in the plot to divide our estates, mules, lands and household furniture."[4]

Secessionist papers also continued to stress their campaign argument that the South, should it submit to Lincoln's election, would be consigned permanently to a position of economic subserviency. Secession, on the other hand, would remove the shackles imposed by a Northern tariff by opening direct trade with Europe, thereby ensuring an era of unexampled prosperity. A Louisiana paper asked: "Why, then, should we desire to consort any longer with a people, so antagonistic to us in feeling, principles and interest? Why, with one effort, not heave off this incubus, which is oppressing our energies, strangling our commerce, and dwarfing the natural growth of our national proportions?" Contending that Southerners were merely "hewers of wood and drawers of water" for Northern businessman, a Georgia paper wrote: "The day of the severance of the slaveholding from the Abolition States, will be the happiest day for the former, and the death knell of Northern prosperity will be sounded."[5]

Journals demanding secession recognized the necessity of speedy action for the success of their movement. If they worked quickly, the radicals could capitalize upon the shock and anger which the South felt in consequence of Lincoln's election. Therefore, the shortest road out of the

Union was best. In the words of South Carolina's Newberry *Conservatist:* "We regard the excitement which is prevailing throughout the Southern country, and especially in South Carolina, as a most wholesome indication. . . . Now is no time for delay. We must *act* at once. . . . He who dallies is a dastard, and he who doubts is damned."[6]

In no case should the South wait to withdraw until after Lincoln's inauguration, secessionist journals warned. A Texas paper explained why delay would be fatal to the South: "She [the South] cannot safely submit to a Black Republican administration a single day. She cannot wait for an overt act, and until the plans of her enemies are fully matured and partially executed. It would be madness to suffer the Army and Navy of the Confederacy to pass into the hands of a Black Republican President." *"We have but three months in which to work,"* stressed a Georgia paper. "On the 4th of March, 1861, we are either *slaves in the Union or freemen out of it.* Let true men and Georgians decide for themselves." Sam Dixon of the Wetumpka (Alabama) *Enquirer* put it more graphically: "If I find a coiled rattlesnake in my path, do I wait for 'his' 'overt act,' or do I smite him in his coil?"[7]

The more extreme Southern-rights papers scorned all suggestions of compromise. It was too late for any adjustment, they argued. The Northern states, they insisted, were no more disposed to make concessions than were the Southern states. Therefore the proposed convention would mean only a fatal delay, and, as one Louisiana paper reminded its readers, "Delay may be death." "The time for conciliatory measures is passed," echoed the Key West (Florida) *Key of the Gulf.* The Southern states, asserted the Charleston *Mercury,* "want *no conference but in the Convention which will assemble to frame the Constitution, and complete the organization of a Southern Confederacy*

. . . The day for new guarantees is gone. Henceforth we are two peoples."[8]

Secessionist papers also rejected the secession of the Southern states by co-operative action, that is, through a unanimous, concerted effort of all the slave states. If unanimity were required before secession could become a reality, secessionist editors believed, then their movement would collapse, for the states of the upper South were almost certain to refuse South Carolina's invitation to join her in leaving the Union. But let one or two states act quickly, and the border slave states also eventually would be forced to secede. "Separate State action," therefore became the motto of extreme secessionist papers. Some of them curiously argued that co-operative secession was unconstitutional, while separate state secession was legal. For example, Alabama's Montgomery *Weekly Mail* said: "It is true that each state may advise or notify any other State or states, that on a given day, she will secede—thus indirectly advising a similar course to the State notified; but any actual 'agreement' or 'compact' to that or any other end, 'without the consent of Congress,' . . . is illegal and rebellious." Showing a similar talent for casuistry, the New Orleans *Daily Delta* branded as treasonous those who would "resist" the Lincoln administration "within the Union." Said the *Delta:* "The States seceding are outside the Union. It may have been an unconstitutional and illegal act to secede; but when they are once out, they are no longer bound by your Constitution. But you stay in the Union, and deliberately propose to violate and disregard the provisions of the compact. It is you who are revolutionary and treasonable."[9]

Even as they advocated secession, some Southern-rights papers betrayed an ambivalence toward the Union. Many commonly substituted such euphemisms as "action" and "resistance" for the unsavory word "secession." And some journals contrived ambiguous and contradictory arguments to prove that secession really was not disunion at all. The Union was dependent upon a strict adherence to the principles of the Constitution, contended a Virginia paper; therefore, since the seceding states were true to those original principles, they were more "Unionist" than the states which remained in the Union: "Is not Secession simply a withdrawing from an attempt to establish a sovereignty over the South? Secession *is not disunion.* It is no cause for disunion." A Louisiana journal wrote: "Secession is not *Disunion*—without the first, we cannot meet our sister States in council; and without secession, the North could not be brought to the true understanding of her perilous position, nor be made to preserve the Union if she could."[10] Other papers contended that the Republicans had "virtually dissolved" the Union by their violations of the Constitution; therefore, the South was blameless for putting a formal end to a Union whose spirit the North already had slain.[11]

Less vehement Southern-rights papers kept the door slightly ajar for some solution which might stop short of disunion. Such journals usually suggested the calling of a Southern convention which would present an ultimatum to the North, demanding the protection of slavery both in the states and in the territories as well as the repeal of the hated Personal Liberty Laws of the North. Apparently few of these journals really expected the North to respond favorably to such an ultimatum, but a negative response, they felt, would place the blame upon the Yankees for the consequent dissolution of the Union. The Little Rock *Old-Line Democrat* wanted an ultimatum, "in order to justify ourselves before the world . . . and let the consequences of their refusal to grant it, fall alone upon the heads of the North." Declared the San Antonio *Daily*

Herald: "Such a course, demanding nothing but what is right, and submitting to nothing clearly wrong, will unite the South, divide the North and conciliate the whole enlightened world in favor of the South, should it be rejected."[12]

Southern Unionist editors fought hard to resist the tide of emotionalism that followed Lincoln's election. Secession, they reiterated, was unjustified because of the mere election of one whose principles Southerners despised. The South must hold calmly to the Union, resist the siren cry of the fire-eaters, and all might yet be well. Such papers usually showed great faith in the conservatism of the masses, both North and South. "Our people," admitted a Virginia editor, "have already been carried to great lengths by hot-headed demagogical party leaders; but when the question of union or disunion comes to be bruited, those leaders will find the people will not go with them." Observing that, "with very few exceptions," North Carolina's newspapers were "eminently conservative" in the wake of Lincoln's election, a paper in that state asserted: "In this the public Press, instead of forming public opinion, reflects it, for nine out of ten of the voters of North Carolina are for the Union, and dead against the movements of South Carolina and Georgia."[13]

The South would gain nothing by seceding, some Unionist papers argued; on the contrary, the Southern states would lose their share of the national establishment. The Milledgeville (Georgia) *Southern Recorder* defined secession as, "the giving up by a State of all interest in our National Government . . . a quit claim title to all interests in the National Treasury—the Navy—the Army—the national store houses—the arsenals—the manufactory of arms and munitions of war, and last but not least the entire public domain outside the State." All this would be relinquished for nothing, felt Unionist editors, because peaceable secession was a mirage. There was no right of secession, only of revolution, and revolutions were seldom accomplished without the shedding of blood. "We cannot get rid of the North by secession," said a Tennessee paper, "Try the experiment when we may, the dreams of visionaries will soon be dispelled by contact with stern realities." "The State that secedes must pass through a baptism of blood," warned a North Carolina journal.[14]

Increasing numbers of Unionist newspapers—most notably in the upper South—believed that Lincoln might prove acceptable to the South. Some discovered in old Lincoln speeches evidences of conservatism on the slavery question. Said the Knoxville *Whig:* "Mr. Lincoln himself is no doubt a sincere lover of his country. He is to-day, what he has always been, an OLD CLAY WHIG, differing in no respect—not even upon the subject of *Slavery,* from the Sage of Ashland." "The probability is," predicted the Norfolk (Virginia) *Herald,* "that he will administer the Government with strict impartiality; or if anything, be more regardful of the interests of the South than Southern Presidents usually have been." The Clarksville (Tennessee) *Jeffersonian* expected Lincoln to be "moved by an earnest desire to conciliate the whole people, and make a popular administration." Some argued that Southerners could not possibly know what course a Republican administration would follow until it had assumed power. Those secessionists who continually wailed about the horrors of submission, said the Kosciusko (Mississippi) *Chronicle,* "have about as much idea of the principles upon which a Republican Government should be constructed, as an ant has of building a fireproof Court house." Lincoln at least should have the chance to prove his acceptability to the South, "submissionist" journals contended.[15]

Nor was the South lost if Lincoln proved untrue to Southern interests, asserted Unionist editors. The Republi-

cans were in the minority in the Senate and lacked a sufficient majority in the House to organize that chamber
without Democratic votes. Hence, the Congress would join
with an equally hostile Supreme Court to block any attempt of Lincoln to implement the Chicago platform.
Thus frustrated, the Republican party probably would become plagued by internal dissensions, a development which
would work to the South's distinct advantage. It might or
might not be true, said the Unionists, that in a few years
the Republicans would gain control of all three branches
of the government. But if Republicans should fall to
fighting among themselves, the Unionist papers pointed
out, there was a distinct possibility of a strong Democratic
comeback in 1862 and 1864. In any event many Unionist
journals agreed with North Carolina's Hillsborough *Recorder* which asked: "Is it wise so long to anticipate evils
very likely never to occur, and plunge into others still more
dire and immediate?"[16]

Unfortunately for the Unionist position, the continuing
debate over secession did not take place in a political
vacuum; developments in the lower South soon swept
Unionist editors down the road toward disunion. Three
days after the election a newspaper in Tennessee observed: "Occurrences, yet unrevealed, must shape the
course of newspapers, and we must 'wait for the wagon.' "

The wagon was not long in coming. Already, there was
intense excitement in South Carolina. In Charleston the
palmetto flag went up over the office of the *Mercury* to the
loud applause of those watching. Secessionists such as Keitt
and Rhett egged-on the crowds in Columbia with their
fiery rhetoric. Several of the state's most important federal officeholders, such as Judge A. D. Magrath, Collector
W. F. Colcock, and Senators James P. Chestnut and
James H. Hammond, resigned their positions. And militia
units all over the state stepped up their preparations for war.

Accurately reading the public mind before the election, the South Carolina legislature had voted to remain in session until the results were known so that it could act quickly in case Lincoln won. Shortly after learning the outcome, the legislature of the Palmetto State ordered the election of a secession convention and set December 17 as the date for that body's assemblage. The other states of the "Gulf Squadron" were also feverish with secessionist activity. Before the end of November, the states of Alabama, Mississippi, Georgia, Florida, and Louisiana had taken steps preparatory to dissolving their connections with the Union. In Texas, when Unionist Governor Sam Houston refused to summon a special session of the legislature, secessionists held, on December 3, an irregular meeting which ordered an informal election of delegates to a secession convention.[17]

Secessionist papers joyously reported the disunion developments in the Southern states. "Georgia Moving!" "Ten Thousand Cheers for Florida!" "Alabama All Right —Convention Called!" read typical headlines of the secessionist journals. Other news often was crowded off the pages.[18]

The surging tide of secessionism further emboldened fire-eating journals of the lower South to threaten Unionists of all degrees. "Is not the cry of wait for ANY ACT not only disgraceful to a Southerner but TREASON to the soil of his nativity?" asked a Georgia paper. A Florida editor expected the day to come soon when those who advised submission "will be hanged as high as Haman, and we caution those gentlemen, who are in the habit of doing so to be careful, the day is possibly not distant, when such talk will be punished as treason, and it is not improbable, some one of them may adorn the gallows."[19]

Unionist papers nevertheless caustically criticized South Carolina for setting secession in motion. After printing the

"startling news" from the Palmetto State, the Vicksburg
Whig wrote: "Our heart sickens at the rashness of a misguided and demagogue-ridden commonwealth." "We say,
let them go," declared the Charlestown *Virginia Free Press:*
"The Union will be rid of some pestiferous grumblers,
who, like Lucifer, would become tired of the golden streets
and adornments of Heaven itself." Noting that a man
named MacBeth had reportedly urged disunion at a
Charleston political meeting, a Bell paper in Tennessee
wrote: "We look to that unfortunate little State and ex-
claim with MacBeth, 'Out d——d spot.' "[20]

Nevertheless, there was evidence of a weakening of resolve among Southern Unionist papers in the weeks following Lincoln's election. For all their professions of optimism that Lincoln might prove acceptable to the South,
Southern conservative editors shared the fears of their hot-
spur colleagues that Lincoln would betray the South. The
seeds of racial fears which extreme Southern-rightists and
secessionists had broadcast for so long upon Southern soil
now seemed to take root on ground which previously had
proven barren. About two weeks after the election, for example, the New Orleans *Bee* warned whites to look vigi-
lantly after their slaves; many blacks, it explained, had already become excited by news of Lincoln's victory, which,
they seemed to believe, meant that they were about to be
freed. The pro-Douglas Newbern (North Carolina)
Weekly Progress, which had once been inclined to view
reports of Negro insurrections with skepticism, on December 11 carried a report of an alleged uprising in Kentucky.
The editor wrote:

There have been times when both our taste and judgment would
have induced us to pass by such an item, . . . but now we have
fallen upon times when we believe that every *class* should know
their respective positions. Let the slaves know that the first
attempt at revolt will be met with speedy vengeance. And that

every offender will be swung to the first tree. Let them know that
the white men of the South have determined, whether the Union
be dissolved or not, that they shall be obedient, submissive and
quiet, and that they shall continue to serve their owners in the
future as in the past. . . . Let every Southern man who is true
to his section and his rights watch all suspected persons, and
whenever one is found going out of his way to tamper with or to
associate with slaves let him be swung to the nearest tree. These
are desparate [*sic*] means, but then we must recollect that we live
in desparate times. Not only our property but our honor, our
lives and our all are involved.[21]

The growing doubts of Unionist journals were further
reflected in their changing attitudes toward South Carolina.
Even the sharpest critics of the Palmetto State now warned
the North to let her go in peace. Very few Unionist papers now advocated the coercion of a seceded state. Should
Lincoln attempt forcibly to restrain South Carolina from
seceding, warned the Richmond *Whig*, "he would at once
unite the whole Southern people in resistance, and produce
a universal conflagration." Though deploring precipitate
action, the West Baton Rouge (Louisiana) *Sugar Planter*
wrote: "If the administration of Mr. Lincoln in any manner interferes with those States [which secede], can the others, who may not agree with them, stand idly by and witness
the outrage? Certainly not. Every Southern sword will leap
from its scabbard to avenge an insult to a Southern State,
be she in the right or wrong."[22]

The Unionist press further betrayed a growing belliger-
ence toward the North in its insistence upon a redress of
Southern grievances. Like many moderate Southern-rights
journals, Unionist sheets now often advocated state, South-
wide, or national conventions through which Southerners
could present their demands. Some wished to present the
North with an ultimatum. If the South's demands were rejected, threatened the Memphis *Daily Appeal*, "we will
shake from the soles of our feet the dust of the Federal

Government and dissolve our political ties with it, having at home the undivided cooperation of a united South, and abroad the sympathy of the foreign civilized world."[23] Such papers continued to criticize radical Southern-rights journals for insisting upon immediate, separate-state secession. One Georgia proponent of a Southern convention alleged that the secessionists feared the will of the people, and that was why they did not want to wait to hear "from the cross-roads and the groceries" on the question of secession.[24]

The most striking changes in Unionist sentiment occurred in newspapers of the lower South. On November 28 the Alexandria *Louisiana Democrat* observed that Louisiana Unionists no longer desired "Union at any price," but now insisted upon guarantees of Southern rights as a condition of the South's remaining in the Union. On the same date a Virginia paper lamented that in all of Mississippi, only the Vicksburg *Whig* seemed still opposed to secession: "But its cry for 'Union' seems to be lost in the general clamor for resistance." In South Carolina, where every editor urged disunion, papers apparently were liable to criticism if they failed to show sufficient ardor for the cause. The Newberry *Rising Sun* was the subject of a condemnatory resolution passed in a town meeting, not because the paper opposed secession, but because one of its editors refused to join the radical secessionist organization, the Minute Men.[25]

Antisecessionist newspapers in the lower South began deserting their cause with almost incredible alacrity. Only three days after the election of Lincoln a secessionist Georgia paper crowed: "It is truly gratifying to us in these perilous times, to find the Southern Press getting right."[26]

The devastating effect of Lincoln's election upon Unionist journalism was nowhere better revealed than in Alabama. As early as November 22 the Hayneville *Chronicle* reported: "There are not half a dozen papers in the State, so far as we have seen, but warmly advocate the policy of withdrawing from the Union." A week later, the Richmond *Whig* noted that all Douglas papers in Alabama "have either had their Union batteries spiked; or else they have turned with the tide and are as strong disunionists as any of their contemporaries." Still one week later (December 6) the Grove Hill *Clarke County Democrat* said: "We do not know of a Bell paper or a Breckinridge paper in the State but that favors secession at this time."[27] Still, all was not harmony in the Alabama press. Douglas and Bell papers continued to fight the Breckinridge organs as vehemently as before, but they now argued, not against secession, but for "co-operation" with the other Southern states.[28] At least one Alabama editor, Colonel John G. Harvey of the Greensboro *Alabama Beacon,* refused to go with the tide. In July he had been forced by public opinion to give up Douglas for Breckinridge, but he now drew the line at secession. Nevertheless, instead of fighting his critics, he thought it expedient to sell the newspaper to one who would reflect the views of its "older patrons." Under its new editor, W. H. Fowler, the *Alabama Beacon* promptly assumed a secessionist position.[29]

Any of the Union's staunchest editorial defenders in the lower South gave up the fight and became fire-eaters themselves with astonishing speed. For example, J. J. Seibels's Montgomery (Alabama) *Confederation* had called secession "treason" during the campaign, but by December 7 it declared: "We earnestly hope that the day is not far distant when we shall have withdrawn from such an obnoxious and oppressive government, and established a confederacy of the whole of the Slaveholding States." As late as October 31 Seibels's competitor, the Montgomery *Weekly Post,* envisioned great evils for the South if it should secede; yet on November 21 it believe that the South could no longer submit to Northern "aggressions." The Augusta (Georgia)

Daily Constitutionalist, on November 3, saw no reason for the South to secede if Lincoln should win; on November 30, according to the same paper, Lincoln would be intolerable, even if he should prove to be more moderate than expected.[30]

As late as November 10 the Memphis *Daily Appeal* advised its readers to try Lincoln, who "on more occasions than one, declared his intention to meet [*sic*] out equal justice to the South." Yet that same paper, one month later, pronounced the Union virtually ended and declared: "There is an irrepressible conflict existing between the two sections, which it is impossible ever to reconcile."[31]

The New Orleans *Bee*'s metamorphosis from immovable Unionist paper to determined secessionist journal was one of the most interesting examples of the secession syndrome which manifested itself in the Unionist press after Lincoln's election. The *Bee,* on October 5, had declared its loyalty to the Union, "under every conceivable circumstance." It opposed disunion "whether the Presidential election terminates in the choice of Bell, or Douglas, or Lincoln or Breckinridge; whether the next Congress is Black Republican or Conservative; whether Seward counsels irrepressible conflict, or Rhett strives to muster an armed force to prevent Lincoln's inauguration; whether John Brown is canonized in New England, or solemn sanhedrins of Secessionists devote the Union to the infernal Gods. The real Union men have not the slightest idea of breaking up the Confederacy." But on December 14 that same paper wrote: "The North and the South are heterogeneous and are better apart. . . . We are doomed if we proclaim not our political independence."[32] Following Lincoln's election the *Bee* moved gradually, but steadily, toward a secessionist view. Two days after the election it still argued that the South must accept the constitutionally elected Republican President. "Is it not utterly preposterous to pretend that we are cruelly outraged and oppressed?" asked the *Bee:* "Where is the proof of these allegations? . . . Our wrongs are prospective rather than real, nor can they be inflicted so long as ABRAHAM LINCOLN is rendered practically powerless by an adverse Congress." But on the 12th the *Bee's* tone changed, and the journal stressed that it would "go with Louisiana" should that state secede. The next day, the *Bee* approved the calling of a state convention to consider secession and warned again that although it loved the Union, "Louisiana claims the undeviating allegiance of all her sons, and as such we shall not be found wanting in the day of trial."[33]

As if in answer to the question that it had posed on the 8th, the *Bee,* on the 21st, ran a list of twenty-eight past "outrages and aggressions" against the South. A week later, according to the *Bee's* editors, the South must have "plenary guarantees of future safety and equality within the Union, or independence out of it." Moreover, the *Bee* asserted that the entire responsibility for the Union's salvation now lay with the North, which must take the initiative in guaranteeing the South its rights. Finally, on December 4, the *Bee* prepared itself for the final step into the secessionist camp by labeling the debate over the legality of secession an "idle abstraction." Although the *Bee* had often attacked the legality of secession in the past, it now said: "If secession be determined upon, it will be executed upon the principle of safety and self-protection. Whether this principle is to be considered as revolutionary and emanating from 'higher law,' or as deducible directly from the character of the federal compact, are points which will not call for a moment's consideration, and will indeed hardly be heard in the overwhelming magnitude of the measure itself."[34]

Many papers, though they refused to renounce their allegiance to the Union, clearly showed less determination than before to resist the growing army of disunion. Such journals often changed their emphasis simply by giving increased attention to the Republican "threat" and devoting proportionately less space to exposés of secessionist "plots." A change of tone was evident in a number of Unionist papers. The Vicksburg *Whig*, on November 14, wrote an emotional plea for the Union's preservation, declaring: "We shall *submit* to the evils, confessedly great though they may be," and adding: "Its [the Union's] majestic pillars ought not to be overthrown through passions of disappointed demagogues and politicians, or the more sincere but equally dangerous schemes of open revolutionists." A month later the *Whig* still denied that there was a right of "peaceable secession" but now emphasized its belief that "the right to throw off an oppressive government, and establish a new one, like the right of self-defence, in our judgment, exists in every nation, and is the right of revolution." Shortly after the election a pro-Douglas Virginia paper admitted that it was downcast by the Republican success but said: *"Let us try Abraham Lincoln."* The same paper, two weeks later, had second thoughts about remaining in the same Union with the Northern people who assertedly had desecrated the Constitution, repudiated the Bible, and denied God: "Infidels, free-lovers, amalgamationists, they are, and as such can make the Devil himself grow pale over their acts of wickedness." The paper did not espouse secession, but its determination to accept Lincoln was clearly on the wane: "We ask, then, if such a party is to rule the country, how can the people of the South endure the Union with them? What is there in such a Union but dishonor, degradation and ruin?" One of the staunchest Unionist journals in Arkansas seemed certain enough of its position in November when it scathed the "high priests" of disunion who "would fain sacrifice the country" and who were urging the people on "to madness and ruin," but, in

December, the same journal mused: "We are satisfied that
the wisest man in the South can not, to-day, lay his hand
upon his heart, and, as an honest and truthful man, say
what is the best policy for the South to adopt and pursue."[35]

Several developments accounted for the growing radicalism of newspapers of the lower South between the election
of Lincoln on November 6 and the secession of South
Carolina on December 20. Moderate Southern-rights and
Unionist editors looked upon the North's decisive vote for
Lincoln, in disregard of all warnings from the South, as
evidence of a growing Northern ill will toward Southerners and their institutions. The Republican party's vote
totals in several key states had risen spectacularly over
those of the previous election—by 120,000 in Pennsylvania,
76,000 in Illinois, 45,000 in Indiana, and 30,000 in New
Jersey. Southerners regarded such statistics as a calculated
affront to their section. According to the Augusta (Georgia) *Chronicle and Sentinel,* the Northern vote was "a
manifestation of that spirit of intolerance, of hatred, of
hostility, of fanatic anti-slavery feeling, with which we
cannot live in peace." The same journal later explained
that its changing views on the Union were not the result of
Lincoln's election, *"per se,"* but: "Our opposition is to the
animus of the North, as exhibited in the passage of Liberty Bills, and finally in the election of an irrepressible
conflict representative, as the Chief Executive of these
States." The New Orleans *Bee* answered the question,
"Why has the election of Lincoln so altered the opinion of
conservative Southerners in favor of Secession?" by pointing out that before the election Southern Unionists had
believed that Northern conservatism would defeat Lincoln. Even if Lincoln were to win, Southern conservatives
had believed, his plurality in the North would be so small
that he would be unable as President to implement the
Republican platform. "But," continued the *Bee,* "the result

proved astounding. It showed the tremendous power and popularity of Black Republicanism. . . . What could be alleged against such convincing and irrefragable proof of Northern unsoundness? With what shadow of reason could Southern men be advised to submit and await the possible events of the future when abolitionism had swept every Northern Commonwealth, and had even displayed unexpected and growing power in some of the slaveholding States themselves?"[36]

Southern conservative papers were further disenthralled when some Northern newspapers, politicians, and preachers scorned the granting of concessions or guaranties to the South and derided the region's threats of secession. The Southern reaction is somewhat difficult to understand, since in the first few weeks following the election relatively few Northerners advocated a policy of coercion. Thurlow Weed, editor of the Albany (New York) *Evening Journal* and Republican party "boss," suggested a plan to reinstate the old Missouri Compromise with its 36° 30' line. Even Horace Greeley took a cautious position. "Whenever a considerable section of our Union shall deliberately resolve to go out," wrote Greeley's *Tribune,* "we shall resist all coercive measures designed to keep it in. We hope never to live in a republic whereof one section is pinned to the residue by bayonets." Some Northern papers nevertheless expressed militant opposition to disunion. William Cullen Bryant's New York *Post,* for example, branded all secessionists as traitors. The New York *Times,* Hartford *Courant,* and Chicago *Tribune* were among other journals which had similar views.[37] Although such newspapers were in the minority of Northern sheets, the Southern press chose to accentuate the negative opinions, rather than the more numerous positive ones. "The tone of the Northern press, rostrum and pulpit," said a formerly moderate Georgia paper, "should convince all southern

men that the hour for dissolution is come and that it is as
inevitable as the fulfillment of the decrees of God." A
New Orleans paper wrote: "It is almost impossible to believe that if the Northern press was actually aware of the
imminent danger of secession, it would use the language of
recklessness or defiance."[38]

Unionist journals were further disillusioned when the
national government demonstrated little energy or resolution in its efforts to bring about a solution to sectional
differences. Congress proceeded almost routinely to appoint
its Committees of Thirteen and Thirty-three to consider
the crisis wrought by Lincoln's election. The cabinet was
divided, with Howell Cobb, Jacob Thompson, and John
B. Floyd of the South urging President Buchanan to follow
an indulgent Southern policy, while Northern members
Joseph Holt, Lewis Cass, and Jeremiah Black demanded
an unequivocal antisecession stand. The beleaguered
President was too old and too tired to bring the full powers of his office to bear upon the sectional crisis. Speaking
to the new Congress on December 4, Buchanan greatly
disappointed and confounded many Southern editors with
his illogical thesis: The South, he said, had no constitutional right to secede; yet, should it do so, the federal
government had no constitutional power to coerce it back
into the Union.[39] After Buchanan's pitifully inept oration,
Southern Unionists realized that there would be no magic
words from the White House to aid their cause.

Nor were conservative Southern newspapers immune to
the emotionalism which swept their section in the wake of
Lincoln's election. In the heat of the campaign many
Unionist papers undoubtedly had stretched their convictions in arguing that Lincoln and the Republicans posed
little or no danger to Southern institutions. Now, after the
election, the cries of "No submission" which went up from

increasing numbers of Southerners could scarcely fail to affect the entire press. Some papers completely reversed themselves on secession; others changed subtly, sometimes only in tone. The changes in newspaper attitudes toward the Union were most dramatic in the Gulf states, where secession feeling ran highest; they were least pronounced in the upper South, where pro-Union opinions still dominated. Generally speaking, moderate Breckinridge papers succumbed to secession fever first. Douglas papers usually gave in next. Bell journals were ordinarily the most reluctant of all the party journals to "let the Union slide."

As winter approached, there was a feeling among many conservative Southerners that a power too great to combat was drawing the South out of the Union. The Baton Rouge *Gazette and Comet,* an unstinting supporter of the Union both before and after the election, betrayed a growing pessimism and listlessness when it commented upon the defection to the secessionist camp of the pro-Bell New Orleans *Crescent:* "The Crescent has changed; the press and the politicians have changed. Whether the people have changed or not, remains to be seen, when the great question is submitted to them. If they are in favor of breaking the Union, of course it will be done. . . . A much worse condition than that in which we shall enter the year '61, can hardly be imagined." "We feel like giving up the contest, and letting matters take their course," confessed a Unionist paper in Virginia. Conservative men still talked about preserving the Union, but they spoke as defeated men. There can be little doubt that the belligerent diatribes of the secessionist press were in large measure responsible for the demoralization of Unionists. One Arkansas Unionist wrote in his diary: "The Newspapers come loaded with such a howl of . . . denunciation, such threats of disruption of the government and such shouts of preparation against the North that it puts us to thinking where a peaceable citizen who has a family to protect can retreat to."[40]

On December 12 a Unionist paper in North Carolina wrote: "Madness seems to rule the hour, and fearful forebodings cloud the prospect. More than human wisdom is required to lead us out of difficulty." There was little time for recourse to a higher wisdom; South Carolina seceded one week later.[41]

VIII

The Great, Grand, Noble
Deed is Done

THERE was hardly any suspense in South Carolina over whether the Palmetto State would secede. Even the most politically naïve citizen knew that his state would soon haul down the Stars and Stripes; the only question was when. The legislature, moving cautiously in order not to alienate the other slave states, originally had set the election of delegates to a secession convention for January 8, with the convention to meet one week later. So strong was the public demand for more expeditious action, however, that the legislature moved up the election to December 6 and the convening date to December 17. The convention met at Columbia on the appointed date but was delayed slightly when the threat of a smallpox epidemic caused the delegates to shift their deliberations to Charleston. There, on December 20, the convention voted unanimously to dissolve South Carolina's ties with the United States. The Charleston *Mercury* was so far from being surprised that it required only five minutes to get an "extra" on the streets announcing the momentous event.[1]

Ecstatically reporting their state's withdrawal from the

Union, South Carolina's newspapers displayed such headlines as:

> GLORIOUS INDEPENDENCE!
> SOUTH CAROLINA FOREVER
> THE SECESSION ORDINANCE!
> PASSED DECEMBER 20, 1860

The editor of the Columbia *Daily Southern Guardian* rejoiced in the news that South Carolina was no longer "a
member of the Confederacy known as the United States."
His excitement was so great, he said, that he could scarcely
calm himself enough "to write any comments upon this
consummation." The "twentieth day of December," predicted the Charleston *Mercury*, would be "inscribed among
the calends of the world" as "an epoch in the history of
the human race." The Camden *Weekly Journal* declared:
"THE UNION IS DISSOLVED! . . . THE GREAT, GRAND, NOBLE
DEED IS DONE, AND THE DECISION OF DECEMBER 20TH, 1860,
AT CHARLESTON, SOUTH CAROLINA, CAN NEVER BE REVERSED."
The editors of the Charleston *Courier,* once the unsparing
critics of Rhett's extremism, celebrated "the event of the
century . . . in a becoming manner at the *Courier* office,"
with "patriotic and refreshing entertainment."[2]

Secessionist papers in the other states of the lower South
heaped unrestrained praise upon the Palmetto State. They
recognized that the prompt action of South Carolina had
virtually ensured the secession of the entire Gulf Squadron
and the creation of a Southern Confederacy. A Mississippi
newspaper wrote: "Brave South Carolina: Long enduring
South Carolina! . . . It leads the van of the great army of
the Southern Confederacy." A Texas journal considered
South Carolina's example "worthy of all emulation." "Let
us do likewise," urged a Florida paper, "and with our
banner thrown proudly to the breeze proclaim our inde-

pendence. Other states will soon follow, and similar interests and institutions will lead all to combine against a common foe." Thus would the reluctant slave states of the upper South be drawn into the perimeter of a great Southern nation.[3]

In the upper South, where public opinion still opposed secession, some Southern-rights papers gently chided South Carolina for acting hastily, but their aggressive, even belligerent, defense of the Palmetto State belied their criticism. Some might question South Carolina's wisdom, admitted the Raleigh *State Journal,* "but let no one dare to question her purity of intention. . . . She stands *alone* on this great continent the professed champion of Southern honor. Who first will strike her—who first take [his] stand by her side?"[4]

Southern Unionist papers were angered and disappointed by South Carolina's revolutionary action. They accused the seceding state of ignoring the wishes of her Southern neighbors and of precipitating a needless crisis at a time when the issues might still be settled by compromise. In going out of the Union, "without even passing the compliments of the season" with the other slave states, South Carolina assertedly had endangered further negotiations with the North and, thereby, had endangered the peace. Furthermore, according to Unionist journals, the Palmetto State's leaders had not sincerely regarded the election of Lincoln as a threat to slavery but had used it as an excuse for achieving their lifelong ambition of destroying the Union. South Carolina's rash act, said the Charlestown *Virginia Free Press,* "is beginning to excite disgust every where, and is fast destroying the sympathy which naturally existed among Southern men." A Tennessee paper wrote: "The ill-advised precipitation of South Carolina in rushing out of the Union . . . thus inviting and almost forcing a collision with the Federal Authorities is generally deprecated and condemned by conservative men in all of the border States."[5]

Southern secessionist editors did not boast idly when they said that other states soon would follow South Carolina out of the Union. Even before the Palmetto State acted, Mississippi and Alabama elected pro-secession conventions, both of which were to convene on January 7. Florida followed suit, calling its convention for January 3. Secessionist delegates also triumphed in Georgia's convention election held on January 2. Louisiana chose a secessionist convention on January 7, and Texas did the same one day later, in spite of Governor Houston's opposition. By the second week of January seven states of the lower South had either cut their ties with the Union or had indicated clearly their intentions of doing so.[6]

Unionist newspapers viewed the rapid advance of secessionism with grave concern. Adding to their apprehension was the growing shadow of war. South Carolina, having severed her federal connections, demanded that the United States government abandon the three federal forts at Charleston and withdraw all troops from South Carolina soil. President Buchanan refused these demands, and on the night of December 26, Major Robert Anderson, who commanded the federal troops at Charleston, slipped his men from vulnerable Fort Moultrie on the mainland into the more defensible Fort Sumter, in Charleston harbor. South Carolina's Governor Francis W. Pickens thereupon seized the abandoned Moultrie. On January 9, when the merchant ship *Star of the West* attempted to reinforce Anderson, she was driven off by fire from Charleston's batteries.[7]

Southern-rights papers placed upon Buchanan all blame for the shocking developments at Charleston. The President allegedly had broken his promise to maintain the status quo at Charleston. Major Anderson's surreptitious

move to Sumter and Buchanan's deceitful attempt to reinforce him clearly presaged an attempt to coerce South
Carolina, these papers further asserted.[8]

Unionist papers, on the other hand, considered South
Carolina's occupation of Fort Moultrie and her attack
upon the *Star of the West* as proof of that state's determination to draw the entire South into bloody revolution. They
agreed with the Richmond *Whig* which wrote:

We have never had a doubt that it was the deliberate purpose of
South Carolina, by some rash, illegal steps, to involve all her
sister Southern States in the calamity of civil war. She is not content to be allowed to go out of the Union peaceably. Her object
is to "drag" other States with her, and involve them all in a common and terrible conflict with the General Government. Her
self-conceit and her selfishness know no bounds. But will Virginia
become 'hitched on,' a miserable dependant [*sic*], to her tail? We
shall see.[9]

Unionist journals commended the President's determination to hold Fort Sumter. "We do not see how the
President can order Fort Sumter to be surrendered or
abandoned," said the Raleigh *North Carolina Standard*.
Some thought that the government should not have given
an inch, and criticized Buchanan for allowing Moultrie to
be abandoned to South Carolina. Most, however, approved
Anderson's action; indeed, the Major became something of
a hero to a few Unionist papers of the upper South. A
Virginia paper, for example, praised Anderson's skill in
accomplishing his strategic *"coup de main."* A North
Carolina journal admired the Major's "judicious step,"
which it believed was "calculated to prevent a collision,
and not to produce one."[10]

The growing friction between South Carolina and the
federal government gave a new sense of urgency to the old
newspaper dispute over coercion. After Lincoln's election
a great majority of Southern newspapers had come out

unequivocally against maintaining the Union by force. After South Carolina seceded and inaugurated a belligerent policy toward the federal government, a few Unionist papers were so embittered against the state that they hinted their approval of coercion. The Raleigh *Register* on December 26 argued that no national administration could allow a state to seize its property with impunity and concluded: "Let her stand alone to enjoy all the rich rewards due to her arrogant and obstinate course." South Carolina was trying to drag the whole South "into the vortex of revolution," asserted a Virginia paper, but her people should be left "to accept the consequences of their own act."[11]

Most antisecession papers nevertheless continued to warn the federal government not to attempt coercion. Said the Nashville *Republican Banner:* "As much as we love the Union of these States, and as little as we sympathize with the schemes of those Southern men who have been plotting for years the disruption of the government . . . we say 'let the Union slide' rather than attempt to preserve it 'forcibly.' " A coercive policy, argued Unionist papers, must result ultimately in a gigantic war between the sections. The Little Rock *Arkansas State Gazette* spoke the conviction of many such journals: "South Carolina has gone; let her go; and wo [*sic*] to the administration, or the power, that attempts to force her back into the Union against her will! The Southern States may not be united now, but an attempt to coerce South Carolina will not only unite the Southern States, but the Southern people, as one man."[12] By January only a very few Southern Unionist editors still dared to suggest coercion.[13]

Although they opposed a federal policy of force, many Southern Unionist papers continued to believe that peaceable secession was impossible. The growing aggressiveness of the lower South, together with a hardening of pro-coercion opinion in the North, reaffirmed for many editors the probability of war. On January 15 an Arkansas journal wrote: "The conflict between the sections of the country becomes more and more intense. The wisest men in the land can see no peaceful solution to our difficulties, nor are we sanguine enough to hope for any good results from them—or indeed anything but disaster and dire calamity and distress." A North Carolina newspaper, on February 5, predicted war within six months if the sectional differences were not resolved. A Virginia paper was even more pessimistic; in early January it allowed only sixty days of peace before holocaust would descend upon the land. Peaceable secession, the same journal said, was a "delusion" and an "absurdity." The Des Arc (Arkansas) *Constitutional Union* believed in mid-January that war was "tolerably certain to ensue."[14]

And the war, if it should come, would be a lengthy, costly, and bloody conflict, Unionist papers argued. The South might win such a war, some editors said, but it would be a pyrrhic victory. Not only would there be many casualties, they warned, but military despotism would replace government by the people. The Salisbury (North Carolina) *Daily Banner* predicted: "Fire and sword will devastate the land—the unhappy and heavily burthened people will become more or less servile, and for the sake of peace and the hope of safety, they will consent to the rule of ambitious tyrants."[15]

Americans could avoid internecine war only by agreeing to compromise their differences, Unionist journals asserted. If the nation's conservative, Union-loving men could but overcome the extremist minorities in both sections, they could restore harmony by negotiation. The Raleigh *North Carolina Standard* suggested that all would be well if only five-hundred public men from both sections could be "transported or confined in dungeons for six months."[16]

Unionist papers of the upper South looked first to Congress for the coveted compromise. Unfortunately, the sectional chasm between North and South proved too great for that body to bridge. Senator John J. Crittenden proposed a plan which provided for the extension of the Missouri Compromise line (36° 30') to the Pacific. Slavery was to be prohibited north of that line but protected south of it. In addition, new states could either adopt or outlaw slavery; the Fugitive Slave Act would be strengthened and slaveholders reimbursed for escaped slaves; the foreign slave trade would be suppressed; and slavery would be protected in the Southern states as well as the District of Columbia. These proposals constituted the minimum demands of even many Southern Unionists. But most Republican leaders were opposed to any compromise that would allow the further expansion of slavery. Indeed Lincoln admonished a Republican member of the House: "Entertain no proposition for a compromise in regard to the extension of slavery. The instant you do, they have us under again; all our labor is lost, and sooner or later must be done over." The Republican members of the Senate Committee of Thirteen, following Lincoln's lead, voted unanimously against the Crittenden plan, and although the Senate continued to debate the Kentucky senator's proposed amendment—with several variations—it never had a chance to be adopted.[17] Nevertheless Unionist newspapers of the upper South were grasping at straws, and almost all of them professed strong support for this plan.[18]

By February even the Unionist press of the upper South had given up on Crittenden's plan and had, instead, come out in support of the Washington Peace Conference, called by the Virginia legislature. Twenty-one states were represented when the delegates assembled on February 4; however the convention's prospects for success were clouded at the outset by the absence of eight Southern states, six of which met at Montgomery—also on February 4—to create the Confederacy. Although the peace convention showed few signs of ameliorating the sectional dispute during its lengthy deliberations, many Unionist editors persisted throughout the month of February in believing that ultimately it would restore the Union.[19]

Some Unionist journals nevertheless failed to hide their pessimism. The Wellsburg (Virginia) *Herald* predicted that the stalemate would continue until after Lincoln's inauguration, at which time "all the compromises will probably resolve themselves into the 'saltpetre' argument. Any other Government but the American wo'd have resorted to it long ago."[20]

Buoyed by the growing success of their movement secessionist newspapers vehemently rejected all suggestions of compromise. North Carolina's Charlotte *Bulletin* wrote: "We spit upon every plan to compromise, come from what source it may. A Southern man who would now offer to compromise with the Northern States is a traitor to the South, and ought to be branded, if possible, with a more prominent mark than was placed upon the murderer CAIN. May he be accursed forever." The rejection of the Crittenden plan by the Republicans gave secessionists a strong argument against further attempts by Southerners to save the Union. They now charged, with some justification, that the North was unwilling to concede even the minimal demands of the South. Therefore, they asked, why should any "true Southerner" wait a moment longer to advocate secession?[21]

Secession advocates continued to assert that the abolition of slavery was the real aim of the Republican party and they stressed the dire economic, political, and social damage which, allegedly, such a step would wreak upon the South. Some saw in the experience of other nations proof for their thesis that abolition would prove ruinous. The Wilmington (North Carolina) *Journal,* for example, found a lesson for the South in the recent history of Spain's former colonies in America. Freedom for blacks in those colonies not only had "degraded the white man almost to the level of his natural inferiors," but in virtually every case it had also caused deep economic depression. "Capital has fled, employment is gone," lamented the *Journal.* Pro-Confederate papers also appealed to the sense of revulsion which white Southerners invariably felt when they contemplated the social and political equality which blacks supposedly would attain if they were emancipated. An Arkansas editor admonished his readers: "Think for a moment . . . how would you like to have a buck negro come to the polls and tell you to stand back and let him vote? How would you like to sit on a jury with a negro, and how would you like to have a negro give testimony against you; in a word how would you like to have him associate with you and your family as an equal? Disgusting beyond description!" A secessionist Georgia paper subtly invoked the deepest fears of its female readers as it sought to enlist them for its cause:

We appeal to the women of the land. If they would keep our fair South free from the curse of negro equality; would keep forever the slave in the kitchen and cabin, and out of the parlor; would wish a national Capitol, where they will not be elbowed by negroes in the galleries of its Senate, and see negro delegates . . . sitting with the dignitaries of the land; if they would avoid that worse than Egyptian curse of flies, the vast population of impudent free negroes occupying the pavements, and getting the best seats everywhere; if they (the mothers of the States) have sons who can vote, let them record their names on the roll of liberty to-day; if the daughters have brothers or friends who hesitate, let them give them a blue rosette, a smile, and a ticket to—VOTE FOR SECESSION.[22]

As the secession movement gained momentum, extreme Southern-rights papers made increasingly bold attacks upon "submissionists," often asserting that at best they were simpletons, at worst, traitors. The Atlanta *Daily Intelligencer*, for example, could understand how Horace Greeley, "the leader of the abolitionists and abolition press of the North," could hold the opinions he held, "taking into account the neglected youth of this abandoned boy, and the school of fanaticism in which he has since been educated," but that paper thought it incredible that Southern editors could write "as vile abolitionism . . . as ever issued from the corrupt pens of Greeley and Garrison." But, the *Intelligencer* continued, should a Northern abolitionist come south "at this excited time," preaching "the doctrines that Southern Abolitionists are publishing in Southern newspapers with impunity, we would not give a dime for his life. He would be strung up to the nearest live oak—and permitted to dance upon nothing. The time has come when this home manufactured Abolitionism must be suppressed." Another Georgia journal called those who advocated caution and restraint "children in politics." A Texas paper was not so charitable; it asserted that the term "submissionist" was too mild for those who still believed in the Union: "Are they not traitors? Traitors to the South, to the equality of the States, and to a constitutional Union?"[23]

It was hardly surprising that secessionist journals sometimes demanded the proscription of certain Unionist newspapers. A leading fire-eating paper of Georgia thought that the Nashville *Democrat* should be prevented from circulating in Georgia. Free discussion of secession had been all right earlier, the editor explained, "but now we have taken the step and incurred the risks and responsibilities of a Revolution, and are just in that critical state of transitive existence which calls for patriotic harmony,

we think the circulation of such papers as the one we have
mentioned a positive crime against the State." In a like
manner, an Alabama paper argued that the *Tennessee
Baptist* ought to be banned from Alabama, because it was
published by "abolitionists" who hoped "insidiously to
propagate objections to and arguments against, *the institutions of the South.*"[24]

Unionist editors often complained about the growing
intolerance of the extreme Southern-rights press. Grumbled
John Maginnis of the New Orleans *True Delta:* "If a voice
of protest is heard like our own it is denounced as the
muttering of an unreasoable discontent." James P. Newcomb, editor of the San Antonio *Alamo Express,* asked:
"Is this still a land where liberty loves to dwell? Where
freedom is allowed to opinions and not denied utterance?
Where men are not to be persecuted for opinion's sake? If
it is, it would be well for those who differ with us to
remember it." The Knoxville *Whig* ran a copy of William
L. Yancey's boast that its editor, William G. Brownlow,
would be hanged in 1861. The prospective victim, who
was no stranger to threats, shrugged off the prediction and
said: "But, come what may, through weal or woe, in peace
or war, no earthly power shall keep me from denouncing
the enemies of my country." Editors under attack for their
"treason to the South" sometimes lost their tempers. The
Nashville *Republican Banner* told of an unnamed Virginian who, under a woodcut of a pistol, wrote: "He who
asserts that we are abolitionists or a black republican, is a
liar to all intents and purposes."[25]

The Unionist journalist who persevered might face both
financial and physical danger. The controversial William W. Holden, editor of the Raleigh *Standard,* lost his
position as state printer because he persisted in attacking
the state's pro-secession Democratic leaders.[26] Moreover, in
March of 1861 the same editor reportedly had just re-

ceived his third challenge "for the present season," apparently because of one of his attacks on secessionists.[27]

Holden, nevertheless, continued to publish without hindrance; at least one Unionist paper in Texas was not so fortunate. One night in early January of 1861 a secessionist mob broke into and smashed the offices of the Galveston *Union*, forcing the German-language paper to publish in a drastically curtailed form for several weeks. The independent La Grange *True Issue* called the incident an outrage and noted that the other Unionist paper in Galveston, the *Civilian and Gazette*, so feared the secessionists that it had not even reported the affair. On the other hand, the once moderate San Antonio *Herald* approved of the *Union*'s destruction because, it said, the journal was an "abolition concern." Actually the editor of the *Union*, B. F. Flake, was himself a slaveowner, whose "abolitionism" consisted of his arguing that Texas should consult the border states before withdrawing from the Union.[28] Small wonder that some Unionist editors gave up the fight. In a letter to Governor John Letcher of Virginia, written on February 18, 1861, A. B. Hendren of the Athens (Alabama) *Union Banner* explained his reasons for quitting the newspaper business: "Situated in the midst of a small community of Union loving men, to whom I flatter myself the 'Banner' has been mainly instrumental in giving tone and character, I would with pleasure be willing to continue an unrelenting warfare against the spirit of secession if my subsequent labors could promise the least encouragement to our cause, but being *the only press* now in Alabama that 'shows its hand' in that particular, I cannot of course expect to survive the mighty powers brought against me."[29]

After the election of Lincoln many secessionist papers denied, as they had during the campaign, that war must necessarily follow secession. No administration, they contended, would be so foolhardy as to invade the South. The Northern people would not allow it; world opinion would discountenance it. "Everything considered, we cannot believe there will be much fighting," said an Alabama paper. Declared a Georgia journal: "So far as civil war is concerned, we have no fears of that in Atlanta." Nor did the Memphis *Daily Appeal* believe that there was a living Northerner who would be so bold "as to dare raise a mailed hand against the Mother of States [Virginia], against the land where Jackson lived [Tennessee], or on the State which contains the ashes of the glorious and beloved Henry Clay [Kentucky]." Georgia's Albany *Patriot* promised to insure with a postage stamp the life of every Southern man killed in a war against the North. According to that same paper, the local women and children, using muskets loaded with "Connecticut wooden nutmegs," could whip every abolitionist who would come to Albany in the next ten years.[30]

While some minimized the chances of war, other secessionist editors grew increasingly truculent in the weeks following Lincoln's election. Many now readily admitted the possibility of armed conflict. Some even seemed to welcome the prospect. It was as if, after years of frustration in trying to solve sectional differences by peaceful means, some editors found attractive the idea of submitting the issues to the arbitration of the God of Wars. They minimized the possibility of defeat, pointing out that Southern men were more skilled in the use of firearms than were the Yankees. Fighting in defense of their homes and firesides, Southerners would be invincible, they argued. The New Orleans *Daily Delta* saw no reason to fear a war for freedom: "There is not a country of the civilized world which has not been compelled to pass through desolating wars and bloody revolutions." Good might even come from such a struggle, some believed. Though the Richmond *Dispatch* still hoped for a preservation of the Union, it wrote on December 15: "But, as we have before said, better dissolution, better war, than a perpetuation of the present state of chronic discontent. . . . Out of the chaos some new system may arise."[31]

One after another, the states of the lower South seceded. By the end of January, conventions in Mississippi, Alabama, Florida, Georgia, Louisiana, and Texas had voted their states out of the Union, except that the action in Texas would not become official until the voters had ratified it.[32]

Each secessionist paper joyfully greeted the news of its state's withdrawal from the Union. Many of the editors demonstrated intense emotion like that of the Athens (Georgia) *Southern Banner,* which wrote: "From our inmost soul we thank the God of our fathers for this glorious consummation. Let us all now say Amen! to it, from the mountains to the sea!" Louisiana's secession reminded a fire-eating New Orleans journal of the withdrawal of the children of Israel from Egypt:

Louisiana has joined the Southern exodus; she has passed dryshod through the chasm, she has placed a gulf of storm and water, cloud and darkness, thunder and lightening [*sic*], between herself and Egypt and servitude. Let Pharoah [*sic*] and his hosts follow at their peril.

The Milledgeville (Georgia) *Federal Union* patriotically changed its name to *Southern Federal Union* in honor of Georgia's secession. An Atlanta paper offered copies of Georgia's secession ordinance for ten cents apiece or three for a quarter; the document could be purchased on white satin for two dollars.[33]

Most of the moderate Southern-rights newspapers which had opposed separate-state secession cheerfully bowed to the decisions of their conventions. The Augusta (Georgia)

Daily Constitutionalist even apologized to the fire-eaters for once having opposed them: "We quarrelled with them *then* because we saw that their course would destroy the Union, we thank them *now* that it did."[34]

Occasionally, a paper expressed the hope that secession would help to bring about a "reconstruction" of the Union. For example, the Clarksville (Texas) *Northern Standard* wrote: "The Union is dissolved . . . but may be reconstructed, and we hope will be; and we hope to see the exertions of statesmen to that object—reconstruction." However, a great majority of the secessionist newspapers of the lower South regarded the organization of the Southern Confederacy on February 4 as an irrevocable step. The South must not look back, said an Alabama paper: "To recede is death." To the question "Will Georgia go back?" a journal in that state said: "We answer for one— never, no never. We are out of the foul domination of Black Republicanism, and we say let us stay out, world without end." A like-minded Louisiana sheet wrote: "The sooner the Black Republican Union, the Border States, and the world generally, understand that we are in earnest, and that our separation from a tyrannical government is final, the better it will be for all parties."[35]

The determination of secessionists to shake from their feet the dust of the old Union was complemented by an almost unbounded enthusiasm for the nascent Confederacy. With the formation of the new government there quickly developed a strong sense of Confederate nationalism, built upon the expressed conviction that the South, once freed of its Northern incubus, would immediately assert its superiority, not only over North America, but over the entire Western Hemisphere.

The new nation would far outshine the old, many editors predicted. Indeed, only two months after it had expressed hope for a reconstruction of the Union, the Clarksville

(Texas) *Northern Standard* asserted that, already, "the spirit, vigor, and force of legislation in the new Government, is a half century ahead of that in the old Government." The Memphis *Daily Appeal,* an erstwhile defender of the Union, made a similar judgment: "The new Republic, which is now being erected by Southern patriots, the rival in arts and arms of the northern Government, and surpassing it in its truly republican institutions, *will be the sole evidence on this continent of the capacity of man for self-government."* Some journals were so hard-put to find a modern government worthy of comparison to the new Confederacy that they searched the ancient past for suitable prototypes. The Atlanta *Gate-City Guardian* declared: "We will in a half century, show to the world such a people and such a Government as has not existed since the days of the Theocracy." Alabama's Jacksonville *Republican* had a similar vision of the new nation: "Looming up from the golden portals of the east, the sun throws his broad beams upon the landscapes of the very Eden of the South—the Palestine of a new Republic!" But the new "Eden," at least in the eyes of the Richmond *Enquirer,* would last even longer than the great civilizations of the past. "We may even hope that, in duration, it will exceed the pyramids, which, after the lapse of more than forty centuries, still stand erect and unshaken above the floods of the Nile."[36]

The new nation's geographical boundaries would by no means be limited to the lower South, or even to the continental United States. Among a strong minority there was a revival of the old spirit of Manifest Destiny, but with a Confederate twist. God had ordained the Confederacy, some editors reasoned; therefore he must have preordained that it would become the next empire of the western world. One Texas paper asserted that "the cotton lands of Mexico" would, "in the ordinary course of things," be absorbed by the South. The Confederacy also would annex Cuba, presumably whether or not Spain was agreeable to sustaining the loss of that colony. Indeed, according to the same journal, the natural expansion of the Confederacy would transform the Gulf of Mexico into a Southern "lake," and "the rich resources of Mexico and the South American States can thus be developed for the benefit of the Southern Confederacy, instead of being converted, as they are now, to the profit of England and France." The Wilson (North Carolina) *Ledger* was optimistic that the Confederacy would eventually embrace all of the slave states. But its ultimate vision was nothing short of grandiose. "The next thing we most earnestly desire is the acquisition of all of Mexico and Central America—all territory to the Isthmus *must* be ours; Cuba afterwards, either by negotiation or conquest."[37]

Many Unionist editors of the lower South, unmoved by these secessionists' rhapsodies over the Confederacy's future prospects, resisted secession until after their states had left the Union. Almost on the eve of Mississippi's secession, the Vicksburg *Whig* spoke bitterly of the extremists, both North and South, whose "acrimonious and malicious spirit . . . is rapidly re-acting on the masses." The Rome (Georgia) *Weekly Courier* pledged loyalty to the state but reminded secessionists that it was "vastly easier to get into trouble than to get out of it." The Baton Rouge *Weekly Gazette and Comet,* which for economic reasons believed Louisiana to be "the very last State in the glorious old constellation which should be induced to withdraw," thus addressed its state's secessionist convention: "Gentlemen, we are charitable enough to suppose that madness has made you blind, and that under this influence you know not what you do." In a like manner, the Shreveport *South-Western* begged Louisiana's "men of substance" not to be led astray "by those who would make the people believe that the planets were made of gold and diamonds, and are approachable by railroads and balloons."[38]

Secession grieved the Unionist editors of the lower South as much as it pleased the fire-eaters. Many Unionists made no attempt to hide their disappointment. The Augusta (Georgia) *Chronicle and Sentinel* wrote: "To say that we *rejoice* at such an act would be simple hypocrisy—we can not, and do not, rejoice. We have loved the Union with an affection pure and unselfish—not for any blessings it conferred, but because no pulsation of our heart ever beat, that was not loyal to the *great idea* of our ancestors—Union, Liberty and Fraternity." A Bell paper in Louisiana refused to place all of the blame for the Union's dissolution upon the North. It called both the abolitionists and fire-eaters "vile traitors" and sorrowfully asserted that the Southern people had allowed themselves to be duped and betrayed: "and thus the South has been *paticeps criminis* [*sic*] in this great national calamity. . . . Out upon the demagogues who have wrought this ruin of our glorious republic. May they be execrated and accursed henceforth and forever, and the places which knew them once, know them no more upon the earth." A Mississippi journal with similar views said:

We have lived to hear guns fired in honor of an attempted dissolution of the American Union. Thank God, we had tears to shed; tears of bitter grief and of indignant reproach—alike against the fanaticism of the North, which has given the excuse or apology for the act, and against the wild madness of partisans of the South, who, ever hating the Union, have precipitated the Cotton States into revolution.[39]

Having vented their anger, however, Unionist journals of the lower South usually accepted secession in good grace. Most of them believed that the acts of the secession conventions reflected the will of a majority of the people; therefore, they felt that all citizens should support the new Confederacy. A Constitutional Union paper in Louisiana epitomized the view of most such journals: "We have all embarked in the same ship. No matter how much we may be dissatisfied with her commanders, her equipments or the manner of her launching, *we are on board,* and must take her share of storms and sunshine. . . . Sink or swim, let us all pull together."[40]

Some Unionist editors required a few weeks to get over their anger. For example, the Augusta *Chronicle and Sentinel* at first opposed Georgia's joining the Confederacy and was so disillusioned by the failure of the democratic process to solve sectional problems that it seriously proposed a constitutional monarchy for the South. By February 5, however, the *Chronicle and Sentinel* was willing to join a "temporary Confederacy" for the mutual protection of the Southern states; and on February 13 the paper's metamorphosis was completed when it announced its full support of "the new Republic."[41]

A minority of Unionist editors of the lower South continued to denounce secession after their states had left the Union. Although the Tuscumbia *North Alabamian* had "acquiesced" in secession, it still "disapproved" of it; and after the state had joined the Confederacy, its editor expressed regret that he had favored the co-operationist delegates for the Alabama convention. When the fire-eating Tuscumbia *Constitution* suggested that the *North Alabamian*'s editor should leave the Confederacy if he disliked it, the editor replied: "If all were to leave who are dissatisfied, we fear the balance would soon have to leave or do worse, for they would have few left on whom they could safely rely for self-protection." Mississippi's Corinth *Advertiser* was still demanding a "reconstruction" of the Union on February 9. A Constitutional Unionist in Texas promised, on March 1, to resist the new order of things, not forcibly, but with the pen: "And so long as freedom of opinion is tolerated, we shall boldly and fearlessly give expression to our honest convictions, however distasteful they may be to tyrants and usurpers."[42]

John Maginnis of the New Orleans *True Delta,* one of the most unyielding critics of the Confederacy, showed his contempt for the new Southern government even before it was born. While Louisiana's delegates met at Montgomery with the representatives of the other seceded states for the purpose of creating the Confederacy, Maginnis commented:

We want to see the Yanceys, the Toombes [*sic*], the Rhetts, the Jeff. Davises and the mighty swarm of equally brilliant aspirants for fame and high office at the head of such a government; and we should enjoy the sight still more were it not for the disagreeable recollection that for all their dancing this state must, in the nature of things, be a large contributor for the music. Then comes the reckoning when the banquet's over; but never mind, sufficient unto the day is the evil thereof.

Later he referred to the Confederate officials as "the Montgomery provisionals" and to their government as "the provisional abortion at Montgomery." When at last, the Louisiana secession convention broke up on March 22, almost two months after it had voted the state out of the Union, the *True Delta* wrote: "In our inmost heart, this morning, we sincerely do thank God that the ignorant, factious and republic-destroying gang, recently belching and spitting out treason, profligacy and waste, in Baton Rouge, is scattered."[43]

By February many newspapers in Virginia, North Carolina, Arkansas, and Tennessee were advocating secession. Moreover, Union supporters in those states demonstrated a growing pessimism. Crittenden's plan, which embodied the minimum demands of most Southerners, had been decisively rejected by the Republicans. The leaders of the cotton states had proceeded with their plans to organize the new Southern Confederacy, and the revolt of the lower South took on an air of permanence. In addition, when the cotton states seceded, their congressmen and senators resigned and returned home. This destroyed the most emphasized of all Unionist arguments, which contended that the Republicans were powerless to harm the South because the Democrats controlled Congress. By February 1 the Republicans were very much in the congressional driver's seat.

Most Unionist editors continued to oppose secession in February only because they had reason to believe that a compromise of sectional differences was still possible. The Washington Peace Conference, still proceeding with its secret deliberations, was the principal reason for their optimism. Unionist editors of the upper South believed that if they could impede the growth of secessionism in their states until the peace conference could perform its miracles, the sections might still be reunited. Consequently, such editors labored hard to defeat the secessionist delegates in convention elections held in Virginia, Arkansas, North Carolina, and Tennessee. In each of these states the Unionists won. Tennessee voted against calling a convention at all, and Arkansas, Virginia, and North Carolina each elected Unionist majorities to their conventions.[44]

Antisecessionist papers regarded the convention victories in the upper South as an auspicious sign of the Union's impending salvation. The Trenton (Tennessee) *Southern Standard* wrote: "Secession has received a terrible blow in this State. 'Glory be to God in the highest, peace on earth and good will towards all men.' The prospects for a compromise are also greatly increasing." The Charlestown *Virginia Free Press* was pleased that Virginia had refused to be "precipitated" into rebellion and further wrote: "We look to the Peace Convention now in Washington to reestablish union, fraternity, and concord in our glorious and hitherto prosperous Republic." Another Virginia paper also was cheered by the results of the election, but it warned the friends of the Union not to relax: "The monster of disunion in the desperation of its death agony, is still capable of making mischief. Watch the tail until the sun goes down, then burn the carcass and scatter the ashes, as the only security."[45]

These shouts of "victory" were really but the death rattle of editorial Unionism in Virginia, Arkansas, North Carolina, and Tennessee. The most faithful among Unionist papers in these states now placed stern conditions upon their Unionism. Only a few months before, many such journals were contending that the South had suffered nothing at the hands of the North. Now, they demanded a "restoration" of the South's "rights." "She [the South] wants her rights in the Union, if possible," said a Virginia paper: "It now remains for the North . . . to make a peaceful adjustment of difficulties." The Little Rock *Arkansas State Gazette* declared: "Redress will be asked for our grievances, and if not granted, fully and entirely, a formal separation will take place. This is inevitable." A solution must be found by March 4—the date of Lincoln's inauguration—warned the Van Buren *Press,* or Arkansas would be forced to secede. Others called for military preparations in case negotiations with the North proved fruitless.[46]

Some Unionist papers had already joined outright the growing band of secessionist journals in the upper South. On January 8 the Newbern (North Carolina) *Weekly Progress* declared the Union dissolved and called upon the whole South to arm itself in defense of "our honor." After the Crittenden Plan had been rejected by Congress, the Fayetteville *Arkansian* announced: "The Union no longer exists. The ties of love and friendship between the North and South are severed. . . . And now our only and last appeal is, to God and our right arms." The Des Arc *Constitutional Union* agreed with the *Arkansian,* asserting on January 18 that the secession of the lower South had left Arkansas no choice but to secede. The editor deplored the necessity of

following after the departed states, "yet being 'native here
and to the manor born,' we are with them forever."[47]

There was evidence that some conservative papers found
the transition from Unionist to secessionist positions painful. For example, a North Carolina journal which until
recently had defended the Union carried in the same issue
contradictory poems—"Oh God, Preserve My Country" and
"The Southern Marseillaise." The former beseeched the
Lord to protect the Union,

> 'Till through the land is heard,
> Brothers meet as brothers always,
> Both in deed and heart and word.

The other sounded a different note:

> Sons of the South, awake to glory!
> Hark! hark! what myriads bid you rise.
> Your children, wives, and grandsires hoary,
> Behold their tears and hear their cries.
> . . . .
> To arms! to arms! ye brave,
> Th' avenging sword unsheath!

The Jonesborough (Tennessee) *Union* flayed those who
still believed that the Union was salvageable, but its masthead continued to proclaim: "WE JOIN NO PARTY WHICH DOES
NOT CARRY THE FLAG, AND KEEP STEP TO THE UNION." According to its neighbor, the Jonesborough *Express,* the *Union*
changed opinions so often that it should append the words
"corrected weekly" to its column entitled "Our Present Position."[48]

Although the Unionist papers of Virginia, Arkansas,
North Carolina, and Tennessee seemed to be moving toward a secessionist viewpoint, many of them still cast a
jaundiced eye at the new Southern Confederacy. They continued to harbor rancor toward the "precipitators" of the
lower South. Some doubted the stability of any Union of

which South Carolina was a member. Such journals also were reluctant to join the Confederacy because they feared that it would be dominated by the Gulf states. In such a nation, they said, only the voice of "King Cotton" would be heard. The Fayetteville *Arkansian* suggested that Arkansas would get more political offices in an alliance with the Indian nations than in a Confederacy dominated by South Carolina. Said Parson Brownlow's Knoxville *Whig:* "We can never live in a Southern Confederacy, and be made hewers of wood and drawers of water for a set of aristocrats, and overbearing tyrants." If Tennessee joined the Confederacy, declared the Parson, the *Whig* would advocate East Tennessee's secession from the rest of the state and the formation of an independent "STATE OF FRANKLAND."[49]

Most of the editors who foresaw a dissolution of the Union and who opposed joining the Southern Confederacy wished to establish a "Border" or "Middle" Confederacy. Such a Union theoretically would include all of the slave states of the upper South. It would remain aloof from both the Northern Union and the Southern Confederacy.[50] During the spring, as secessionism was intensified in Virginia, Arkansas, North Carolina, and Tennessee, talk of a third confederation decreased in those states. As anger toward the North increased, the idea of being "hitched to South Carolina" apparently became less distasteful.

In spite of mounting evidence to the contrary, many Unionist papers professed to see signs in the North of a growing moderation on sectional questions. They especially emphasized conciliatory speeches made by Seward and other Republicans in Congress. These orations were said to be manifestations of a great change which was taking place in the North. A North Carolina paper read into them "a returning sense of justice at the North." And a Virginia journal wrote: "We firmly and honestly believe that the Union will be restored, and peace and prosperity revived. . . . The skies may be darkened for a while, but there is light ahead. This is too great, too happy, and too prosperous a country for patriotism to permit its sacrifice on the unhallowed altar of reckless ambition. The stars and stripes will yet wave over a united people."[51]

But Unionist journals were mistaken in contending that sectionalism was declining in the North. Republicans in Congress steadfastly rejected every proposal for compromise. And, although Seward spoke moderately on sectional issues, several other Republican congressmen and senators used the strongest invective in denouncing the South. In addition, many Northern state legislatures passed belligerent resolutions denying the right of the South to secede and endorsing a policy of coercion.[52]

Moreover, Lincoln, the President-elect, gave few indications during the winter that he took the secession movement seriously. After the election many Southern Unionist papers had professed restrained confidence in Lincoln. From November to February, however, the President-elect said almost nothing publicly about the sectional crisis, and Unionist papers of the upper South began to criticize him for his policy of silence. A word from the head of the Republican party, said the Lynchburg *Virginian,* "will do more to conciliate the South, and tranquilize the country, than all else at present." Another Virginia paper wrote: "The conduct of Mr. Lincoln, the President elect, in not writing or saying something to assist in quelling the present agitation and indignation excited by the election of a sectional candidate by a sectional party, cannot be justified."[53]

In February, Lincoln finally broke his silence with a series of speeches, delivered on his inaugural trip to Washington. In these impromptu addresses he reaffirmed his support of the Chicago platform and facetiously dismissed Southern grievances.[54] Secessionist journals reacted predictably to the reports of Lincoln's remarks. Typical was the Richmond *Examiner,* which called Lincoln a "beastly figure," and further asserted: "No American of any section has read the oratory with which he has strewn his devious road to Washington, condensed lumps of imbecility, buffoonery, and vulgar malignity, without a blush of shame."[55]

Unionist newspapers of the upper South also were angered by Lincoln's cavalier treatment of Southern demands and by his apparent inability to grasp the seriousness of the sectional crisis. Many now admitted that their former confidence in the "Black Republican" leader had been misplaced, and some now hurled at Lincoln insults that would have been worthy of Robert Barnwell Rhett. The Charlotte *North Carolina Whig* reported Lincoln's speeches and wrote: "Famous as Kentucky has ever been for the size and quality of her live stock, she evidently overdone herself when she gave birth to Abraham Lincoln. . . . We have heard of small men, and seen some, but the 'rail-splitter' is a little in advance of any that we have ever seen or read of." Tennessee's Clarksville *Chronicle* called Lincoln a "soulless and brainless demagogue" and likened him to Nero, who fiddled while Rome burned. That paper further asserted: "If he be an honest man . . . he must be a consummate fool; and if he be a man of talents, then he is a consummate knave." Continuing in the same vein, the Staunton (Virginia) *Vindicator* wrote of Lincoln:

His speeches on his tour . . . have been a display of the most vulgar and ill-bred tastes, more alike to buffoonery of the clown than the logic of the statesman. In stead of rising to the dignity of his exalted position, he indulges in the most disgusting and silly electioneering harangues, and exposes his ignorance both of the science of letters as well as the rules of rhetoric. When the people so far forget themselves as to place such a man at the head of a great nation like ours, we almost become skeptical as to their capacity for self-government.[56]

On inauguration eve most Unionist editors of the upper South were greatly discouraged. The lower South was gone, and a "reconstruction" involving the seceded states seemed impossible. The best hopes for compromise had virtually vanished, and the incoming President was so oblivious to the danger that he was telling jokes on his way to Washington. A North Carolina journal expressed the feeling of many Unionist papers of the upper South when it said: "We are unable to give our readers any hope this week for the preservation of the Union. So far as we can see there is not the least hope left that the Peace Conference will do anything at all."[57] Few such editors expected much reassurance of their fading faith in the Union from Lincoln's inaugural address. Fewer still shared the optimism of the Raleigh *Register* which, on March 3, stated its belief that Lincoln would yet disappoint the abolitionists of his party and grasp "the awful responsibility of the position in which he is placed, and the opportunity which he has of being the savior instead of the destroyer of this great nation."[58]

IX

The Agony Is Over

SOUTHERN newspapers thoroughly reported and discussed Lincoln's inaugural address. The new President sought both to allay Southern fears and to establish the federal authority over the seceded states. Lincoln firmly denied the right of secession. "No state upon its own mere motion, can lawfully get out of the Union," he said. He further argued that, legally, the Union remained unbroken, in spite of the action of the lower South, and he promised to enforce the laws of the nation in all of the states. He then delivered what seemed to many Southerners to be a direct threat against South Carolina: "The power confided to me will be used to hold, occupy, and possess the property and places belonging to the Government and to collect duties and imposts."[1]

On a more conciliatory note, Lincoln appealed to Southern Unionism on the basis of mutual interest. He said: "Physically speaking, we cannot separate. We cannot remove our respective sections from each other, nor build an impassable wall between them. A husband and wife may be divorced, and go out of the presence and beyond the reach of each other; but the different parts of our country cannot do this. They cannot but remain face to face, and intercourse, either amicable or hostile, must continue between them." The President finished his speech with an emotional appeal to the Southern sense of kinship with the North:

I am loath to close. We are not enemies but friends. Though passion may have strained, it must not break our bonds of affection. The mystic chords of memory, stretching from every battlefield and patriot grave to every living heart and hearthstone all over this broad land, will yet swell the chorus of the Union when again touched, as surely they must be, by the better angels of our nature.[2]

Lincoln's inaugural received no praise from the newspapers of the seceded states. The "mystic chords of memory" had long since become crashing cacophonies as far as those states were concerned, and their newspapers looked with contempt upon Lincoln's efforts to renew the "bonds of affection" by appealing to the common past of the sections. "There is nothing in this school boy production except the threat of coercion," said an Atlanta journal, "There will, then, as they must have it, be war." A New Orleans paper called the President's style "vulgar," and further wrote: "We are compelled to regard it [Lincoln's inaugural] as a very inferior production, whether considered as a literary, logical or statesmanlike production. The language is mean, involved and inconclusive, evidently such as only persons of very imperfect education would employ."[3]

Secessionist editors of the upper South were no less critical of Lincoln's oration than their colleagues within the Confederacy. They dismissed as hypocrisy the President's appeal for sectional brotherhood and denounced his promise to assert the national authority over federal property and to continue collecting duties in all Southern ports. Many papers in the upper South regarded the President's message as a clear warning that federal troops and ships were about to be used to subdue the Confederacy. The Nashville *Union and American* said: "No man can read the Inaugural, without coming to the conclusion *that it is a declaration of war against the seceded States,* and in less than thirty days, if its avowals are carried out, we shall have the clangor of resounding arms, with all its concomitants of death, carnage and woe." The Richmond *Dispatch* declared: "The Inaugural Address of ABRAHAM LINCOLN inaugurates civil war. . . . The sword is drawn and the scabbard thrown away." The formerly Unionist Wilmington (North Carolina) *Daily Herald* warned: "There is no mitigation of Lincoln's fanaticism in this Inaugural Address, and, painful as it may be to the American people, they might as well open their eyes to the solemn fact that war is inevitable."[4]

Secessionist newspapers of the upper South discounted Lincoln's conciliatory remarks. They believed that he had included soft assurances only to make the upper South swallow the hard pronouncement of a coercive policy. A North Carolina paper observed: "It [the inaugural] uses honeyed words enough but concedes nothing, and indicates coercion beyond all reasonable doubt." Said another North Carolina journal: "It is deceptive. It coats with the semblance of peace and friendship what smells of gore and hate."[5] Slave states of the upper South must not be deceived, disunionists argued, but must hasten to join their sister states of the Southern Confederacy. War could be avoided only if the fifteen slave states were to present a solid front in opposition to the new administration's apparent policy of force. A Virginia paper wrote: "There is but one way to prevent universal war and destruction too horrible to contemplate, and that one course is for Virginia and every border slave State *at once* to unite with the States of the South, and proclaim to the North that no interference, whatever, will be tolerated for a moment."[6]

Some Unionist papers of the upper South, on the other

hand, saw in Lincoln's more conciliatory words new hope for the Union. Although they noted Lincoln's pledge to uphold the national authority and his denial of the right of secession, they considered the speech to be, on the whole, surprisingly moderate. Such journals blamed the President's more threatening statements upon the exigencies of office. The Salisbury *Carolina Watchman* said: "We cannot see what else he could have said, after just taking the oath of office." Others asserted that Lincoln had taken no more of a coercive position than had Buchanan in his state-of-the-Union message. Thus, a Virginia paper asked: "Why should any one have expected more from Mr. Lincoln than from Mr. Buchanan? Can any one answer this question? And yet every one seems to have done so."[7]

A few Unionist papers of the upper South enthusiastically greeted the President's inaugural. Parson Brownlow, who had recently grown critical of Lincoln, wrote in his Knoxville *Whig:* "We endorse the entire Address, as one of the best papers of the kind we have seen, and we commend it for its temperance and conservatism." The Nashville *Republican Banner* called the speech "mild and conservative," and expressed the belief that if civil war were to ensue, it would not be Lincoln's fault. William W. Holden of the Raleigh *North Carolina Standard* confessed that he was as hostile to Lincoln "as any reasonable man in the South"; nevertheless, he strongly endorsed the President's inaugural address:

It is not a war message. It is not strictly speaking, a Black Republican message; for while he recognizes slavery in the States as perpetual, and as never to be interfered with in any way by the abolitionists, he deliberately refrains from pressing the main principle of his platform, to wit, the exclusion of the South from all the Territories of the Union. It is not unfriendly to the South.[8]

Most Unionist papers of the upper South appraised Lincoln's inaugural cautiously. They often expressed disap-

proval of the President's address but were still willing to
wait for a more tangible sign of his hostility toward the
South. Such papers believed that there would be plenty of
time to act later, if Lincoln should prove treacherous. An
Arkansas journal called Lincoln's message "wishy-washy,"
but it also admitted that the President could hardly have
been expected to encourage revolution. "We for one, are
willing to give him a trial." Lincoln was too "practical" to
attempt coercion, said a Tennessee paper; therefore, the
upper South should not rush out of the Union on account
of the strong words spoken by the President at his inauguration.[9]

Significantly, many of those papers which had been
among the Union's best defenders in previous months now
seemed ready to give up the struggle. They were unable to
share the optimism of those who discounted Lincoln's
threats against the seceded states. They agreed with the
secessionist view that Lincoln's inaugural was virtually a
declaration of war against the South. Consequently these
papers demonstrated both a growing hostility toward Lincoln and a new cordiality toward the cotton states. The
Charlotte *North Carolina Whig* said of Lincoln's speech:
"It cannot fail to excite a shudder in the most stoical
bosom." Showing more faith in future historians than was
warranted, the editor further predicted:

The people of the South understand this matter perfectly, and
whoever in after days shall write the history of these times, will
find no difficulty in affixing the blame where it justly belongs. We
are waiting the signal that shall call us to arms. And when the
sword is taken from the scabbard, we hope it may never again be
sheathed until the rights of the South are acknowledged and
respected.

The Richmond *Whig* conceded that the Gulf states had
acted rashly; "but, considering them erring sisters entitled
to our sympathies and our aid in an emergency, Virginia

can never consent, and will never consent for the Federal Government to employ coercive measures towards them."[10]

Lincoln's policy in the month following his inauguration seemed to confirm the opinion of the more sanguine Union papers. He carefully avoided a showdown with South Carolina by refusing to send reinforcements to Fort Sumter. Moreover, on March 19 the Associated Press reported that the evacuation of Sumter would take place the next day. On the same day, the President dispatched a mission to Charleston to determine the condition of the fort and to ascertain the attitude of South Carolina's people toward the Union. Ward Lamon, one of the members of the Charleston mission, assured Governor Pickens on March 25 that Lincoln shortly would order Fort Sumter's evacuation. In addition, Secretary of State William H. Seward, from mid-March to April 8, repeatedly assured Confederate commissioners in Washington that the federal troops would be withdrawn from the Charleston fort.[11]

Major Anderson's troops failed to move, however, and the apparent vacillation of Lincoln perplexed and confused Southern editors. A Georgia paper probably spoke the thoughts of many editors when it wrote: "The conduct of the Lincoln Administration is a mystery and a riddle to every one, both friend and foe. They profess to be desirous of avoiding civil war, and yet talk as coolly of collecting the revenue in the seceded States as if they believed there would be no resistance to such a measure. They have promised . . . to withdraw from Fort Sumter, but they still remain there. . . . What are we to think of this shuffling policy between peace and war?"[12]

Some secessionist papers of the upper South nevertheless believed the reports of Sumter's impending evacuation. But this did not sway them from their opinion that the border slave states must secede. Indeed, some believed that an evacuation of the fort would actually aid the secession movement. The Memphis *Avalanche* wrote on March 15: "The evacuation of Fort Sumter and determination not to collect revenue of the Government within the seceded States will add strength to the cause of secession. It will be virtually admitting that the Union is dissolved, and a recognition of the doctrine of secession, and will, therefore, add strength to the course of disunion." The Clarksville (Virginia) *Tobacco Plant* considered the plan to evacuate the fort a ruse designed to lull the slave states of the upper South into submission. That paper wrote:

Must Virginia forget, clean forever, her children of the South, and sink down a sullen slave to Lincolnism? Must she give up the glorious future which awaits her connection with the Gulf States, and wait, wait, pause, until the chains of tyranny are forged and the rod of oppression made for her and her children's children; or will she, in the spirit of Revolutionary resistance to wrong, nobly resolve to follow, as she is now too late to lead, the holy crusade for liberty, equality and independence.[13]

Secessionist papers of the upper South redoubled their efforts on behalf of disunion in the weeks following Lincoln's inaugural. Although conventions in Virginia, North Carolina, Tennessee, and Arkansas had decided against secession, advocates of disunion in those states were increasingly confident of the ultimate success of their cause. They pointed to the failure of the Washington Peace Conference as final proof of the North's unwillingness to compromise sectional differences. It was evident, such papers argued, that the conflict between the free and slave states was indeed an irrepressible one. They further contended that there was no longer a question of whether the border states would leave the Union; it only remained to be revealed when they would secede. Arkansas's Fort Smith *Daily Times and Herald* said: "The Southern States—we mean all south of Mason and Dickson's [sic] line, will and must ultimately unite in one Confederacy. It is as certain as the laws of gravitation." The Richmond *Examiner* predicted: "The inexorable necessity and sequence of events will take Virginia out of the Northern, and place her in the Southern Union. *The only real question concerns the day she will go.*"[14]

Exponents of secession in the upper South were also encouraged by the rapid growth of their movement among Constitutional Unionists. Cheered by this trend, a secessionist journal in North Carolina admonished its readers: "Don't give up the ship. Stand to your guns. Recruits are coming daily. The very flower of the opposition are with us now. One more effort against Black Republican rule and the day is ours."[15] Secessionist editors shrewdly cajoled conservatives in an effort to win them over to the side of revolution. They asserted that the Union was already permanently dissolved; therefore, they said, the old theoretical arguments over disunion no longer applied. The Staunton (Virginia) *Vindicator* wrote: "We must either identify ourselves with the North or the South. The question of Union or Disunion is dead and buried. Dissolution has already taken place." Opined the Memphis *Daily Appeal:* "Lincoln only announced a philosophical truth, when he proclaimed that this Government could not exist half slave and half free. . . . Secession means nothing more nor less than a severance from the Black Republic of the North and a union with the white man's Confederacy of the South." The Richmond *Examiner* asserted: "Submission is revolution; Secession will be conservatism."[16]

Secessionist papers reserved stronger methods of persuasion for refractory conservatives. They continued to accuse Unionists of treason to the South. For example, on March 16, the Memphis *Avalanche* alleged: "The Memphis *Bulletin* is *not* at present an avowed straight-out, downright Black Republican paper, but it is fast becoming such. Some sort of wiley [*sic*] temptation, we know not what, seems to have allured it into the most bewildering snares, and it is now slowly but surely marching into the Black Republican party." Another Memphis secessionist paper warned the public to beware of those who counseled submission: "Lincoln now has apologists; in a few months more he will have advocates."[17]

Other pressures upon Union advocates were of a more personal nature. The editor of the Nashville *Republican Banner* admitted that a loss of friends and readers had forced him to examine and re-examine his stand against secession; yet, he was convinced of the correctness of his position and refused to change it. The Lynchburg *Virginian*'s editor was so upset over disagreements with friends concerning the question of disunion that he would have retired from political journalism, he said, had he not felt it a duty to continue. When secessionists failed to win over a Union paper by other means, they sometimes bought it. On March 9 the Memphis *Avalanche* announced the purchase of the Memphis *Enquirer*. And, on April 4, the Charlestown *Virginia Free Press* wrote: "The Secessionists of the State, not content with *three* Disunion newspapers in the city of Richmond, have also bought the Whig from Messrs. Bondurant and Co."[18]

Occasionally, in Unionist areas, it was the secession advocates who felt pressure. The Charlotte *North Carolina Whig* admitted on March 26 that several of its readers had canceled subscriptions since its decision to support disunion. On April 3 the Raleigh *State Journal* denounced as disgraceful the strong antisecession demonstrations in Raleigh and promised to continue advocating revolution, regardless of the pressure that might be brought to bear upon its editor. "Nowhere in this State, if any where in the Country, does there exist such a state of feeling against Southern Rights men as in Raleigh."[19]

Unionist papers were much encouraged by Lincoln's apparent decision to evacuate Fort Sumter. Such a step, they reasoned, would remove the principal threat of war between the sections. If civil war could be avoided, the secession movement would be checked and, eventually, the Union might be restored. In an article headed "Secession On Its Back," an Arkansas journal informed its readers of Sumter's impending evacuation and predicted that such a move by the government would give "the death blow to secession in this State—and we are soon to have peace and quiet throughout the land." A Virginia paper, noting reports that Lincoln planned to relinquish Sumter, said: "We shall be most delightfully disappointed at the new Administration's commencing its official dealings with the seceded States with such a wise, proper and laudable act." A North Carolina Union advocate wrote: "Let this policy be carried out, and we predict that the secession fever will die out in a short while, not only in the border States, but in those that have seceded." A Tennessee paper believed that the seceded states "will, after a few years of independent existence, return to the glorious Union of our Fathers."[20]

Lincoln's dilatory policy regarding Fort Sumter temporarily restored the waning faith in the Union of many other antisecessionist journals of the upper South, and, by the end of March, many of them were rededicating themselves to resist disunion. In late March the Little Rock *Arkansas State Gazette* declared: "We will not believe in a final and irrevocable dissolution of the Union until that fact has been consummated beyond all doubt and hope." "North Carolina will not secede from the Union for existing causes," averred the Raleigh *North Carolina Standard* on April 3. Tennessee's Clarksville *Jeffersonian* said: "We believe that the continuance of this Union under which we have prospered so much and achieved such greatness and renown, is entirely compatible with the rights of every section and the true interests of every individual citizen."[21] Some Unionist papers renewed their attacks upon the theory of secession. For example, on March 22, the Harrisonburg *Virginia Citizen* wrote:

When the question of the secession of a State from the American Union was first broached, there was not an individual in all the land with a thimble full of brains who believed it to be within the range of the rights reserved to the States. . . . But time wore on. Contentions grew apace; and now, strange to say, a large proportion of the Southern people not only *endure* but actually *embrace* the unclean thing; and all who do not fall down and worship at the altar of the newly found goddess, are branded as miscreants and traitors! It has become not only a legal but an excellent thing—It is good for all sorts of complaints, and is as easily applied as ever was the "Poor Man's Plaster." Old men roll it under their tongues as a sweet morsel, and children play with it as familiarly as little girls dandle their dolls upon their knee.[22]

Hopes for the Union's resurrection were short-lived. The Washington Peace Conference collapsed in March. Some Unionist editors next supported a convention of the border states as a means of saving the peace, if not the Union, but they usually were vague on the specific steps such a convention might take and their hearts clearly were not in the new movement.[23]

By early April the news from Washington had begun to sound ominous once again. Advocates of the Union had based their recent optimism upon the reports that Lincoln would give up Fort Sumter and probably Fort Pickens in Florida. Actually, the President had not yet made up his mind on a firm course of action regarding Sumter. He had ordered Pickens reinforced on March 11, but it was April 16 before the fort was actually relieved. Throughout March, Lincoln put off making a decision on Fort Sumter, while he continued to seek some middle ground on which could be preserved both the peace and the Union. In early March the President seemed willing to relinquish Sumter, if the Union could be preserved in the transaction. But, by the end of the month, he was disillusioned with Southern Unionism—the strength of which he had previously overestimated—and, by April 4, he had reached his decision to resupply Major Anderson and retain the fort.[24]

Lincoln's decision on Sumter was not kept secret, and the news spread quickly to the Southern press. Secessionist and Unionist papers alike reacted with alarm to the reports of a federal attempt to relieve the Charleston fort. This information "broke upon the ear of the public like the alarm of the fire bell at night," said the Memphis *Avalanche*. Most journals of the upper South reaffirmed their belief that war must follow any attempt to reinforce Sumter. Indeed, many editors now argued that war between the sections was inevitable. "War is at hand," said a North Carolina paper on April 11. A Virginia journal warned: "The most reliable intelligence from Washington warrants the belief of immediate war upon the seceded states."[25]

Meanwhile, on April 10, the Confederate Secretary of War, L. P. Walker, ordered General P. G. T. Beauregard, who commanded the Confederate forces at Charleston, to present an ultimatum to Major Anderson, demanding the surrender of Fort Sumter. If Anderson refused, Beauregard was to open fire and reduce the fort. Anderson rejected the ultimatum, but, at the same time, admitted that a shortage of food would compel his surrender within "a few days." The last part of the Major's reply made the Confederates pause. The officials at Montgomery hoped to avoid firing the first shot of a civil war. Their strategy was to achieve a peaceful separation, if possible, and, if it proved impossible to save the peace, they wanted the federal government to commit the first act of war. On the other hand, Sumter was more than just a thorn in Jefferson Davis's flesh; it had become the symbol of federal authority in the seceded states and therefore must be taken, if the Confederacy expected to command the respect of either the border slave states or the outside world. Since the impetuous South Carolinians threatened to act if the Confederacy did not, Davis's government had to move quickly, or run the risk of losing the initiative at Charleston to local hotheads. At Secretary Walker's order, Beauregard, on the night of April 11–12, demanded of Anderson that he specify the date and time of his evacuation. Anderson replied to the three aides who delivered the message that he would evacuate by noon on the fifteenth, "should I not receive prior to that time controlling instructions from my Government or additional supplies." Beauregard's aides considered this answer unsatisfactory, since word had already come of the imminent arrival of the Sumter relief expedition. Thus, at 3:30 A.M., on April 12, they informed Anderson that the bombardment would begin in one hour.[26]

Both the best hopes of secessionist journals and the worst fears of Unionist papers were confirmed when at 4:30 A.M., April 12, Confederate batteries opened fire on Fort Sumter. After absorbing a bombardment of forty hours, Major Anderson surrendered the fort.

Within hours of the first shot at Charleston the telegraph carried news of the action to papers all over the South. Not surprisingly, secessionist papers of the upper South were jubilant. In their opinion the outbreak of hostilities between federal and Confederate forces at Charleston would break the back of Unionism in the border slave states and would cement public opinion in those states on the side of secession. They demanded unity. A Memphis paper wrote: "*Now* we can have no political differences; *now* we can have no *Union* men; *now* we must have a united and harmonious South, giving counsel and courage to each other, to bear up the banner of *independence* fearlessly and onward." The Raleigh *State Journal,* which recently had complained of Unionist pressures in North Carolina's capital city, charitably promised not to "retaliate upon those who have been denouncing us. This is a time when the people should forget past differences and come now to the sacred altar of their country and there *now to stand or fall together*."[27]

The secessionist press in Virginia, North Carolina, Tennessee, and Arkansas insisted that their states must secede without further delay. "Is Virginia to act now?" asked the Richmond *Examiner:* "When the tocsin has sounded and the gun is booming, shall Virginia turn her thumbs in silent motion as an old toothless woman? Is Virginia a suckling, powerless babe, then? Is she to be spit upon? Let her people answer." In a like manner, the Nashville *Union and American* wrote: "Are we but the bastard sons of the heroes who here won for our State, the glorious distinctive appellation of 'THE VOLUNTEER STATE'?" On May 1 another secessionist paper in Tennessee asked:

How long will Tennessee remain in Abe Lincoln's Union? Our people are getting impatient. The Legislature has been in session nearly a week, and the Ordinance of Secession has not passed! . . . To see Tennessee out of the Union is now the acme of our ambition. For these long many years, amid abuse and slander, we have labored and toiled for this great object; and when it shall have been attained, we expect to experience emotions akin to those which filled the bosom of Columbus when he discovered the land for which his weary being had so long yearned.[28]

Unionist newspapers were stunned by the news of Sumter's bombardment. A few of them blamed the Confederates for the outbreak of hostilities. The Nashville *Republican Banner* at first praised Major Anderson for standing his ground against Confederate General P. G. T. Beauregard and predicted that the assailants of the fort would meet with "fearful retribution." Parson Brownlow called the assault upon the fort "cowardly," and asserted: "The war at Charleston was begun by the Seceded States."[29]

Other conservative journals reacted cautiously at first. The Fayetteville (North Carolina) *Observer* advised South-

erners to wait for further particulars on the events at
Charleston: "The stake is too great to rush into disunion
and civil war upon the strength of telegraphic dispatches."
Many hoped that the Union would yet be saved, although
they could suggest no plan by which this could be accomplished. The Raleigh *North Carolina Standard* called upon
the border states to act as peacemakers between North and
South and to "maintain their rights in the Union." The
Lynchburg *Virginian* balked at the prospect of war and
wrote: "Rather would we address ourselves to the reason
and conscience of our countrymen; that they might ere this
tragedy go farther, set themselves to the work of restoring
peace."[30]

Unfortunately, peace—the wish of the Unionist press—
proved to be beyond restoring. On April 15 Lincoln issued a
proclamation calling out the militia "of the several States
of the Union, to the . . . number of seventy-five thousand,"
to suppress the rebellion in the Southern states. The border
slave states were included in this general demand for
troops; therefore, they too must furnish men to subdue their
rebellious neighbors to the south.[31] Unionist papers in Virginia, Arkansas, Tennessee, and North Carolina generally
were outraged more by Lincoln's proclamation than they
had been by the outbreak of hostilities. Papers which had
been slow to fix the blame for Fort Sumter now attacked the
President for dealing deceitfully with the Confederacy.
They defiantly rejected Lincoln's proclamation. Said the
Richmond *Whig:* "The only fitting reply from Virginia is
a levy *en masse* of every man able to bear arms, to fight for
our altars and firesides." Another conservative Virginia paper promised that Virginia would respond "in a different
manner from that he [Lincoln] seems to anticipate." William W. Holden, the staunchest Unionist editor in North
Carolina, now declared: "The proclamation of Mr. Lincoln
has left to the people of the border States no alternative but

resistance or unconditional submission. . . . It is a war which could not have been avoided. It has been forced upon us. We must fight!"[32]

A great majority of Unionist papers in Virginia, Arkansas, Tennessee, and North Carolina demanded immediate secession following Lincoln's call for troops. Most of these papers also demanded that their states join the Southern Confederacy. The Athens (Tennessee) *Post,* which had satirized the Confederate government as late as April 15, called, on April 26, for "a prompt union and defensive alliance of the entire South." To the question, "where is North Carolina to go?" the Raleigh *Register* answered, *"into the Confederacy of the South*—into the Confederacy formed by the men who are now marching to drive back the Goths and Vandals from Maryland and Virginia." The *Register* proudly reported that it had raised the Confederate flag over its office in a ceremony accompanied by "patriotic airs by some of the pupils from the Blind Asylum." Similarly, the Richmond *Whig,* long a defender of the Stars and Stripes, reported on April 18 that it had replaced the American flag over its office with the state flag of Virginia.[33]

Still vestiges of the old antisecessionism clung to the new converts to disunion. The Raleigh *North Carolina Standard,* for example, predicted a long civil war and added: *"We have told our readers from the first that secession meant civil war and the destruction of civil liberty."* In like manner the Little Rock *Arkansas State Gazette* wrote: "Speaking for ourself [sic] we are opposed to the doctrine of secession, but the right to rebel against an oppressive government is one upon which all agree. Peaceable secession has proven to be what we thought it from the first—an impossibility. As well expect to pull a stout man's arm from its socket in his shoulder without pain as to sever the Union without violence." The Raleigh *Weekly Ad Valorem Banner* advocated secession and resistance but also declared:

It does not necessarily follow that because we secede we shall join the Southern Confederacy. . . . We are sorry to hear that the flag of the Southern Confederacy has been hoisted over Fort Macon. That Fort does not belong to the Southern Confederacy, and that flag has no business there. We hope the Governor will order it down. Give us the Stars and Stripes, which are ours, and which we love, and we will fight under them to the death.[34]

A few Unionist editors stubbornly continued their fight against secession after the outbreak of war between the sections. The New Orleans *Daily True Delta,* although it finally accepted secession after Sumter was attacked, remained critical of the Confederacy. De Witt C. Roberts, a Northern newspaperman who resided in New Orleans at the time of Louisiana's secession, later praised the *True Delta* which "alone of all New Orleans journals did not go over hand and foot to the enemy." According to Roberts, that paper finally was forced to use restraint in attacking the Confederate government, "but it never acted cordially with the party it opposed." Roberts further recalled:

At various times during the sixteen months of rebel rule over the city the office was in danger of being demolished by the angry mob, and it was only by the firmness and courage of its proprietor, John McGinnis [*sic*], the knowledge that he had a store of small arms and a piece of artillery in the office, the full conviction that he and his friends would use them, and the fact of his paper being the Irish organ which saved his office from destruction.[35]

At least one editor of the lower South refused even to soften his assault upon disunionism. On April 15 James P. Newcomb of the San Antonio *Alamo Express* published "what purports to be 'war news.'" Newcomb wrote: "It is all right for the South to raise thousands of troops and ready them for a premediated attack . . . but if the U.S. government quietly dispatches a few war vessels there is a terrible outrage committed upon the peace of the country and a fearful panic ensues." Newcomb was unrelenting in his criticism of Confederate leaders. Five days after the attack upon Fort Sumter he accused the "Charlestonians" of starting a war "upon the question of supplying sixty men . . . with pork and beans for a few days." The controversial editor finally went too far. On May 13 he issued an "extra" satirizing the capture of a small detachment of federal troops by Texas Confederates off the coast of Texas. That night a mob composed of Knights of the Golden Circle and Confederate Rangers broke open the *Express* office, destroyed its press, and set fire to the building. Newcomb later recalled: "The morning light displayed the charred ruins of the *Alamo Express,* the last Union paper in Texas."[36]

Diehard Unionist papers were somewhat more numerous in the upper South than in the Gulf states. Several papers in Western Virginia steadfastly resisted disunion and approved the separatist movement which ultimately led to the creation of the new state of West Virginia.[37] Parson Brownlow of the Knoxville *Whig* was the most famous (or infamous) of the Southern Unionist editors who continued to resist secession after the war had begun. He declared that if he were given the choice of going to hell or joining the Confederacy, it would probably take him a week to decide which he would choose. The Parson promised to give up the fight against secession after Tennessee left the Union, and he announced that his paper would henceforth devote its columns to "Literary, Agricultural and Miscellaneous matter, including the war news of the day." But Brownlow's pen proved to be incapable of restraint, and he continued to denounce the Confederacy until his arrest in October 1861. Unrepentant to the end, the Parson, in his last number, republished the articles which were the basis for the charges brought against him, so that it would be clear to all that he had retracted nothing.[38]

Although a handful of courageous editors fought on against secession, a vast majority of the conservative newspapers in the states of Virginia, Arkansas, North Carolina, and Tennessee joined with disunion journals in welcoming the secession of those states. Indeed, their enthusiam often was as great as that of the most "ultra" Southern-rights papers.[39]

Newspapermen who, a few weeks before, had defended the Union dropped their pens and rushed off to war in such numbers as to jeopardize the operations of the press. The editor of North Carolina's Wadesborough *Argus* wrote: "Our partner, our son, and our pressman, have gone to the war. Until their return, we shall be compelled to issue the *Argus,* in its present reduced form. . . . While we write the shrill notes of the fife are sounding in our ears, and the spirit-stirring drum makes us feel as, when we were younger we were wont to feel." The Harrisonburg (Virginia) *Rockingham Register and Advertiser* said that half of its office force had "deserted us and joined the standard of its country."[40] A scarcity of help contributed to the collapse of many newspapers. About six weeks after the war began, the Hillsborough (North Carolina) *Recorder* wrote: "In consequence of the absence of Editors or workmen, or both, who have volunteered in defence of our homes, and the discouragements thrown in their way by the prostration of business, we miss from our table several of our Exchange papers." The *Recorder* then listed seven journals in North Carolina alone that had recently discontinued publication.[41]

Papers that had once appealed to the South's feeling of brotherhood with the North now pronounced the gulf between the two sections to be unbridgeable. The Petersburg (Virginia) *Daily Express* declared the Union to be so far gone that "one hundred millions of federal soldiery, led on by a thousand BONAPARTES could not restore it." "When peace comes," said the Clarksville (Tennessee) *Jeffersonian,* it will be on the basis of two established governments." The Charlotte *North Carolina Whig,* a late convert to

secessionism, probably failed to realize that it was painting
a strangely prophetic picture when it wrote:

And now to the North let us say, wage your irrepressible conflict
with fire and sword, until you have depopulated our towns, demolished our houses, devastated our fields, laid waste our forests,
and deluged our land in fraternal blood, and still your object is
unattained. This can only be bought at the price of our total
extermination. But you will reap as the reward of your unholy
war a bitterness of antipathy against you, which centuries will
fail to wipe out of the remembrance of our children's children.[42]

Lincoln's decision to reinforce Sumter and his subsequent
call for volunteers accomplished that which the secessionists
had been unable to achieve with their propaganda campaign. With few exceptions, the papers of the states that
would compose the Confederacy now believed in seceding
from the Union. Papers that lately had blamed the South's
difficulties upon fire-eaters or submissionists now laid the
awful responsibility for fraternal war upon Lincoln. A
North Carolina journal said: "The mask has fallen and the
Black Republican administration stands forth in all its
hideous deformity. . . . A free people unwilling to submit
to wrong and oppression and fighting for their rights are to
be butchered by the power of this great government." In a
like manner a Georgia paper placed all of the blame for the
war upon Lincoln and was certain that "impartial history"
would do likewise.[43]

Since according to the Southern press the South's cause
was just, it followed that Providence would smile upon the
Confederacy in the coming conflict. The Raleigh *Democratic Press* predicted that for every Southern soldier who
would fall in Lincoln's "war of extermination," "a dozen
of the dastardly marauders will be made to bite the dust.
We have right and justice on our side—and with these we
can reverently and with clear consciences invoke the aid of
the God of Battles, with a firm faith that he will prosper

the Right." Religious editors, most of whom had eschewed politics throughout most of the crisis, agreed with the political press that a just God must absolve the South of responsibility for the war and aid Confederate arms. With the Raleigh *Church Intelligencer* they thanked God "that we are the party aggrieved, that we stand upon our defence, that we fight for our altars and our homes, and that we may, therefore, in all humility and sincerity pray to Him for the success of our arms." Should the North persist in its determination to coerce the South, wrote the *North Carolina Presbyterian,* "there can be no doubt on which side truth, righteousness and victory will be found." Another journal assured its readers: "God will fight the battles of such a host [of Southerners]—who have mustered together in his name. The end may be far off, and the road to it rugged and bloody, but we shall see it and rejoice."[44]

With the secession of Virginia, Arkansas, North Carolina, and Tennessee, most newspapers in those states experienced relief as well as exultation. The intrastate struggles over secession were over; the tension was broken. Alienated friends could be friends once again. And the excitement of martial spectacle overcame the reservations that many had professed about the wisdom of secession. A Tennessee newspaper must have expressed the feeling of many when it wrote: "The Agony is Over." Unfortunately for the South, and the nation, the real agony was just beginning.[45]

X

Newspapers and Telegraphs Have Ruined the Country

In mid-April 1860, virtually all newspapers of the future Confederate states believed in preserving the Union, provided that Southern "rights," as they conceived them, could be protected. One year later all but a handful of the same journals had endorsed the Confederacy. During most of the intervening twelve months the Southern press was divided on the question of secession. Papers which believed that the Union was salvageable held the upper hand in the pre-election period. But a combination of events—notably the alleged abolitionist conspiracy in Texas, the election of Lincoln, the secession of South Carolina and the lower South, and the failure of compromise—shifted the initiative to the disunion publicists and led to a gradual breakdown of Unionist journalism, until, with few exceptions, the press in eleven Southern states became a unit in favor of withdrawal.

On the whole, Unionist papers courageously defended the Union and stubbornly resisted the mounting pressures of the secessionists. Their efforts to maintain a reasonable approach in examining the issues contrasted sharply with the frankly emotional appeal of disunionist journals. Their stark warnings that economic deprivations would accompany disunion made considerably more sense than did the visionary assurances of fire-eaters that a Confederate South would become a Garden of Eden. Furthermore, the Unionist editors' predictions of a long, bloody civil war proved to be tragically accurate, while the disunionists' denials that war would follow secession seem, in retrospect, to have been irresponsible.

There were several reasons for the demise of Unionist journalism in the South after Lincoln's election. The nationalism of most Unionist editors, while sincere, lacked the depth indicated by their pre-election language. Like their Southern-rights counterparts, Unionist editors feared a Republican administration, though some failed to realize the depth of their fears until after the election. In the days following Lincoln's triumph at the polls, as some Northern journals taunted and threatened the South and as the states of the lower South took firm, irrevocable steps preparatory to leaving the Union, Southern Unionist papers increasingly found it necessary to decide between the Confederacy and the Union. Since nearly all editors pledged first allegiance to their states, there was usually no question which side they would support when it became impossible to remain loyal to both national and state governments.

Unionist papers also labored at a disadvantage because of the approach which they used in defending the Union. In their efforts to stir the national patriotism of Southerners, such papers frequently stressed the past glories of a united nation and the nationalism of such Southerners as Andrew Jackson and George Washington. But such nostalgic appeals to the past seemed irrelevant to many Southerners in 1860–1861. The excitement of the times seemed to call for action instead of reflection; for political innovation instead of political preservation. In such an atmosphere the initiative lay with the secession advocates, since their party alone had a program of action.

Moreover, the Union advocates' appeal to logic and reason was at best uninspiring to alarmed and angry Southerners; at worst, it seemed cowardly to a people who believed in the redemption of offended honor by means of the code duello. Most Southerners regarded the election of a Republican President by Northern votes as a direct, calculated insult to their section. With the South's honor allegedly at stake, most Southern Unionist editors soon forgot their earlier quarrel with secessionists over the legality of secession. Papers which before the election had argued that secession was illegal suddenly discovered in the "universal right of revolution" a convenient rationale for their post-election conversions to disunionism.

Other editors apparently struck their Unionist banners because their cause lacked the support of their readers. Unionist papers found it increasingly difficult to maintain financial solvency. On the eve of the Civil War a rural editor in Virginia's Blue Ridge country illustrated the difficulty facing Union advocates when he asked: "Will the people of Southwestern Virginia sustain us in our efforts to keep up a paper devoted to their best interests? There are but three or four Union papers, now, in the State, the balance are for plunging us into civil war; the secession of Virginia will accomplish their design. Unless the people support their Union men and Union papers, all is lost, and the people may prepare for war, for come it will, unless they act in this matter." If prospective subscribers were unable to pay money, the editor said, farm produce would be acceptable: "All the money we need is just enough to buy our paper and ink."[1] Papers that stayed with the old ship *Union* too long experienced numerous cancellations of subscriptions. In view of the fine line which many editors walked between solvency and bankruptcy, such pressures must have caused many editors to change their positions on the Union.

Stronger pressures also weakened the determination of many editors to defend the Union. Secessionist editors frequently hurled charges of disloyalty and abolitionism at papers that resisted disunion and questioned whether such journals should be permitted to publish in the South. There were enough violent acts and menacing threats against Southern newspapers in 1860–1861 to cause many editors with Unionist proclivities to repent of their "heresies." Most of those who could not give up their Unionism gave up their papers. Such a man was James W. Hunnicutt, editor of the Fredericksburg (Va.) *Christian Banner,* who suspended operations shortly after the Virginia convention passed the secession ordinance. In explaining his action, Hunnicutt wrote: "We saw and felt that the liberty of the press, the liberty of speech, and the rights of freemen were all wrested from us, and that the withdrawal of patronage would ultimately force us to discontinue the publication of the 'Banner' and we determined after the publication of the number of May 9, 1861 to close our office."[2] Secessionist editors justified the suppression of freedom of the press on the ground that the South was fighting for its very way of life and could ill afford dissension among its people.

Concern over the possible abolition of slavery probably was the most basic reason why Southern newspapers shifted from Unionist to secessionist positions. Lincoln's election was unacceptable to most Southern editors, because they feared that he, or one of his successors, would abolish slavery in the Southern states, and not simply prevent its extension into the territories. Moreover, Southerners were convinced that abolition would be but the first in a chain of events that would spell disaster for the South. The Republican leaders, whose contact with Negroes in most cases was limited, could separate slavery the political issue from slavery the social issue, as indeed they demonstrated when they wrote their party platform. But Southerners, most of whom had daily contact with Negroes, were unable to make such a distinction. To the average Southerner in 1860 it was the slave code, rather than a physical separation of the races, that ensured his continued domination of the black man. Eliminate that code, and a Pandora's Box of evils would innundate the South. In the Southen view, the Republican dislike of slavery would culminate eventually in abolition; abolition would result in enforced social equality; social equality would lead to intermarriage, the natural consequence of which would be amalgamation; and amalgamation would seal the collapse of the South's civilization.

Thus Southern editors of all political persuasions frequently raised before their readers—sometimes subtly, sometimes bluntly—the specter of a South racially degraded at the hands of callous Northern Republicans. Shortly after Georgia had seceded, a newspaper in that state wrote: "The institution of African Slavery produced the Secession of the Cotton States. If it had never existed, the Union of the States would, to-day, be complete." Far from faulting either the South or its peculiar institution, however, the same journal asserted that slavery had produced in the South "a degree of perfection equal to that of any age in the history of the world." It was the Northern "Puritans" whose "lust of power, envy, and hatred" of slavery had left proud Southerners no alternative but secession. To remain in a Union presided over by Abraham Lincoln not only would lead to the eventual abolition of slavery but also to the degradation of the South's idyllic society. A Louisiana journal said of Lincoln and his cronies: "They will be the most moderate of national men in their professions, without abating a jot of the ultimate purpose of forcing the extinction of slavery. . . . It is for these future, progressing, insidious, fatal results, more than from an 'overt act' of direct oppression, that the triumph of Black Republicanism . . . is to be profoundly deprecated by every Southern man of every shade of party opinion." This view was typical of the Southern-rights press throughout the secession period, but, in this case, it was expressed by the New Orleans *Picayune,* one of the most dedicated Unionist journals in the South.[3]

Most other conservative papers in the South harbored misgivings similar to those expressed by the *Picayune*. Such journals therefore were able to argue with conviction on behalf of the Union's perpetuation only so long as the slave states remained a unit within the Union to block in Congress any Republican attempt to tamper with the institution of slavery. After the withdrawal of the Gulf states, many Unionist editors saw little chance of preventing the "progressive, insidious, fatal results" so gloomily predicted by the *Picayune*.

Since even their most conservative journals charged the Republicans with plotting to subvert the white race in the South, it is difficult to see how Southern readers could have maintained anything resembling an objective, balanced view of Lincoln and his party. Had a majority of the South's newspapers maintained even a modicum of integrity in reporting Northern views in general, and the Republican party's slavery intentions in particular, the South's "Republicanphobia" almost certainly would have been less virulent than it was, although all symptoms of the disease probably would not have disappeared.

The Southern monopoly over news distribution in the South greatly facilitated the task of secessionist editors. Southeners read in Southern papers what Northerners supposedly thought and said, and even the most dedicated Unionist journals often revealed their strong anti-Northern biases in their selection and treatment of the news. By printing one-sided and often inflammatory accounts of develop-

ments in the sectional dispute, it was relatively easy for secessionist editors to capitalize upon the fears and prejudices
of their readers. In the absence of contradictory Northern
arguments, most Southerners apparently had little trouble
believing the allegations of Southern secessionist papers
that the North had one great desire—to abolish slavery—
and that Lincoln scarcely could wait to appoint Negro officeholders, encourage Negro uprisings against whites, and enforce social as well as civil equality. Such exaggerations of
the Republican position by the secession publicists helped
their movement to overcome the native conservatism and
historic nationalism of the Southern people.

A few moderate editors deplored the failure of Southern
newspapers to report sectional issues objectively. An Arkansas paper, for example, blamed the press in both sections of
the country for the secession crisis. "How can two sections
of our country ever hope to be at peace so long as the journals of the country continue to make such flings at them?
We cannot censure the Northern press only, for we, unfortunately have many of the same factious spirit in the
South. And it is from such sources we have most to fear." A
Tennessee journal showed exceptional insight when, at the
height of the sectional crisis, it blamed the alienation of the
sections upon newspapers. "There is not in the South one
journalist in forty that knows any thing of the real state of
society at the North, or of the ebb and flow of the currents
of public opinion." Nor did newspapers of the North have a
better understanding of Southerners, the paper continued.
"Yet, each indulges in constant crimination and labors incessantly to mislead and prejudice the people of the respective sections. And even now, when the country is trembling
on the verge of dissolution, the warfare of misrepresentation
and abuse is carried on with redoubled violence by the vul-
tures who thrive and fatten on popular prejudice. We

would rather be the lowest thing that crawls the earth than rear our children on bread obtained by such means."[4]

Unfortunately, most Southern editors had no such qualms about earning their bread by feeding upon the biases of their readers. Such an approach was deeply ingrained in Southern journalism. Perhaps it would have been asking too much to expect of Southern newspapers during the secession crisis more responsible behavior than they were able to exemplify in calmer times. Nor, perhaps, could Southern editors have been expected to act more reasonably than others in their society, such as ministers and politicians, who were similarly responsive to public opinion. But this does not absolve Southern journalism of its share of the blame for the most fateful step that the South ever took. Avery Craven has written: "Wars do not have simple causes, and differences have to be emotionalized before they get beyond the ability of the democratic process to handle them."[5] The isolation of the Southern press from any influences that might have restored to it a national perspective and its intensely partisan nature helped make Southern newspapers the perfect vehicles to emotionalize both real and imaginary sectional differences.

At the outset of the secession crisis one Virginia paper commented: "Newspapers and Telegraphs have ruined the country. Suppress both and the country could be saved now."[6] Perhaps a disruption of communications alone would not have saved the Union; the disagreement over slavery would have remained. But, without the press, the task of those who divided the nation would have been infinitely more difficult.

APPENDIX, NOTES, BIBLIOGRAPHY, INDEX

Appendix

ALABAMA

Breckinridge Papers

Abbeville *Banner*
Abbeville *United South*
Auburn *Sketch Book*
Bellefonte *Era*
Benton *Weekly Herald*
Blountsville *Pioneer*
Cahaba *Gazette*
Camden *Register*
Camden *Republic*
Canebrake *Gazette*
Carrollton *Courier*
Carrollton *West Alabamian*
Chambers *Tribune*
Cherokee *Coosa River Argus*
Claiborne *Southern Champion*
Clayton *Banner*
Conecuh *Spartan*
Dallas *Gazette*
Eufala *Spirit of the South*
Eutaw *Observer*
Fayette *Democrat*
Florence *Gazette*
Greensboro *Alabama Beacon*
Greensboro *Gazette*
Greenville *South Alabamian*
Grove Hill *Clarke County Democrat*
Hayneville *Chronicle*

Huntsville *Advertiser*
Huntsville *Democrat*
Jacksonville *Republican*
Jasper *Advertiser*
Linden *Jeffersonian*
Marion *Commonwealth*
Marshall *News*
Mobile *Mercury*
Mobile *Tribune*
Montgomery *Weekly Advertiser*
Montgomery *Weekly Mail*
Moulton *Democrat*
Newton *Times*
Opelika *Weekly Southern Era*
Prattville *Southern Statesman*
St. Clair *Diamond*
Selma *Issue*
Shelby *Chronicle*
Somerville *Democrat*
Sumter *Democrat*
Talledega *Democratic Watchtower*
Troy *States Rights Advocate*
Tuscaloosa *Observer*
Tuscumbia *Constitution*
Tuskegee *Democrat*
Union Springs *Gazette*
Wedowee *Democrat*
Wetumpka *Spectator*

(Alabama papers, continued)
Douglas Papers

Athens *Herald*
Cahaba *Slaveholder*
Dadeville *Banner*
Dadeville *Democrat*
Decatur *Times*
Elba *States Rights Democrat*
Fayetteville *Banner*
Gainesville *Independent*
Guntersville *Independent*
Huntsville *Advocate*
Mobile *Register*
Montgomery *Confederation*
Pickinsville *Journal*
Prattville *Autauga Citizen*
Selma *Alabama State Sentinel*
Troy *Advertiser*
Tuscumbia *States Rights Democrat*
Uniontown *Herald*
Wetumpka *Enquirer*

Bell Papers

Athens *Union Banner*
Athens *Limestone News*
Centreville *Enquirer*
Eutaw *Whig*
Greenville *Southern Messenger*
Hayneville *Watchman*
Huntsville *Independent*
Lafayette *Sentinel*
Livingston *Messenger*
Marion *American*
Mobile *Advertiser*
Montgomery *Weekly Post*
Selma *Reporter*
Talladega *Alabama Reporter*
Tallapoosa *Times*
Tuscaloosa *Monitor*
Tuskegee *Republican*

Independent Papers

Autauga *Citizen*
Canebrake *Herald*
Jacksonville *State Rights Democrat*

ARKANSAS

Breckinridge Papers

Arkadelphia *Arkansaw Traveler*
Batesville *Sentinel*
Brownsville *Prairie Democrat*
Camden *Star*
Des Arc *Citizen*
Clarendon *Democratic Standard*
El Dorado *Bulletin*
Fayetteville *Arkansian*
Fort Smith *Times*
Helena *Note-Book*
Helena *States-Right Democrat*

Jacksonport *Herald*
Lake Village *Chicot Press*
Little Rock *Old-Line Democrat*
Little Rock *True Democrat*
Madison *Journal*
Magnolia *Magnolian*
Monticello *Sage of Monticello*
Napoleon *Planter*
Ozark *South-Western*
Warren *Sunbeam*
Washington *South Arkansas Democrat*
Fort Smith *Thirty-Fifth Parallel*

(Arkansas papers, continued)
Douglas Papers

Lawrence *Union*
Little Rock *National Democrat*
Pine Bluff *Independent*
Pocahontas *Advertiser and Herald*
Van Buren *Press*
Washington *Telegraph*

Bell Papers

Batesville *Balance*
Helena *Shield*
Little Rock *Arkansas State Gazette*
Camden *Ouachita Herald*

Independent Papers

Arkadelphia *Ouachita Christian Advocate*
Harmony Springs *Theocrat*
Searcy *Eagle*

FLORIDA

Breckinridge Papers

Apalachicola *Times*
Cedar Keys *Telegraph*
Fernandina *East Floridian*
Jacksonville *Standard*
Key West *Key of the Gulf*
Lake City *Herald*
Marianna *Patriot*
Madison *Messenger*
Monticello *Friend*
Newmansville *Dispatch*
Ocala *Companion*
Pensacola *Observer*
Pensacola *Tribune*
Quincy *Republic*
San Augustine *Examiner*

Tallahassee *East Floridian*
Tampa *Peninsular*

Bell Papers

Lake City *Independent Press*
Marianna *West Florida Enterprise*
Miconopy *Peninsular Gazette*
Milton *Courier*
Pensacola *Gazette*
Quincy *Florida Express*
Tallahassee *Sentinel*

Douglas Papers

Jacksonville *Mirror*

GEORGIA

Breckinridge Papers

Albany *Patriot*
Americus *Southwestern News*
Athens *Southern Banner*
Atlanta *Daily Intelligencer*
Atlanta *Locomotive*
Augusta *Dispatch*
Augusta *True Democrat*

Bainbridge *Argus*
Brunswick *Southern Advocate*
Calhoun *Platform*
Cartersville *Express*
Clarkesville *Herald*
Columbus *Corner-Stone*
Columbus *Sun*
Columbus *Times*

(Georgia papers, continued)
Cuthbert *Reporter*
Dalton *Times*
Griffin *Middle Georgian*
Griffin *Southern Democrat*
Macon *Daily Telegraph*
Macon *Examiner*
Marietta *Advocate*
Marietta *Southern Statesman*
Milledgeville *Federal Union*
Ringgold *Journal*
Rome *True Flag*
Savannah *Daily Morning News*
South-Western News
Stone Mountain *Independent Press*
Thomasville *Reporter*
Valdosta *Watchman*
Waresboro *Georgia Forester*
Waynesboro *Independent South*

Douglas Papers

Atlanta *Confederacy*
Augusta *Daily Constitutionalist*
Cassville *Standard*
Columbus *Daily Star*
Minden *Herald*
Rome *Southerner*
Savannah *Evening Express*

Bell Papers

Americus *Republican*
Athens *Post*
Athens *Southern Watchman*
Atlanta *National American*
Augusta *Chronicle and Sentinel*
Bainbridge *Southern Georgian*
Columbus *Enquirer*
Covington *Times*
Dahlonega *Mountain Signal*
Frederick *Examiner*
Griffin *American Union*
Hamilton *Harris County Enterprise*
LaGrange *Reporter*
Macon *Daily Citizen*
Macon *Journal and Messenger*
Milledgeville *Southern Recorder*
Rome *Weekly Courier*
Savannah *Republican*
Sumter *Republican*
Thomasville *Enterprise*

Independent Papers

Gainesville *Air-Line Eagle*
Lawrenceville *News*
Madison *Visitor*
Newman *Independent Blade*
Sandersville *Central Georgian*

LOUISIANA

Breckinridge Papers

Alexandria *Democrat*
Arcadian *Bayou Sara Ledger*
Attakapas *Register*
Baton Rouge *Daily Advocate*
Bellevue *Bossier Banner*
Bossier *Jeffersonian*

Caddo *Gazette*
Claiborne *Advocate*
Clinton *Spirit of the South*
False River *Pointe Coupée Democrat*
Floyd *Louisianian*
Houma *Ceres*
Iberville *Gazette*

(Louisiana papers, continued)
Madison *Journal*
Minden *Advertiser*
Monroe *Register*
New Orleans *Courier*
New Orlean *Daily Delta*
New Orleans *Sentinel*
New Orleans *Catholic Standard*
Opelousas *Courier*
Plaquemine *Gazette and Sentinel*
Plaquemine *Rice Planter*
St. James *Acadian*
Sparta *Southern Banner*
Tensas *Gazette*
Vermilionville *Echo*
Winnfield *Sun*

Douglas Papers

Baton Rouge *Little Giant*
Clinton *Feliciana Democrat*
Homer *Iliad*
Lake Providence *True Issue*
LaFourche *Union*
Madison *Democrat*
Massillon *Banner*
Mount Vernon *Southern Times*
Natchitoches *Union*
New Orleans *Bee*
New Orleans *Deutsche Zeitung*
New Orleans *States Rights Democrat*
New Orleans *True Delta*
Red River *National Democrat*
Sparta *Jeffersonian*
Winnfield *Southern Sentinel*

Bell Papers

Abbeville *Meridional*
Alexandria *Constitutional*
Clifton *National American*
Comte *Times*
Franklin *Union Bell*
Houma *Civic Guard*
Jefferson *Journal*
Marksville *Central Organ*
Morehouse *Advocate*
New Orleans *Commercial Bulletin*
New Orleans *Crescent*
New Orleans *Daily Picayune*
New Orleans *Louisiana Staats Zeitung*
New Orleans *Mirror*
New Orleans *Louisiana Signal*
Opelousas *Patriot*
Shreveport *South-Western*
St. Charles *Meschasebe*
St. James *Messenger*
St. Martinville *Courier de la Teche*
Thibodaux *Gazette*
West Baton Rouge *Sugar Planter*

Independent Papers

Baton Rouge *Weekly Gazette and Comet*
Concordia *Intelligencer*
Covington *Wanderer*
Lake Providence *Herald*

MISSISSIPPI

Breckinridge Papers

Aberdeen *Sunny South*

Columbus *Mississippi Democrat*
Corinth *Cross City*

(Mississippi papers, continued)

Enterprise *East Mississippi Democrat*
Gallatin *Mississippi Mirror*
Handsboro *Democrat*
Holmes County *Weekly Democrat*
Jackson *Intelligencer*
Jackson *Mississippian*
Jackson *Patriot*
Kemper *Democrat*
Liberty *Amite Democrat*
Monticello *Journal*
Natchez *Mississippi Free Trader*
Oxford *Intelligencer*
Oxford *Mercury*
Paulding *Eastern Clarion*
Pontotoc *Examiner*
Port Gibson *Southern Reveille*
Quitman *Chickashay Advertiser*
Randolph *Democrat*
Ripley *Advertiser*
Vicksburg *Sun*
Woodville *Republican*

Douglas Papers

Aberdeen *Conservative*
Columbus *Expositor*
Corinth *True Democrat*
Lauderdale *Meridian*

Macon *Beacon*
Vicksburg *Evening Citizen*

Bell Papers

Brandon *Republican*
Canton *American Citizen*
Columbus *Eagle*
Corinth *Union Guard*
Enterprise *Union Advocate*
Fulton *Southern Herald*
Holly Springs *Constitutional Union*
Jacinto *Tishomingo Patriot*
Jackson *Daily News*
Kosciusko *Chronicle*
Liberty *Advocate*
Marion Station *Eastern Sentinel*
Natchez *Courier*
Raymond *Hinds County Gazette*
Starkville *Oktibbeha Advertiser*
Upson *Pilot*
Vicksburg *Whig*

Independent Papers

Fayette *Times*
Hazlehurst *Copiah News*
Holmesville *Independent*
Magnolia *Grant Trunk Magnolian*
Woodville *Wilkinson Gazette*

NORTH CAROLINA

Breckinridge Papers

Asheville *News*
Charlotte *Bulletin*
Charlotte *Western Democrat*
Fayetteville *Daily Courier*

Fayetteville *North Carolinian*
Goldsboro *Daily Rough Notes*
Goldsboro *Tribune*
Hillsboro *Plaindealer*
Murfreesboro *Citizen*
Newbern *Enquirer*

(North Carolina papers, continued)

Raleigh *Democratic Press*
Raleigh *Standard*
Salisbury *Banner*
Tarboro *Mercury*
Tarboro *Southerner*
Warrenton *News*
Western *Sentinel*
Wilmington *Daily Journal*
Wilson *Star of Freedom*
Winston *Sentinel*

Douglas Papers

Charlotte *True Democrat*
Newbern *Daily Progress*
Raleigh *National Democrat*
Washington *States and Union*

Bell Papers

Murfreesboro *Albemarle Southron*
Asheville *Advocate*

Beaufort *Union Banner*
Charlotte *North Carolina Whig*
Fayetteville *Observer*
Franklin *Observer*
Goldsboro *North Carolina Independent*
Hillsborough *Recorder*
Kinston *American Advocate*
Raleigh *Register*
Salem *People's Press*
Salisbury *Carolina Watchman*
Scotland Neck *News*
Wadesborough *North Carolina Argus*
Washington *Dispatch*
Washington *Times*
Wilmington *Daily Herald*

Independent Papers

Greensboro *Times*
High Point *Reporter*
Raleigh *Spirit of the Age*
Rutherford *Enquirer*

SOUTH CAROLINA

Breckinridge Papers

Abbeville *Independent Press*
Anderson *Intelligencer*
Beaufort *Enterprise*
Camden *Weekly Journal*
Charleston *Daily Courier*
Charleston *Mercury*
Columbia *Daily South Carolinian*
Columbia *Daily Southern Guardian*
Greenville *Democrat*
Greenville *Patriot and Mountaineer*

Lancaster *Ledger*
Lexington *Flag*
Newberry *Conservatist*
Newberry *Rising Sun*
Orangeburg *Southron*
Pickens *Keowee Courier*
Spartanburg *Carolina Spartan*
Spartanburg *Express*

Douglas Papers

Edgefield *Advertiser*

TENNESSEE

Breckinridge Papers

Bolivar *Democrat*
Brownsville *Southern Atlas*
Chattanooga *Advertiser*
Chattanooga *Reflector*
Clarksville *Jeffersonian*
Cleveland *Banner*
Gallatin *Examiner*
Jackson *Southern Intelligencer*
Jonesboro *Union*
Knoxville *Register*
Lewisburg *Messenger*
Memphis *Avalanche*
Murfreesboro *News*
Nashville *Union and American*
Paris *Sentinel*
Shelbyville *True Union*
Sparta *Chieftain*

Douglas Papers

Fayetteville *Lincoln Journal*
Grand Junction *Quid Nunc*
Memphis *Daily Appeal*
Nashville *National Democrat*
Shelbyville *True American*
Somerville *Democrat*

Bell Papers

Alexandria *Independent*
Athens *Post*
Chattanooga *Gazette*
Clarksville *Chronicle*
Dover *Journal*
Franklin *Review*
Gallatin *Courier*
Huntingdon *Carroll Patriot*
Jackson *West Tennessee Whig*
Jasper *Sequatchie Herald*
Jonesboro *Express*
Knoxville *Whig*
Lebanon *Herald*
Lexington *Dispatch*
Maury *Press*
Memphis *Bulletin*
Memphis *Daily Enquirer*
Murfreesboro *Rutherford Telegraph*
Nashville *Patriot*
Nashville *Republican Banner*
Springfield *Speculator*
Trenton *Southern Standard*

Independent Papers

Memphis *Argus*
Nashville *Gazette*

TEXAS

Breckinridge Papers

Austin *State Gazette*
Bellville *Countryman*
Bonham *Era*
Brenham *Texas Ranger*
Brownsville *Flag*
Clarksville *Northern Standard*

Columbia *Democrat and Planter*
Corpus Christi *Ranchero*
Corsicana *Navarro Express*
Dallas *Herald*
Galveston *Civilian and Gazette*
Galveston *Crisis*

(Texas papers, continued)
Galveston *Weekly News*
Gonzales *Enquirer*
Gonzales *Intelligencer*
Hallettsville *Lone Star*
Henderson *Times*
Houston *Southerner*
Houston *Telegraph*
Jacksboro *White Man*
Jasper *Clarion*
Jefferson *Herald and Gazette*
La Grange *Democrat*
Lavaca *Gulf Keys*
Liberty *Gazette*
Marshall *Texas Republican*
Matagorda *Gazette*
Meridian *Bosque Times*
New Braunfels *Zeitung*
Palestine *Trinity Advocate*
Paris *Press*
Rusk *Enquirer*
Sabine Pass *Times*
San Antonio *Herald*
San Antonio *Ledger and Texan*
San Augustine *Express*
Seguin *Mercury*

Sulphur Springs *Independent Monitor*
Sumpter *Valley*
Tyler *Reporter*
Tyler *Sentinel*
Victoria *Texian Advocate*
Waco *Democrat*
Weatherford *White Man*

Bell Papers

Austin *Southern Intelligencer*
Belton *Independent*
Columbus *Colorado Citizen*
Fort Worth *Chief*
Marshall *Harrison Flag*
McKinney *Messenger*
Quitman *Clipper*
San Antonio *Alamo Express*
Weatherford *News*

Independent Papers

Goliad *Messenger*
Indianola *Courier*
La Grange *True Issue*
Mount Pleasant *Union*
Waco *South West*

VIRGINIA

Breckinridge Papers

Abingdon *Democrat*
Alexandria *Sentinel*
Barbour *Jeffersonian*
Bedford *Democrat*
Blue Ridge *Republican*
Charlestown *Independent Democrat*
Charlottesville *Jeffersonian*

Clarke *Journal*
Clarksburg *Register*
Culpepper *Republican*
Danville *Appeal*
Essex *Rural Southerner*
Fairmont *True Virginian*
Fincastle *Valley Sentinel*
Front Royal *Gazette*
Halifax *Echo*
Kanawha *Valley Star*

(Virginia papers, continued)
Leesburg *Democrat Mirror*
Lewisburg *Chronicle*
Lynchburg *Republican*
Madison *County Eagle*
Martinsburg *Virginia Republican*
New Market *Spirit of Democracy*
Norfolk *Southern Argus*
Petersburg *Daily Bulletin*
Port Royal *Gazette*
Prince William *Democrat*
Richmond *Anzeiger*
Richmond *Enquirer*
Richmond *Examiner*
Rockbridge *Democrat*
Romney *Argus*
Sales *Register*
Shenandoah *Spirit of Democracy*
Warrenton *Flag*
Weston *Herald*
Wheeling *Union*
Winchester *Virginian*
Woodstock *Tenth Legion*
Wytheville *Telegraph*

Douglas Papers

Charlestown *Spirit of Jefferson*
Fincastle *Democrat*
Frederick City *Union*
Fredericksburg *Recorder*
Harrisonburg *Rockingham Register and Advertiser*
Harrisonburg *Valley Democrat*
Lexington *Valley Star*
Middlebourne *Plaindealer*
Morgantown *Virginia Weekly Star*
Mount Vernon *Guardian*

Petersburg *True Democrat*
Piedmont *Independent*
Ravenswood *Chronicle*
Richmond *Index*
Staunton *Vindicator*
Wheeling *Staats Zeitung*

Bell Papers

Abingdon *Virginian*
Alexandria *Gazette*
Charlestown *Virginia Free Press*
Charlottesville *Review*
Culpepper *Observer*
Fredericksburg *Christian Banner*
Grafton *Guardian*
Harrisonburg *Virginia Citizen*
Leesburg *Washingtonian*
Lynchburg *Virginian*
Parkersburg *Gazette*
Petersburg *Daily Express*
Petersburg *Intelligencer*
Pruntytown *Visitor*
Richmond *Whig*
Staunton *Spectator*
Warrenton *Whig*
Winchester *Republican*

Lincoln Papers

Wellsburg *Herald*
Wheeling *Daily Intelligencer*

Independent Papers

Clarksville *Tobacco Plant*
Portsmouth *Transcript*
Richmond *Dispatch*
Shepherdstown *Register*
Williamsburg *Gazette*

Notes

Notes to Introduction

1. U.S. Census Office, *The Seventh Census of the United States: 1850,* xxxviii, lxv; Joseph C. G. Kennedy, *Preliminary Report on the Eighth Census,* pp. 130–131, 211–213. Because of the great fluctuations in the numbers of papers throughout the period covered by this study, the census figures should not be regarded as being absolutely correct; nevertheless, they are adequate for purposes of comparison.
2. Kennedy, *Preliminary Report on the Eighth Census,* pp. 211–213.
3. *Ibid.,* pp. 130–131, 211–213.
4. Frank L. Mott, *American Journalism,* p. 303.
5. Richmond *Dispatch,* October 20, 1860; Allan Nevins, *The Emergence of Lincoln,* II, 323.
6. Kennedy, *Preliminary Report on the Eighth Census,* pp. 211–213. Labeling a journal "political" did not mean that it excluded all subjects but politics from its columns, far from it. Southern readers were interested in many topics, and political sheets indulged their readers' tastes by printing a wide variety of nonpolitical material, much of which was clipped from other papers. Foreign news, business items, obituaries, scientific and pseudo-scientific articles, human interest stories, sports, and local news and gossip received considerable attention in Southern political newspapers. Nevertheless, political news predominated in such papers.
7. James M. Lee, *History of American Journalism,* p. 284.
8. This unflattering description was of the Canebrake *Herald* and the Autauga *Citizen.* Montgomery *Advertiser,* quoted in Natchez *Mississippi Free Trader,* July 23, 1860.
9. Milledgeville *Southern Federal Union,* February 12, 1861; Jacksonville (Ala.) *Republican,* December 20, 1860; San Antonio *Ledger and Texan,* June 9, 1860; Montgomery (Ala.) *Universalist Herald,* January 1, 1861. See also Fernandina *Weekly East Floridian,* December 19, 1860; Grove Hill (Ala.) *Clarke County Democrat,* January 3, 1861.
10. Charlestown *Spirit of Jefferson,* cited in Alexandria *Gazette,* May 8, 1860; Wadesborough *North Carolina Argus,* April 11, 1861.

11. Milledgeville (Ga.) *Federal Union,* February 14, 1860; Newbern (N.C.) *Weekly Progress,* April 17, 1860; Clarksville (Tex.) *Northern Standard,* October 20, 1860.
12. Alexandria *Gazette,* January 7, 1861; Athens *Southern Banner,* February 2, 1860.
13. Shepherdstown *Register,* July 21, 1860.
14. Little Rock *True Democrat,* July 14, 1860; Raleigh *North Carolina Christian Advocate,* July 31, 1860.
15. William B. Hesseltine, ed., *Three Against Lincoln: Murat Halstead Reports the Caucuses of 1860,* p. 51.
16. Ralph A. Wooster, *The Secession Conventions of the South,* pp. 18, 32, 54, 70, 86, 106, 127, 143, 159, 177, 197.

Notes to Chapter I

1. Avery O. Craven, *The Growth of Southern Nationalism, 1848–1861,* pp. 303–311; C. Vann Woodward, *The Burden of Southern History,* pp. 63–68; Henry T. Shanks, *The Secession Movement in Virginia, 1847–1861,* pp. 66, 85; Nevins, *The Emergence of Lincoln,* II, 98–112.
2. Craven, *The Growth of Southern Nationalism,* pp. 317–320; Ollinger Crenshaw, "The Speakership Contest of 1859–1860," *Mississippi Valley Historical Review,* XXX, 323–338; Nevins, *The Emergence of Lincoln,* II, 112–124.
3. Dwight L. Dumond, *The Secession Movement, 1860–1861,* pp. 26–34; Craven, *The Growth of Southern Nationalism,* pp. 309–310; Nevins, *The Emergence of Lincoln,* II, 107–112.
4. This term refers to the amorphous political body, which included former Know-Nothings, Whigs, and those dissident Democrats who were disenchanted with the Buchanan wing of their party but who could not stomach the popular sovereignty of Stephen A. Douglas. This loosely drawn coalition later formed the Constitutional Union party and nominated John Bell for President, but in early 1860 it was usually referred to as "the Opposition."
5. Albany *Patriot,* February 9, 1860.
6. Camden *Weekly Journal,* January 3, 1860.
7. Carrollton *West Alabamian,* February 29, 1860.
8. Albany *Patriot,* March 8, 1860. Other papers calling either explicitly or implicitly for secession during the winter and spring of 1860 were: Newberry (S.C.) *Conservatist,* February 14, March 6; Matagorda (Tex.) *Gazette,* January 11, 1860; Atlanta *Daily Intelligencer,* April 7, 1860; Des Arc (Ark.) *Citizen,* January 4, 1860; Bellevue (La.) *Bossier Banner,* January 27, March 2, 9, 1860. The *Bossier Banner* was one of the most extreme papers, and one of the worst edited. It is a gold mine of malapropisms; for example, on January 27, 1860, the *Banner* declared: "Our institutions have been cinctured [*sic*] and defied resentment; our honor and integrity has

[*sic*] been insulted and abused; until it behooves the spirit of resentment to encase [*sic*] itself from its dormant hiding place."

9. Spartanburg *Carolina Spartan,* March 8, 1860. The *Carolina Spartan* is one of those papers which are difficult to classify. After the John Brown raid it advocated secession, but by early 1860 it followed a somewhat less militant line. See also Little Rock *Old-Line Democrat,* September 15, December 15, 1859; Macon (Ga.) *Daily Telegraph,* February 4, 1860.

10. False River *Pointe Coupée Democrat,* December 24, 1859. See also Fort Smith (Ark.) *Times,* April 12, 1860; Newbern (N.C.) *Weekly Progress,* January 10, 1860; Nashville *Union and American,* March 31, 1860; Columbia (S.C.) *Daily Southern Guardian,* April 16, 1860; Fernandina *East Floridian,* April 12, 1860; Tallahassee *Floridian and Journal,* February 4, 1860.

11. Dumond, *The Secession Movement,* pp. 26–28; Shanks, *The Secession Movement in Virginia,* pp. 97–99.

12. Charleston *Mercury* (triweekly ed.), February 9, 1860. See also Raleigh *Democratic Press,* December 24, 1859; Jackson *Weekly Mississippian,* January 25, 1860; Camden (S.C.) *Weekly Journal,* March 13, 1860; Richmond *Semi-Weekly Examiner,* February 3, 1860; Marshall *Texas Republican,* February 18, 1860.

13. Dumond, *The Secession Movement,* p. 25; John W. Du Bose, *The Life and Times of William Lowndes Yancey,* I, 358–366.

14. La Grange *True Issue,* January 6, 1860.

15. Atlanta *Daily Intelligencer,* April 12, 1860.

16. Edgefield (S.C.) *Advertiser,* February 1, 1860; Fernandina *East Floridian,* January 12, 1860; Spartanburg (S.C.) *Carolina Spartan,* January 19, 1860; Charleston *Daily Courier,* March 17, 1860; Abbeville (S.C.) *Independent Press,* February 24, 1860; Columbus *Mississippi Democrat,* January 28, 1860; Florence (Ala.) *Gazette,* February 22, 1860; Little Rock *Old-Line Democrat,* January 19, 1860; Macon (Ga.) *Daily Telegraph,* February 8, 1860; Richmond *Enquirer,* December 9, 1859; St. Augustine (Fla.) *Examiner,* March 3, 1860; Charleston *Mercury,* January 2, 12, March 2, 1860; Sumter (S.C.) *Watchman,* February 22, 1860; Asheville (N.C.) *News,* January 19, 1860.

17. Fayetteville (N.C.) *Observer,* February 13, 1860; Vicksburg (Miss.) *Weekly Vicksburg Whig,* January 25, 1860; Richmond *Whig,* January 24, 1860; Greensboro (N.C.) *Times,* February 4, 1860.

18. Nevertheless, some disunionist papers opposed "nonintercourse," because they thought it impractical and because they disapproved of any policy which might achieve a temporary settlement between the North and the South. The Camden (S.C.) *Weekly Journal,* March 13, 1860, argued: "These spasmodic remedies may temporarily effect, but they cannot, and never can effectually destroy the canker worm gnawing at the root. The knife of dissolution is all that can save us—the axe must be applied at the roots, and the

Upas taken up, or its pestiferous odors will continue to poison and destroy." See also Albany (Ga.) *Patriot,* February 23, 1860; Des Arc (Ark.) *Citizen,* January 4, 1860.

19. West Baton Rouge (La.) *Sugar Planter,* February 11, 1860; Clarksville (Tenn.) *Jeffersonian,* March 14, 1860; Clarksville (Tenn.) *Chronicle,* March 9, 1860; Alexandria (Va.) *Gazette,* March 15, 1860; Corsicana (Tex.) *Navarro Express,* February 4, 1860; Clarksville (Tex.) *Northern Standard,* February 4, 1860; Richmond *Whig,* February 8, 1860; Lynchburg *Virginian,* January 30, 1860. This proposal received its weakest support in the border states. In Virginia, for example, virtually every newspaper west of the Alleghenies and most papers in the east opposed it. Those Virginia papers which did support the proposed conference disavowed any secessionist intentions. Shanks, *The Secession Movement in Virginia,* p. 99.

20. San Antonio *Daily Herald,* March 24, 1860.

21. Canton *American Citizen,* February 18, 1860; San Antonio *Daily Herald,* March 24, 1860; Little Rock *Arkansas State Gazette,* February 25, 1860. See also Nashville *Republican Banner,* March 29, 1860; Raymond (Miss.) *Hinds County Gazette,* February 8, 1860; Harrisonburg (La.) *Independent,* January 4, 1860; Little Rock *Arkansas State Gazette,* February 25, 1860; New Orleans *Bee,* February 1, 1860; Knoxville (Tenn.) *Whig,* February 11, 1860.

22. Richmond *Dispatch,* February 11, 1860.

23. Little Rock *True Democrat,* March 31, 1860.

24. Richmond *Whig,* January 27, 1860; Little Rock *True Democrat,* March 31, 1860; La Grange (Tex.) *True Issue,* January 27, 1860; St. Augustine (Fla.) *Examiner,* February 18, 1860; Vicksburg (Miss.) *Weekly Vicksburg Whig,* January 11, 1860.

25. Richmond *Dispatch,* January 6, 1860, January 26, 1861.

26. Lynchburg *Virginian,* January 30, 1860; Alexandria *Gazette,* January 3, 1860; Vicksburg *Weekly Vicksburg Whig,* January 4, 1860. See also Richmond *Whig,* January 4, 1860; La Grange (Tex.) *True Issue,* March 16, 1860; San Augustine (Fla.) *Examiner,* February 18, 1860.

27. Clarksville *Northern Standard,* February 4, 1860, February 2, 1861.

28. Both the Alabama and Mississippi legislatures passed resolutions which called for secession conventions in those states in the event of a Republican victory in November. Clarence P. Denman, *The Secession Movement in Alabama,* pp. 77–79; Percy L. Rainwater, *Mississippi: Storm Center of Secession,* pp. 105–106; Fayetteville *North Carolinian,* April 23, 1860; Raleigh *Democratic Press,* February 20, 1860; Macon (Ga.) *Daily Telegraph,* April 7, 1860; Baton Rouge (La.) *Weekly Gazette and Comet,* March 25, 1860; Matagorda (Tex.) *Gazette,* February 22, 1860; Jackson *Weekly Mississippian,* January 25, 1860; Bellevue (La.) *Bossier Banner,* March 2, 1860; False River (La.) *Pointe Coupée Democrat,* January 14, 1860; Nashville *Union and American,* January 8, 1860; Fort Smith (Ark.)

Times, November 24, 1859; Montgomery (Ala.) *Daily Confederation,* December 8, 1859; Clarksville (Tenn.) *Jeffersonian,* April 4, 1860; Dallas *Herald,* April 25, 1860; Opelika (Ala.) *Weekly Southern Era,* March 27, 1860; Columbus *Mississippi Democrat,* quoted in Ripley (Miss.) *Advertiser,* February 29, 1860; Helena (Ark.) *States Rights Democrat,* quoted in the Fayetteville *Arkansian,* February 10, 1860; Corsicana (Tex.) *Navarro Express,* April 28, 1860; Richmond *Dispatch,* April 9, 1860. The *Dispatch* already was in retreat from its extreme Unionist position of February 11. On April 9 it warned that a Republican triumph would surely "provincialize the South," and "this state of things must inevitably dissolve the Union, unless the South shall have lost all pride, all manliness, and be willing to submit unconditionally."

29. Jackson *Weekly Mississippian,* March 20, 1860. See also Des Arc (Ark.) *Citizen,* February 8, 1860; Augusta (Ga.) *Daily Constitutionalist,* January 12, 1860; San Antonio *Ledger and Texan,* April 18, 1860; Columbus *Mississippi Democrat,* January 14, 1860; Raleigh *Democratic Press,* January 21, 1860; Leesburg (Va.) *Democratic Mirror,* February 22, 1860.

30. Natchez *Mississippi Free Trader,* January 9, 1860; False River (La.) *Pointe Coupée Democrat,* May 12, 1860.

31. Raleigh *North Carolina Standard* (semiweekly ed.), January 7, 1860. See also Newbern (N.C.) *Weekly Progress,* January 10, 1860; Montgomery (Ala.) *Daily Confederation,* April 3, 1860. William W. Holden, the *Standard's* editor, did a *volte-face* after the Charleston debacle. Blaming the fire-eaters for purposely breaking up the Democratic party in order to achieve a dissolution of the Union, he came to oppose secession in the event of the election of a Republican, and he maintained his Unionist position until after Fort Sumter was attacked in April 1861. Horace W. Raper, "William Woods Holden (1818–92) and the Peace Movement in North Carolina," *North Carolina Historical Review,* XXXI, 493–516.

32. Columbia *Daily South Carolinian,* quoted in Spartanburg (S.C.) *Carolina Spartan,* March 15, 1860; Macon (Ga.) *Daily Telegraph,* March 6, 1860.

33. Wadesborough *North Carolina Argus,* February 23, 1860; Vicksburg (Miss.) *Weekly Vicksburg Whig,* February 1, 1860; Augusta (Ga.) *Chronicle and Sentinel,* January 11, 1860; Charlotte *North Carolina Whig,* March 13, 1860; Fayetteville *Arkansian,* February 10, 1860.

34. Hillsborough *Recorder,* February 22, 1860.

35. Columbus *Enquirer,* February 14, 1860.

36. Petersburg *Intelligencer,* quoted in Hillsborough (N.C.) *Recorder,* January 25, 1860.

37. Augusta *Chronicle and Sentinel,* April 14, 1860. A similar view was expressed by the Milledgeville (Ga.) *Southern Recorder,* January 24, 1860.

38. Matagorda *Gazette,* January 11, 1860.

39. Washington *Dispatch,* quoted in Hillsborough (N.C.) *Recorder,* April 11, 1860.
40. San Antonio *Daily Herald,* March 31, 1860.

Notes to Chapter II

1. Richmond *Dispatch,* April 14, 1860.
2. Natchez *Mississippi Free Trader,* January 7, 1860.
3. Columbus *Mississippi Democrat,* March 3, 1860.
4. Wilmington *Daily Journal,* May 1, 1860. See also Atlanta *Daily Intelligencer,* April 26, 1860; Macon (Ga.) *Daily Telegraph,* April 13, 1860; Opelousas (La.) *Courier,* January 7, 1860; Alexandria *Louisiana Democrat,* February 20, 1860; Nashville *Union and American,* March 28, 1860; Marshall *Texas Republican,* February 4, 1860; Raleigh *North Carolina Standard* (semiweekly ed.), March 14, 1860; Florence (Ala.) *Gazette,* May 9, 1860; Paulding (Miss.) *Eastern Clarion,* April 18, 1860; Corpus Christi (Tex.) *Ranchero,* March 10, 1860; Jacksonville (Ala.) *Republican,* April 19, 1860.
5. Austin *State Gazette,* April 14, 1860; Fayetteville *Lincoln Journal,* March 1, 1860. See also Clarksville (Tex.) *Northern Standard,* April 28, 1860; Marshall *Texas Republican,* April 7, 1860; Hayneville (Ala.) *Chronicle,* April 12, 1860; Columbus *Mississippi Democrat,* February 11, 1860; Opelika (Ala.) *Weekly Southern Era,* March 27, 1860; Gallatin (Tenn.) *Examiner,* February 11, 1860.
6. Clarksville *Jeffersonian,* January 11, 1860; Fayetteville *North Carolinian,* January 14, 1860.
7. Dallas *Herald,* January 11, 1860. See also Greensboro *Alabama Beacon,* December 30, 1859; Montgomery (Ala.) *Daily Confederation,* April 18, 1860.
8. Charleston *Mercury,* April 6, 1860; Newberry *Conservatist,* January 31, 1860.
9. Edgefield *Advertiser,* April 4, 1860. See also Pickens *Keowee Courier,* March 31, 1860; Lancaster *Ledger,* February 8, 1860; Charleston *Courier,* March 10, 1860, noted in Lillian A. Kibler, "Unionist Sentiment in South Carolina in 1860," *Journal of Southern History,* IV, 348.
10. Spartanburg *Carolina Spartan,* February 23, 1860; Newberry *Rising Sun,* quoted in the *Carolina Spartan,* February 23, 1860.
11. Atlanta *Daily Intelligencer,* March 31, 1860. See also Alexandria *Louisiana Democrat,* February 20, 1860.
12. Milledgeville *Federal Union,* April 3, 10, 1860; Richmond *Enquirer,* April 17, 1860. See also Tallahassee *Floridian and Journal,* April 7, 1860; Little Rock *Old-Line Democrat,* January 19, 1860; Savannah (Ga.) *Daily Morning News,* April 12, 1860.
13. George F. Milton, *The Eve of Conflict: Stephen A. Douglas and the Needless War,* pp. 343, 344; Gerald M. Capers, *Stephen A. Douglas: Defender of the Union,* pp. 186–188; Roy F. Nichols, *The Disruption of American Democracy,* pp. 221, 222.

14. Columbus *Mississippi Democrat,* March 3, 1860; Newberry *Conservatist,* April 10, 1860.

15. False River *Point Coupée Democrat,* March 3, 1860.

16. Camden *Republic,* December 1, 1859; Matagorda *Gazette,* February 29, 1860.

17. Spartanburg *Carolina Spartan,* March 8, 1860; St. Augustine *Examiner,* April 11, 1860; Marshall *Texas Republican,* April 21, 1860.

18. Opelika *Weekly Southern Era,* April 17, 1860. For similar anti-Douglas statements see Montgomery (Ala.) *Weekly Advertiser,* May 9, 1860; Abbeville (S.C.) *Independent Press,* February 24, 1860; Tallahassee *Floridian and Journal,* April 14, 1860; Carrollton *West Alabamian,* April 4, 1860; Plaquemine (La.) *Gazette and Sentinel,* May 5, 1860; Jackson *Weekly Mississippian,* April 10, 1860; Milledgeville (Ga.) *Federal Union,* April 17, 1860; Corsicana (Tex.) *Navarro Express,* March 31, 1860.

19. Bellevue (La.) *Bossier Banner,* March 2, 1860; Columbus *Mississippi Democrat,* April 7, 1860; Matagorda (Tex.) *Gazette,* April 18, 1860.

20. Memphis *Daily Appeal,* April 17, 1860; Augusta (Ga.) *Daily Constitutionalist,* March 30, 1860; Greensboro *Alabama Beacon,* February 24, 1860.

21. Augusta *Daily Constitutionalist,* April 11, 1860; New Orleans *Bee,* March 23, 1860. See also Memphis *Daily Appeal,* April 17, 1860; Montgomery (Ala.) *Daily Confederation,* March 21, April 24, 1860; Van Buren (Ark.) *Press,* May 11, 1860; Newbern (N.C.) *Weekly Progress,* April 11, 1860.

22. S. S. Fairfield to Stephen A. Douglas, May 19, 1860, quoted in Rainwater, *Mississippi: Storm Center of Secession,* p. 129.

23. Holly Springs *Herald,* quoted in the Nashville *Republican Banner,* March 25, 1860. See also Atlanta *Daily Intelligencer,* April 14, 18, 1860; Raleigh *Democratic Press,* April 30, 1860; Galveston (Tex.) *News,* March 3, 1860; Fayetteville *Arkansian,* February 10, 1860; Fort Smith (Ark.) *Times,* March 15, 1860; West Baton Rouge (La.) *Sugar Planter,* February 11, March 31, April 14, 1860; La Grange (Tex.) *True Issue,* February 24, 1860.

24. Talladega *Alabama Reporter,* April 19, 1860. See also Columbus (Ga.) *Enquirer,* March 13, 1860; Lynchburg *Virginian,* March 7, 1860; Clarksville (Tenn.) *Chronicle,* August 19, 1859; Milledgeville (Ga.) *Southern Recorder,* April 3, 1860; Fayetteville (N.C.) *Observer,* February 27, 1860; Vicksburg (Miss.) *Weekly Vicksburg Whig,* April 11, 1860.

25. Clarksville *Chronicle,* March 23, 1860; Knoxville *Whig,* March 10, 1860; Lynchburg *Virginian,* January 26, 1860. See also Augusta (Ga.) *Chronicle and Sentinel,* March 7, 1860; Wadesborough *North Carolina Argus,* April 19, 1860; Talladega *Alabama Reporter,* April 19, 1860.

26. Knoxville *Whig,* April 7, 1860; Canton *American Citizen,* April 14, 1860.

27. Columbus *Enquirer,* March 6, 1860; Augusta *Chronicle and Sentinel,* April 7, 1860; Raleigh *Register,* March 1, 1860; Lynchburg *Virginian,* March 5, 1860; Richmond *Whig,* April 7, 1860; Raymond (Miss.) *Hinds County Gazette,* March 21, 1860. See also Rome (Ga.) *Weekly Courier,* April 6, 1860; Nashville *Republican Banner,* March 31, 1860; Talladega *Alabama Reporter,* April 5, 1860; Milledgeville (Ga.) *Southern Recorder,* April 3, 1860; Charlotte *North Carolina Whig,* April 24, 1860.

28. Nichols, *The Disruption of American Democracy,* pp. 288–292.

29. Hesseltine, ed., *Three Against Lincoln,* p. 51.

30. *Ibid.,* pp. 3–110; Nichols, *The Disruption of American Democracy,* pp. 292–307; Capers, *Stephen A. Douglas,* pp. 202–204; Milton, *The Eve of Conflict,* pp. 432–442.

31. Wheeling *Daily Intelligencer,* May 4, 1860; Lynchburg *Virginian,* May 6, 1860; Salisbury *Carolina Watchman,* May 8, 1860; Wadesborough *North Carolina Argus,* May 10, 1860. See also Nashville *Republican Banner,* May 2, 1860; Charlestown *Virginia Free Press,* May 17, 1860; Clarksville (Tenn.) *Chronicle,* May 4, 1860; Natchez (Miss.) *Courier,* May 3, 8, 30, 1860.

32. Knoxville *Whig,* July 7, 1860. For similar "obituaries" see Rome (Ga.) *Weekly Courier,* May 25, 1860; Augusta (Ga.) *Chronicle and Sentinel,* May 2, 1860.

33. Vicksburg *Weekly Vicksburg Whig,* July 4, 1860; Fayetteville *Observer,* quoted in Wadesborough *North Carolina Argus,* May 10, 1860. See also Nashville *Republican Banner,* May 3, 1860; Wilmington (N.C.) *Herald,* June 22, 1860, quoted in Hillsborough (N.C.) *Recorder,* July 4, 1860; Talladega *Alabama Reporter,* May 10, 1860; Charlestown *Virginia Free Press,* May 24, 1860; Richmond *Whig,* May 10, 1860; Rome (Ga.) *Weekly Courier,* June 22, 1860; Lynchburg *Virginian,* May 3, 1860.

34. Athens (Tenn.) *Post,* May 4, 1860; Alexandria (Va.) *Gazette,* May 11, 1860; Vicksburg (Miss.) *Weekly Vicksburg Whig,* June 27, 1860; Canton (Miss.) *American Citizen,* June 23, 1860; Baton Rouge (La.) *Weekly Gazette and Comet,* May 13, 1860; Fayetteville (N.C.) *Observer,* June 25, 1860; Clarksville (Tenn.) *Chronicle,* May 18, 1860; Memphis *Daily Enquirer,* June 10, 1860.

35. Rome *Weekly Courier,* June 1, 1860. See also Augusta (Ga.) *Chronicle and Sentinel,* May 13, 1860; Milledgeville (Ga.) *Southern Recorder,* May 8, June 12, 1860; Richmond *Whig,* May 26, June 8, 1860.

36. Carrollton *West Alabamian,* May 9, 1860.

37. Dallas *Herald,* May 16, 1860; False River *Pointe Coupée Democrat,* May 5, 1960; New Orleans *Daily Delta,* May 2, 1860. See also Plaquemine (La.) *Gazette and Sentinel,* May 12, 1860; Des Arc (Ark.) *Citizen,* May 12, 1860; Bellevue (La.) *Bossier Banner,* May 25, 1860; Jacksonville (Ala.) *Republican,* May 3, 1860; Florence (Ala.) *Gazette,* May 23, 1860; Natchez *Mississippi Free Trader,* May 24,

1860; Opelika (Ala.) *Weekly Southern Era,* May 19, 1860; Grove Hill (Ala.) *Clarke County Democrat,* May 6, 1860; Fernandina *East Floridian,* May 10, 1860; Carrollton *West Alabamian,* May 23, 1860; Tallahassee *Floridian and Journal,* May 19, 1860; Savannah (Ga.) *Daily Morning News,* May 4, 5, 8, 1860; Hayneville (Ala.) *Watchman,* June 9, 1860; Columbus *Mississippi Democrat,* May 5, 1860; Little Rock *Old-Line Democrat,* May 24, 1860; Charleston *Mercury* (triweekly ed.) , May 19, 1860; Prattville (Ala.) *Southern Statesman,* June 2, 1860; Fort Smith (Ark.) *Times,* May 10, 1860; Richmond *Enquirer,* May 8, 1860; Danville (Va.) *Appeal,* quoted in Richmond *Enquirer,* May 8, 1860; Madison County (Va.) *American Eagle,* quoted in Richmond *Enquirer,* May 8, 1860; Marshall *Texas Republican,* June 9, 1860.

38. Corsicana *Navarro Express,* May 19, 1860; Spartanburg *Carolina Spartan,* May 10, 1860; Newberry *Conservatist,* May 8, 1860; Savannah *Daily Morning News,* May 5, 1860.

39. Tyler *Reporter,* May 16, 1860; Columbus *Mississippi Democrat,* May 19, 1860; False River *Pointe Coupée Democrat* (French ed.) , May 12, 1860. For other veiled threats of secession see Ft. Smith (Ark.) *Times,* May 10, 1860; Oxford (Miss.) *Mercury,* quoted in the Natchez *Mississippi Free Trader,* June 18, 1860; Opelousas (La.) *Courier,* May 26, 1860; Corsicana (Tex.) *Navarro Express,* May 12, 1860; Albany (Ga.) *Patriot,* May 17, 1860. Only occasionally did a Southern-rights paper say something good about Douglas. One such paper, the Wilmington *Journal,* wrote: "As between Mr. Douglas' position and the positions of several other leading Democrats, we much prefer theirs to his, but Mr. Douglas' position is certainly better than that of Bell, and incomparably better than that of Lincoln." May 31, 1860.

40. Matagorda *Gazette,* May 9, 1860; Claiborne *Southern Champion,* May 25, June 1, 1860; Newberry *Rising Sun,* May 9, 1860; Fernandina *East Floridian,* May 10, 1860.

41. Opelika *Weekly Southern Era,* June 9, 1860; Savannah *Daily Morning News,* May 4, 1860. See also Hayneville (Ala.) *Watchman,* June 9, 1860; Charleston *Mercury* (triweekly ed.) , May 19, 1860; Fernandina *East Floridian,* May 17, 1860.

42. Newberry (S.C.) *Conservatist,* May 29, 1860; Columbus *Mississippi Democrat,* May 5, 1860; Dallas *Herald,* May 23, 1860; Plaquemine (La.) *Gazette and Sentinel,* May 19, 1860; Albany (Ga.) *Patriot,* May 24, 1860; New Orleans *Daily Delta,* May 5, 1860; Little Rock *Old-Line Democrat,* May 24, 1860; Hayneville (Ala.) *Watchman,* June 9, 1860; Benton (Ala.) *Weekly Herald,* May 12, 1860; Charleston *Mercury* (triweekly ed.) , May 19, 1860; Opelika (Ala.) *Weekly Southern Era,* May 19, 1860; Vicksburg (Miss.) *Sun,* May 28, 1860.

43. Montgomery *Weekly Advertiser,* May 16, 1860; Savannah *Daily Morning News,* May 17, 1860; Spartanburg *Carolina Spartan,* May 31, 1860.

44. Greensboro *Alabama Beacon,* May 11, 1860. See also Fayetteville (Tenn.) *Lincoln Journal,* May 10, 1860; Petersburg (Va.) *Press,* quoted in Richmond *Whig,* May 7, 1860; Raleigh *North Carolina Standard* (semiweekly ed.) , May 12, 1860; Harrisonburg (Va.) *Rockingham Register and Advertiser,* May 18, 1860; Van Buren (Ark.) *Press,* May 18, 1860; Huntsville (Ala.) *Advocate,* quoted in the Montgomery (Ala.) *Daily Confederation,* May 12, 1860.

45. Memphis *Daily Appeal,* May 9, 1860. See also Van Buren (Ark.) *Press,* May 18, 1860; Fayetteville (Tenn.) *Lincoln Journal,* May 24, 1860; Montgomery (Ala.) *Daily Confederation,* May 5, 26, 1860; Athens (Ala.) *Herald,* May 11, 1860, quoted in San Antonio *Ledger and Texan,* June 2, 1860; Du Bose, *William Lowndes Yancey,* I, 376.

46. New Orleans *Bee,* May 3, June 11, 1860; Victoria *Texian Advocate,* quoted in Matagorda (Tex.) *Gazette,* May 16, 1860.

47. Greensboro *Alabama Beacon,* May 25, 1860; Van Buren *Press,* May 25, 1860; Harrisonburg *Rockingham Register and Advertiser,* May 18, 1860; Edgefield *Advertiser,* May 30, 1860. See also Memphis *Daily Appeal,* May 10, 1860; Montgomery (Ala.) *Daily Confederation,* May 4, 1860; Athens (Tenn.) *Herald,* May 11, 1860, quoted in San Antonio *Ledger and Texan,* June 2, 1860.

48. Fayetteville (Tenn.) *Lincoln Journal,* June 14, 1860; Memphis *Daily Appeal,* May 5, 1860; Harrisonburg *Rockingham Register and Advertiser,* June 1, 1860; Augusta (Ga.) *Daily Constitutionalist,* May 6, 1860.

49. Wilmington (N.C.) *Daily Journal,* May 3, June 4, 1860; Milledgeville (Ga.) *Federal Union,* May 22, 1860; San Antonio *Ledger and Texan,* May 19, 26, 1860; Clarksville (Tenn.) *Jeffersonian,* May 9, 23, 1860; Alexandria *Louisiana Democrat,* June 13, 1860; Clarksville (Tex.) *Northern Standard,* June 2, 1860; Macon (Ga.) *Daily Telegraph,* May 8, 1860.

50. Norfolk *Southern Argus,* May 4, 1860; Greenville *South Alabamian,* July 7, 1860; Hayneville *Chronicle,* April 26, 1860. See also St. Augustine (Fla.) *Examiner,* May 19, 1860.

51. Macon *Daily Telegraph,* May 4, 1860. See also Wilmington (N.C.) *Daily Journal,* May 5, 1860; Nashville *Union and American,* May 4, 1860.

52. Pensacola *Observer,* quoted in the St. Augustine (Fla.) *Examiner,* May 26, 1860; Atlanta *Daily Intelligencer,* May 7, 1860; Wilmington *Daily Journal,* May 2, 1860. See also La Grange (Tex.) *True Issue,* May 18, 1860; San Antonio *Ledger and Texan,* May 12, 1860.

53. Milledgeville *Federal Union,* May 15, June 26, 1860; Clarksville *Northern Standard,* June 9, 1860; Little Rock *True Democrat,* May 19, 1860. See also Nashville *Union and American,* May 8, 1860; Fayetteville *Arkansian,* June 8, 1860; Atlanta *Daily Intelligencer,* May 8, 1860.

54. Fayetteville *North Carolinian,* May 12, 1860; Atlanta *Daily Intel-*

ligencer, May 7, May 24, June 21, 1860. See also La Grange (Tex.) *True Issue,* June 1, 1860.

Notes to Chapter III

1. Hesseltine, ed., *Three Against Lincoln,* pp. 143–148; Nevins, *The Emergence of Lincoln,* II, 244–251.
2. Hesseltine, ed., *Three Against Lincoln,* pp. 148–160; Nevins, *The Emergence of Lincoln,* II, 252–254.
3. Reinhard H. Luthin, *The First Lincoln Campaign,* pp. 136–167; Hesseltine, ed., *Three Against Lincoln,* pp. 160–184; Nevins, *The Emergence of Lincoln,* II, 254–260.
4. Wheeling *Daily Intelligencer,* May 19, 1860.
5. Shepherdstown *Register,* May 26, 1860; New Orleans *Picayune,* quoted in Marshall *Texas Republican,* June 9, 1860.
6. Charles Lanman, *Dictionary of the United States Congress, Containing Biographical Sketches of its Members from the Foundation of the Government.* For references to this work see Charleston *Courier,* May 19, 1860, and Bellevue (La.) *Bossier Banner,* June 1, 1860.
7. Wilmington *Daily Journal,* June 1, 1860.
8. Des Arc *Citizen,* July 11, 1860.
9. San Antonio *Ledger and Texan,* May 26, 1860; Newbern *Weekly Progress,* May 29, 1860; Alexandria *Gazette,* May 21, 1860. See also Jacksonville (Ala.) *Republican,* May 24, 1860; Richmond *Whig,* May 21, 1860; Talladega (Ala.) *Reporter,* May 24, 1860; Shepherdstown (Va.) *Register,* May 26, 1860; Fayetteville (N.C.) *Observer,* May 21, 1860.
10. New Orleans *Sunday Delta,* May 20, 1860; New Orleans *Bee,* May 21, 1860; Charleston *Daily Courier,* May 22, 1860; Macon *Daily Telegraph,* May 29, 1860; Wilmington *Daily Journal,* May 21, 1860.
11. Paulding *Eastern Clarion,* May 23, 1860; New Orleans *Bee* (French ed.) , May 21, 1860.
12. Salisbury *Carolina Watchman,* May 22, 1860. See also Tallahassee *Floridian and Journal,* May 26, 1860; Raleigh *North Carolina Standard* (semiweekly ed.) , May 23, 1860; Leesburg (Va.) *Democratic Mirror,* May 30, 1860; Montgomery (Ala.) *Weekly Advertiser,* June 27, 1860; Corsicana (Tex.) *Navarro Express,* June 2, 1860; Wilmington (N.C.) *Daily Journal,* June 1, 1860; Fayetteville (N.C.) *Observer,* May 21, 1860; Alexandria (Va.) *Gazette,* May 22, 1860; New Orleans *Daily Picayune,* May 30, 1860.
13. Wilmington *Daily Journal,* June 1, 1860; Milledgeville *Federal Union,* May 29, 1860. See also Norfolk *Southern Argus,* May 23, 1860.
14. Clarksville *Northern Standard,* June 2, 1860; Corsicana *Navarro Express,* June 2, 1860. See also Montgomery (Ala.) *Weekly Advertiser,* June 27, 1860; Jackson *Weekly Mississippian,* May 29, 1860; Ft. Smith *Times,* May 24, 1860.

15. Carrollton *West Alabamian,* September 19, 1860; Memphis *Enquirer,* quoted in West Baton Rouge (La.) *Sugar Planter,* May 26, 1860; Newberry *Rising Sun,* October 17, 1860. See also Montgomery (Ala.) *Weekly Advertiser,* May 23, 1860.

16. Harrisonburg (Va.) *Rockingham Register and Advertiser,* June 29, 1860; Fort Smith (Ark.) *Times,* May 31, 1860; Paulding (Miss.) *Eastern Clarion,* May 30, 1860; Richmond *Examiner,* quoted in the Richmond *Whig,* May 25, 1860; Hayneville (Ala.) *Chronicle,* May 17, 1860; Little Rock *True Democrat,* May 26, 1860; Corsicana (Tex.) *Navarro Express,* May 4, 1860.

17. Wilmington *Daily Journal,* May 24, 1860.

18. Hesseltine, ed., *Three Against Lincoln,* pp. 126–127.

19. *Ibid.,* p. 130.

20. *Ibid.,* pp. 131–140.

21. Augusta *Chronicle and Sentinel,* May 13, 1860; Raleigh *Register,* May 12, 1860; Knoxville *Whig,* May 19, 1860. See also Lynchburg *Virginian,* May 14, 1860; Richmond *Whig,* May 11, 1860; Canton (Miss.) *American Citizen,* May 19, 1860; Wadesborough (N.C.) *Argus,* May 17, 1860; Hillsborough (N.C.) *Recorder,* May 16, 1860; Milledgeville (Ga.) *Southern Recorder,* May 22, 1860; Alexandria (Va.) *Gazette,* May 11, 1860; Charlottesville (Va.) *Review,* May 18, 1860; Petersburg (Va.) *Daily Express,* May 12, 1860; Little Rock *Arkansas State Gazette,* June 2, 1860.

22. Parkersburg *Gazette,* quoted in Charlestown *Virginia Free Press,* June 21, 1860; Clarksville *Chronicle,* June 22, 1860. See also Talladega *Alabama Reporter,* June 7, 1860; Augusta (Ga.) *Chronicle and Sentinel,* June 26, 1860; Nashville *Republican Banner,* June 26, 1860; Richmond *Whig,* June 25, 1860.

23. Salisbury *Carolina Watchman,* May 15, 1860; Little Rock *Arkansas State Gazette,* June 2, 1860.

24. Camden *Ouachita Herald,* June 23, 1860.

25. For examples, see Rome (Ga.) *Weekly Courier,* May 18, 1860; Columbus (Ga.) *Enquirer,* May 15, 1860; Fayetteville (N.C.) *Observer,* May 14, 1860.

26. Benton *Weekly Herald,* May 17, 31, 1860; Montgomery *Weekly Mail,* May 11, 18, June 5, July 6, 1860.

27. Abbeville *Meridional,* quoted in Wadesborough *North Carolina Argus,* September 27, 1860.

28. Athens *Southern Banner,* May 17, 1860. See also Richmond *Enquirer,* June 8, 1860; Nashville *Union and American,* June 21, 1860; *True Virginian,* May 12, 1860.

29. Fayetteville (Tenn.) *Lincoln Journal,* May 31, June 7, 14, 1860; Nashville *Union and American,* June 5, 1860.

30. Leesburg *Democratic Mirror,* May 16, 1860; Memphis *Daily Appeal,* May 19, 1860. See also Clarksville (Tenn.) *Jeffersonian,* May 16, 1860; Spartanburg (S.C.) *Carolina Spartan,* May 17, 1860.

31. New Orleans *Daily Delta,* May 31, 1860; Dallas *Herald,* May 23,

1860. See also San Antonio *Ledger and Texan,* May 19, 1860.

32. Charleston *Mercury,* May 23, 1860; Newberry (S.C.) *Rising Sun,* May 16, 1860; Greenville (S.C.) *Southern Enterprise,* May 17, 1860.

33. Hesseltine, ed., *Three Against Lincoln,* pp. 185–264; Nichols, *The Disruption of American Democracy,* pp. 312–318, 332; Dumond, *The Secession Movement,* pp. 77–91; Craven, *The Growth of Southern Nationalism,* pp. 333–334; Emerson D. Fite, *The Presidential Campaign of 1860,* pp. 108–116.

34. Fernandina *East Floridian,* June 21, 1860; Jacksonville *Republican,* June 28, 1860. For other criticisms of Douglas, see Ft. Smith (Ark.) *Times,* June 28, 1860; New Orleans *Daily Delta,* June 22, 1860; Hayneville (Ala.) *Chronicle,* June 23, 1860; Claiborne (Ala.) *Southern Champion,* July 6, 1860; Alexandria *Louisiana Democrat,* July 4, 1860; Jackson *Weekly Mississippian,* July 3, 1860; Clarksville (Tenn.) *Jeffersonian,* June 27, 1860.

35. Augusta *Daily Constitutionalist,* July 1, 1860. See also Fayetteville (Tenn.) *Lincoln Journal,* July 19, 1860; Harrisonburg (Va.) *Rockingham Register and Advertiser,* June 29, 1860; Greensboro *Alabama Beacon,* June 29, 1860; Tuscumbia (Ala.) *States' Rights Democrat,* June 7, 1860; Memphis *Daily Appeal,* July 8, 1860; Harrisonburg (Va.) *Valley Democrat,* quoted in Charlestown *Virginia Free Press,* July 5, 1860.

36. For examples, see Clarksville (Tex.) *Northern Standard,* July 7, 1860; Leesburg (Va.) *Democratic Mirror,* July 11, 1860.

37. Florence *Gazette,* June 27, 1860. See also St. Augustine (Fla.) *Examiner,* July 7, 1860; Atlanta *Daily Intelligencer,* July 3, 1860; Ft. Smith (Ark.) *Times,* July 5, 1860; Grove Hill (Ala.) *Clarke County Democrat,* June 28, 1860; Greenville *South Alabamian,* June 30, 1860; Charleston *Daily Courier,* June 25, 1860; Fayetteville *North Carolinian,* June 30, 1860; Des Arc (Ark.) *Citizen,* June 10, 1860; Nashville *Union and American,* June 26, 1860; Plaquemine (La.) *Gazette and Sentinel,* June 30, 1860; Macon (Ga.) *Daily Telegraph,* June 26, 1860.

38. Wilmington *Daily Herald,* June 25, 1860; Savannah *Daily Morning News,* June 25, 1860; Jacksonville *Republican,* June 28, 1860. See also Fayetteville *Arkansian,* June 30, 1860; False River (La.) *Pointe Coupée Democrat,* June 30, 1860; Norfolk (Va.) *Southern Argus,* July 17, 1860; Prattville (Ala.) *Southern Statesman,* June 30, 1860; Tallahassee *Floridian and Journal,* June 30, 1860; Wilmington (N.C.) *Journal,* June 28, 1860; Milledgeville (Ga.) *Federal Union,* June 26, 1860.

39. Vicksburg *Whig,* quoted in Wadesborough *North Carolina Argus,* July 12, 1860. See also Little Rock *Arkansas State Gazette,* June 30, 1860; Newbern (N.C.) *Weekly Progress,* July 3, 1860.

40. New Orleans *Daily Delta,* June 24, August 30, 1860; New Orleans *Daily Picayune,* July 1, 4, 1860; New Orleans *Bee,* July 4, August 3, 1860.

41. Prattville *Autauga Citizen*, June 28, 1860; Edgefield *Advertiser*, June 27, 1860.
42. For example, Charleston *Mercury*, Newberry *Conservatist*, Spartanburg *Carolina Spartan*, Camden *Weekly Journal*, Abbeville *Independent Press*, Lexington *Flag*, Anderson *Intelligencer*, Columbia *Daily South Carolinian*, Beaufort *Enterprise*, and Winnsboro *Register*.
43. Clement Eaton, *The Growth of Southern Civilization, 1790–1860*, pp. 266, 268.
44. Fayetteville *North Carolinian*, January 14, 1860; Knoxville *Whig*, June 16, 1860.
45. Wilmington *Watchman*, quoted in Wheeling *Daily Intelligencer*, July 9, 1860.
46. Bolivar *Democrat*, quoted in the Norfolk (Va.) *Southern Argus*, August 3, 1860; Greensboro *Alabama Beacon*, July 27, 1860; J. C. Sitterson, *The Secession Movement in North Carolina*, pp. 162–163; Raper, "William W. Holden," *North Carolina Historical Review*, XXXI, 493–494.
47. Raleigh *North Carolina Standard* (semiweekly ed.), July 18, 1860.
48. Clarksville *Jeffersonian*, July 11, 1860; Shelbyville *True Union*, quoted in Fayetteville *Lincoln Journal*, July 26, 1860; Nashville *Republican Banner*, July 20, 1860.
49. Hayneville *Watchman*, July 13, 1860.
50. Montgomery *Weekly Mail*, July 6, 1860; Benton *Weekly Herald*, July 19, 1860.
51. Memphis *Daily Appeal*, July 19, 1860.
52. San Antonio *Ledger and Texan*, July 14, August 4, 1860.
53. Kennedy, *Preliminary Report on the Eighth Census*, p. 211; Baton Rouge (La.) *Daily Advocate*, September 3, 1860.
54. See Appendix I for a list of Southern newspapers with their candidate affiliations for the election of 1860. While it was not possible to ascertain the position of every Southern newspaper, the list includes roughly two thirds of all political journals of the future Confederate states.
55. Nichols, *The Disruption of American Democracy*, p. 334.
56. Nashville *Union and American*, July 24, August 29, 1860; Newbern *Daily Progress*, July 3, 1860; Wilmington *Daily Journal*, August 20, 1860; Fairmont *True Virginian*, August 18, 1860; San Antonio *Ledger and Texan*, August 25, 1860. The famous couplet is from Moore's *Irish Melodies*.
57. Homer *Iliad*, quoted in Newbern *Weekly Progress*, August 7, 1860.

Notes to Chapter IV

1. Robert S. Cotterill, *The Old South*, p. 299.
2. Lynchburg *Virginian*, June 25, August 26, 1860; Montgomery *Weekly Confederation*, August 31, 1860. For reports of other shoot-

ings involving editors, see Corsicana (Tex.) *Navarro Express*, June 16, 1860; Waco (Tex.) *Democrat*, quoted in Indianola (Tex.) *Courier*, November 10, 1860.

3. Opelika (Ala.) *Weekly Southern Era*, July 21, 1860; Matagorda (Tex.) *Gazette*, August 15, 1860; Montgomery (Ala.) *Weekly Mail*, July 13, 1860; Plaquemine (La.) *Gazette and Sentinel*, August 4, 1860; Newberry (S.C.) *Conservatist*, July 24, 1860; Natchez *Mississippi Free Trader*, August 27, 1860; Spartanburg (S.C.) *Carolina Spartan*, September 6, 1860; Florence (Ala.) *Gazette*, August 1, 1860.

4. New Orleans *Daily Delta*, November 7, 1860.

5. Ollinger Crenshaw, *The Slave States in the Presidential Election of 1860*, pp. 74–88; Nevins, *The Emergence of Lincoln*, II, 290–296.

6. Spartanburg *Carolina Spartan*, September 6, 1860. See also Natchez *Mississippi Free Trader*, September 4, 1860.

7. Quoted in Nevins, *The Emergence of Lincoln*, II, 294.

8. Raleigh *Democratic Press*, September 26, 1860. See also Milledgeville (Ga.) *Federal Union*, October 2, 1860; Baton Rouge (La.) *Daily Advocate*, October 15, 1860; Paris (Tenn.) *Sentinel*, October 3, 1861.

9. Hayneville *Chronicle*, July 26, 1860.

10. Richmond *Enquirer*, November 6, 1860; Opelousas *Courier*, September 8, 1860; New Orleans *Courier*, quoted in Tallahassee *East Floridian*, October 11, 1860. See also Kanawha (Va.) *Valley Star*, August 27, 1860; West Baton Rouge (La.) *Sugar Planter*, September 15, 1860; St. Augustine (Fla.) *Examiner*, September 22, 1860; Nashville *Union and American*, October 4, 1860; Richmond *Enquirer*, September 4, 1860; Natchez *Mississippi Free Trader*, October 8, 1860; Athens (Ga.) *Southern Banner*, August 30, 1860.

11. Milledgeville (Ga.) *Federal Union*, July 10, August 14, 21, 28, 1860; Richmond *Enquirer*, July 31, 1860; Athens (Ga.) *Southern Banner*, August 16, 1860; Opelousas (La.) *Courier*, September 8, 1860; Tallahassee *East Floridian*, July 26, 1860; False River (La.) *Pointe Coupée Democrat*, August 25, 1860; Fayetteville *North Carolinian*, September 22, 1860; Marshall *Texas Republican*, September 1, 1860; Natchez *Mississippi Free Trader*, July 30, 1860.

12. Milledgeville *Federal Union*, July 17, 1860; Montgomery *Weekly Mail*, October 5, 1860. See also Grove Hill (Ala.) *Clarke County Democrat*, July 12, 1860; Kanawha (Va.) *Valley Star*, July 23, 1860; Opelika (Ala.) *Weekly Southern Era*, June 19, 1860; Murfreesboro (Tenn.) *News*, October 17, 1860; Norfolk (Va.) *Southern Argus*, July 21, 1860; Wilmington (N.C.) *Daily Journal*, September 21, 1860; Natchez *Mississippi Free Trader*, July 16, 1860; Tallahassee *Floridian and Journal*, October 6, 1860.

13. Murfreesboro *News*, October 17, 1860; Columbus *Mississippi Democrat*, August 18, 1860; St. Augustine *Examiner*, September 15, 1860; Opelika *Weekly Southern Era*, June 16, 1860. See also Baton Rouge

(La.) *Daily Advocate,* September 27, 1860; Dallas *Herald,* October 24, 1860; Montgomery (Ala.) *Weekly Advertiser,* October 3, 1860; Prattville (Ala.) *Southern Statesman,* October 13, 1860; Milledgeville (Ga.) *Federal Union,* September 18, 1860.

14. Tuskegee *Republican,* quoted in Milledgeville (Ga.) *Southern Recorder,* July 31, 1860. See also Fayetteville (N.C.) *Observer,* August 13, 1860; Greenville (Ala.) *Southern Messenger,* June 20, 1860; Hayneville (Ala.) *Watchman,* September 21, 1860; Charlestown *Virginia Free Press,* August 2, 1860; Nashville *Republican Banner,* September 14, 1860; Canton (Miss.) *American Citizen,* September 8, 1860; Knoxville *Whig,* July 21, 1860; Richmond *Whig,* July 26, 1860; Charlotte (N.C.) *Whig,* September 4, 1860; Wadesborough *North Carolina Argus,* August 23, 1860; Hillsborough (N.C.) *Recorder,* September 5, 1860; Augusta (Ga.) *Chronicle and Sentinel,* July 31, 1860; Columbus (Ga.) *Enquirer,* June 26, 1860; Rome (Ga.) *Weekly Courier,* July 20, 1860; Montgomery (Ala.) *Weekly Post,* August 29, 1860.

15. Carrollton *West Alabamian,* September 19, 1860; Vicksburg (Miss.) *Weekly Whig,* September 19, 1860; Columbus *Mississippi Democrat,* September 15, 1860.

16. San Antonio *Alamo Express,* August 25, 1860. Although Bell papers generally softened their attitudes toward Douglas, a few Constitutional Union organs continued to print anti-Douglas editorials. For examples, see Salisbury (N.C.) *Carolina Watchman,* September 11, 1860; Greenville (Ala.) *Southern Messenger,* June 13, 1860; Nashville *Republican Banner,* July 13, 19, 1860.

17. Natchez *Mississippi Free Trader,* July 28, 1860; Matagorda *Gazette,* August 15, 1860. See also Richmond *Enquirer,* September 11, 1860; Plaquemine (La.) *Gazette and Sentinel,* August 11, 1860; Clarksville (Tenn.) *Jeffersonian,* July 14, 1860; Columbus *Mississippi Democrat,* August 11, 1860; Nashville *Union and American,* July 13, 1860; Milledgeville (Ga.) *Federal Union,* October 30, 1860; Baton Rouge (La.) *Daily Advocate,* October 20, 1860; Alexandria *Louisiana Democrat,* August 8, 1860; Florence (Ala.) *Gazette,* August 15, 1860.

18. New Orleans *Bee,* August 24, 1860. See also Fayetteville (N.C.) *Observer,* September 10, 1860; Salisbury (N.C.) *Carolina Watchman,* August 14, 1860; Talladega *Alabama Reporter,* July 26, 1860; Richmond *Whig,* July 24, 1860; Hillsborough (N.C.) *Recorder,* September 19, 1860; Lynchburg *Virginian,* October 3, 1860.

19. Willie M. Caskey, *Secession and Restoration of Louisiana,* pp. 14, 15; Denman, *The Secession Movement in Alabama,* p. 86; Wooster, *The Secession Conventions of the South,* p. 191; Jack B. Scroggs, "Arkansas in the Secession Crisis," *Arkansas Historical Quarterly,* XII, 190.

20. See p. 60.

21. Knoxville *Whig,* August 18, 1860; New Orleans *Bee,* September 22,

1860; Charlestown *Virginia Free Press,* August 9, 1860; Vicksburg (Miss.) *Weekly Vicksburg Whig,* August 22, 1860; Memphis *Daily Appeal,* August 17, 1860; Nashville *Republican Banner,* October 25, 26, 1860; Lynchburg *Virginian,* October 11, 1860; Richmond *Whig,* September 7, October 9, 1860; Augusta (Ga.) *Daily Constitutionalist,* July 26, 1860.

22. Nashville *Patriot,* July 11, 1860. See also Wadesborough *North Carolina Argus,* August 16, 1860; Austin (Tex.) *Southern Intelligencer,* September 5, 1860; Memphis *Daily Appeal,* July 14, 1860; Raymond (Miss.) *Hinds County Gazette,* August 22, 1860; West Baton Rouge (La.) *Sugar Planter,* August 25, 1860.

23. Raleigh *Register,* July 28, August 18, 22, 1860; Richmond *Whig,* September 10, 1860; Clarksville (Tenn.) *Chronicle,* July 6, 1860; Vicksburg (Miss.) *Weekly Vicksburg Whig,* August 8, 1860; Aberdeen (Miss.) *Conservative,* quoted in Nashville *Republican Banner,* July 10, 1860; Knoxville *Whig,* October 20, 1860; Montgomery (Ala.) *Daily Confederation,* June 9, 1860; Huntsville (Ala.) *Advocate,* quoted in Raleigh *Register,* July 28, 1860; Selma (Ala.) *Sentinel,* quoted in Newbern (N.C.) *Weekly Progress,* August 7, 1860; Morgantown (Va.) *Star,* quoted in Charlestown *Virginia Free Press,* July 5, 1860; Little Rock *Arkansas State Gazette,* September 29, October 13, 1860; Alexandria (Va.) *Gazette,* August 3, 1860; Augusta (Ga.) *Daily Constitutionalist,* August 19, 1860; New Orleans *Bee,* August 31, 1860; Augusta (Ga.) *Chronicle and Sentinel,* July 26, 1860; Hayneville (Ala.) *Watchman,* August 10, 1860.

24. Van Buren *Press,* August 24, 1860; Milledgeville *Southern Recorder,* August 14, 1860; New Orleans *Bee,* August 3, 1860. See also Greenville (Ala.) *Southern Messenger,* August 15, 1860.

25. Alexandria *Constitutional,* September 22, 1860; Lynchburg *Virginian,* September 8, 1860; Vicksburg *Weekly Vicksburg Whig,* October 3, 1860; San Antonio *Alamo Express,* August 18, 1860. See also Knoxville *Whig,* July 28, 1860; Charlotte *North Carolina Whig,* October 23, 1860; Tuscumbia (Ala.) *States' Rights Democrat,* September 14, 1860; Canton (Miss.) *American Citizen,* September 15, 1860; Clarksville (Tenn.) *Chronicle,* July 20, 1860; Wilmington (N.C.) *Herald,* quoted in Wadesborough *North Carolina Argus,* September 13, 1860.

26. Jackson *Weekly Mississippian,* October 31, 1860; Rainwater, *Mississippi: Storm Center of Secession,* pp. 152–156; Woodville *Republican,* quoted in Natchez (Miss.) *Courier,* November 2, 1860; Charleston *Mercury,* August 28, 1860, quoted in Charles E. Cauthen, *South Carolina Goes to War, 1860–1865,* pp. 17, 33.

27. Claiborne *Southern Champion,* quoted in Wadesborough *North Carolina Argus,* August 9, 1860; Camden *Register,* quoted in Wadesborough *North Carolina Argus,* August 9, 1860; Houma *Ceres,* quoted in Opelousas (La.) *Courier,* August 18, 1860.

28. Fite, *The Presidential Campaign of 1860,* pp. 174, 175, carries ex-

cerpts from Breckinridge's speech delivered at Ashland, Kentucky. For the full text see Charleston *Daily Courier,* September 22, 1860; St. Louis *Missouri Republican,* September 11, 1860.

29. Jonesborough *Union,* September 22, 1860; Gallatin *Examiner,* September 1, 1860; Norfolk *Southern Argus,* August 9, 1860; Alexandria *Louisiana Democrat,* August 15, 1860; Newberry *Rising Sun,* July 18, 1860. See also Nashville *Union and American,* September 15, 1860; Athens (Ga.) *Southern Banner,* July 12, 1860; Clarksville (Tenn.) *Jeffersonian,* July 4, 1860.

30. Plaquemine *Gazette and Sentinel,* June 28, 1860; Fairmont *True Virginian,* September 1, 1860; Carrollton *West Alabamian,* October 10, 1860. See also Little Rock *True Democrat,* September 1, 1860; Newberry (S.C.) *Conservatist,* July 17, 1860; St. Augustine (Fla.) *Examiner,* September 15, 1860.

31. Florence *Gazette,* August 29, 1860; Milledgeville *Federal Union,* September 11, 1860. See also Clarksville (Tenn.) *Jeffersonian,* August 15, 1860; Raleigh *Democratic Press,* September 26, 1860; Athens (Ga.) *Southern Banner,* October 4, 1860; Paris (Tenn.) *Sentinel,* October 10, 1860; Nashville *Union and American,* August 30, 1860.

32. Wheeling *Daily Intelligencer,* September 28, 1860; Richmond *Dispatch,* July 4, 1860.

33. San Antonio *Alamo Express,* November 5, 1860. See also Vicksburg (Miss.) *Weekly Vicksburg Whig,* October 24, 1860; Canton (Miss.) *American Citizen,* September 29, 1860; Knoxville (Tenn.) *Whig,* September 15, 1860; Tuscumbia *States' Rights Democrat,* August 17, 1860; Fayetteville *Arkansian,* June 23, 1860; Prattville (Ala.) *Autauga Citizen,* October 4, 1860; Talladega *Alabama Reporter,* September 20, 1860; Shreveport (La.) *South-Western,* August 29, 1860.

34. Montgomery *Weekly Advertiser,* September 5, 1860.

35. Clarksville (Tenn.) *Chronicle,* November 2, 1860; Hillsborough (N.C.) *Recorder,* October 31, 1860; Alexandria (Va.) *Gazette,* October 19, 1860; Richmond *Whig,* October 17, 1860; Fayetteville (N.C.) *Observer,* October 29, 1860.

36. Shreveport *South-Western,* September 19, 1860; Alexandria *Constitutional,* October 27, 1860; Raleigh *Register,* November 3, 1860; Richmond *Central Presbyterian,* September 8, 1860. See also Fayetteville (Tenn.) *Lincoln Journal,* August 30, 1860; Richmond *Dispatch,* August 22, 1860; Richmond *Whig,* September 20, 1860; New Orleans *Daily Picayune,* October 21, 1860; Clarksville (Tenn.) *Chronicle,* July 6, 1860; San Antonio (Tex.) *Alamo Express,* August 25, 1860; Augusta (Ga.) *Chronicle and Sentinel,* September 18, 1860; Washington (N.C.) *Dispatch,* quoted in Hillsborough (N.C.) *Recorder,* August 1, 1860.

37. Wadesborough *North Carolina Argus,* October 25, 1860; Charlestown *Virginia Free Press,* November 1, 1860. See also Alexandria (Va.) *Gazette,* October 19, 1860; Raleigh *Register,* September 8,

1860; Memphis *Daily Appeal,* September 27, 1860; Little Rock *Arkansas State Gazette,* September 29, 1860; New Orleans *Bee* (French edition) , September 12, 1860; Montgomery (Ala.) *Weekly Post,* October 31, 1860; Nashville *Republican Banner,* August 5, 1860; Talladega *Alabama Reporter,* August 16, 1860; Raleigh *North Carolina Standard,* July 11, 1860.

38. Montgomery *Confederation,* quoted in Wheeling (Va.) *Daily Intelligencer,* October 13, 1860. See also Charlestown *Virginia Free Press,* August 23, 1860; Clarksville (Tenn.) *Chronicle,* November 2, 1860.

39. Salisbury (N.C.) *Carolina Watchman,* October 16, 1860; Lynchburg *Virginian,* October 17, 1860; Petersburg (Va.) *Intelligencer,* quoted in Hillsborough (N.C.) *Recorder,* August 29, 1860; Charlestown *Virginia Free Press,* August 2, 1860.

40. Fayetteville *Arkansian,* July 7, 1860.

41. Milledgeville (Ga.) *Federal Union,* August 28, 1860; Norfolk (Va.) *Southern Argus,* September 18, 1860; Kanawha (Va.) *Valley Star,* July 23, 1860; Murfreesboro (Tenn.) *News,* September 26, 1860; Nashville *Union and American,* August 7, 1860; Little Rock *True Democrat,* August 25, 1860; Newberry (S.C.) *Conservatist,* August 21, 1860; Montgomery (Ala.) *Weekly Mail,* June 8, 1860; Memphis *Avalanche,* quoted in Montgomery *Weekly Mail,* June 8, 1860; Jacksonville (Ala.) *Republican,* July 12, 1860; Benton (Ala.) *Weekly Herald,* July 26, 1860; False River (La.) *Pointe Coupée Democrat,* September 1, October 13, 1860; Austin (Tex.) *State Gazette,* July 21, 1860; Dallas *Herald,* October 17, 1860; San Antonio *Daily Herald,* August 29, 1860; Baton Rouge (La.) *Daily Advocate,* September 4, 1860; Tallahassee *Floridian and Journal,* July 7, 1860; Albany (Ga.) *Patriot,* August 23, 1860.

42. Norfolk *Southern Argus,* October 3, 1860; Jackson *Weekly Mississippian,* June 27, 1860. See also Atlanta *Daily Intelligencer,* September 26, 1860.

43. Charleston *Mercury* (triweekly ed.) , July 31, 1860; Fernandina *East Floridian,* November 7, 1860; Atlanta *Daily Intelligencer,* October 3, November 1, 1860. See also Wilmington (N.C.) *Daily Journal,* October 11, 1860.

44. Corsicana *Navarro Express,* September 21, 1860; Charleston *Mercury* (triweekly ed.) , July 31, 1860. See also Mobile (Ala.) *Tribune,* quoted in Hayneville (Ala.) *Watchman,* June 15, 1860; Norfolk (Va.) *Southern Argus,* October 3, 1860.

45. Atlanta *Daily Intelligencer,* November 6, 1860.

46. For two exceptions to this generalization, see Raleigh *North Carolina Standard* (semiweekly ed.) , May 23, 1860, and Corsicana (Tex.) *Navarro Express,* April 28, 1860.

47. Columbus *Mississippi Democrat,* August 4, 1860; Little Rock *Old-Line Democrat,* August 30, 1860; Carrollton *West Alabamian,* August 22, 1860; Norfolk (Va.) *Southern Argus,* August 10, 1860;

New Orleans *Daily Picayune,* August 17, 1860; Alexandria (La.) *Constitutional,* August 13, 1860; Charleston *Mercury,* September 12, 1860.

48. Nashville *Republican Banner,* August 30, 1860.
49. Quoted in David Donald, *Charles Sumner and the Coming of the Civil War,* p. 357. Donald has a concise summary of Sumner's lengthy speech.
50. *Ibid.,* p. 357.
51. New Orleans *Daily Picayune,* June 10, 1860; Asheville *News,* June 20, 1860; Milledgeville *Federal Union,* June 19, 1860. See also Norfolk (Va.) *Southern Argus,* June 8, August 13, 1860; Richmond *Dispatch,* June 9, 1860; Leesburg (Va.) *Democratic Mirror,* June 13, 1860; Clarksville (Tenn.) *Jeffersonian,* June 13, 1860; Lynchburg *Virginian,* June 11, 1860; New Orleans *Bee,* June 12, 1860; Fayetteville *Arkansian,* July 7, 1860.
52. Macon (Ga.) *Daily Telegraph,* September 17, 1860; Murfreesboro (Tenn.) October 17, 1860; San Antonio *Daily Herald,* September 28, 1860; New Orleans *Daily Picayune,* September 8, 1860.
53. Austin *State Gazette,* October 13, 1860. See also Edgefield (S.C.) *Advertiser,* June 13, 1860; San Antonio *Daily Herald,* September 28, 1860; Macon (Ga.) *Daily Telegraph,* September 17, 1860.

Notes to Chapter V

1. The most lucid examination of the "Texas Troubles" may be found in Crenshaw, *The Slave States in the Election of 1860,* pp. 89–108. Crenshaw does not attempt to determine whether a plot actually existed, although he seems somewhat dubious and points out that there had been a similar panic in Texas during the presidential election of 1856. A brief but well-balanced account may be found in Nevins, *The Emergence of Lincoln,* II, 306–308. William W. White, "The Texas Slave Insurrection of 1860," *Southwestern Historical Quarterly,* LII, 259–285, and Wendell G. Addington, "Slave Insurrections in Texas," *Journal of Negro History,* XXXV, 408–434, accept the reports, but both articles are gravely weakened by their exclusive dependence for documentation upon Breckinridge newspapers; neither cites contrary reports in Bell papers. See also Herbert Aptheker, *American Negro Slave Revolts,* pp. 353–354.
2. Dallas *Herald,* "Extra," July 11, 1860; Clarksville *Standard,* July 14, 1860; Edmond F. Bates, *History and Reminiscences of Denton County,* pp. 348–349.
3. Dallas *Morning News,* July 10, 1892.
4. *Ibid.*
5. Austin *State Gazette* (weekly ed.), July 14, 1860.
6. Bonham *Era,* July 17, 1860.
7. Houston *Telegraph,* July 21, 1860.

8. Marshall *Texas Republican,* August 11, 1860.
9. Corsicana (Tex.) *Navarro Express,* July 14, August 11, 1860. Perhaps ninety percent of Southern political journals carried the stories of Texas fires; see Atlanta *Daily Intelligencer,* August 18, 1860; Spartanburg (S.C.) *Carolina Spartan,* August 2, 1860; Fernandina *East Floridian,* August 16, 1860; Shepherdstown (Va.) *Register,* August 11, 1860; Prattville (Ala.) *Southern Statesman,* September 1, 1860; Montgomery (Ala.) *Weekly Mail,* August 24, 1860; Anderson (S.C.) *Intelligencer,* August 14, 28, 1860; Clarksville (Tenn.) *Jeffersonian,* August 1, 8, November 7, 1860; Jacksonville (Ala.) *Republican,* August 23, 1860; Nashville *Union and American,* August 21, September 26, 1860; Matagorda (Tex.) *Gazette,* August 22, September 12, 1860; Marshall *Texas Republican,* August 11, 18, 1860; Jackson *Weekly Mississippian,* September 19, 1860; Hayneville (Ala.) *Chronicle,* August 23, October 4, 1860; Opelousas (La.) *Courier,* August 11, 1860; Memphis *Daily Appeal,* August 3, 5, 1860; Van Buren (Ark.) *Press,* August 3, 1860; Sandersville *Central Georgian,* August 8, 1860; San Antonio *Ledger and Texan,* July 28, August 25, 1860; Milledgeville (Ga.) *Federal Union,* August 7, 21, 1860; Charleston (S.C.) *Daily Courier,* August 8, 16, 1860; Asheville (N.C.) *News,* August 9, 1860; Paris (Tenn.) *Sentinel,* October 3, 1860; Richmond *Enquirer,* August 7, October 5, 1860; Little Rock *Old-Line Democrat,* September 6, 1860; Fort Smith (Ark.) *Times,* August 16, 1860; Tallahassee *Floridian and Journal,* August 11, 1860; Columbus *Mississippi Democrat,* September 1, 1860; Natchez *Mississippi Free Trader,* September 10, 17, 1860; Greensboro (N.C.) *Times,* August 11, 1860; Centre (Ala.) *Coosa River Argus,* September 8, 1860; Greensboro *Alabama Beacon,* August 10, 1860; Camden (S.C.) *Weekly Journal,* July 31, August 7, 14, 1860; Abbeville (S.C.) *Independent Press,* August 10, 17, 1860; Newberry (S.C.) *Conservatist,* August 7, 14, September 4, 1860. The towns variously reported to have been victimized were: Dallas, Belknap, Sulphur Springs, Millwood, Birdville, Bonham, Georgetown, Daingerfield, Waxahachie, Kaufman, Gainesville, Mt. Vernon, Denton, Pilot Point, Henderson, Tyler, Quitman, Liberty, Austin, Sherman, Lancaster, McKinney, Belleview, Weatherford.
10. Athens (Ga.) *Southern Banner,* August 2, September 6, 1860; Shepherdtown (Va.) *Register,* September 15, October 20, 1860; Kanawha (Va.) *Valley Star,* August 27, 1860; Macon (Ga.) *Daily Telegraph,* October 8, 1860; Anderson (S.C.) *Intelligencer,* September 18, 1860; Jacksonville (Ala.) *Republican,* August 30, 1860; Prattville (Ala.) *Autauga Citizen,* August 9, 1860; Hayneville (Ala.) *Chronicle,* October 25, 1860; Asheville (N.C.) *News* November 1, 1860; Des Arc (Ark.) *Citizen,* September 12, 1860; Van Buren (Ark.) *Press,* September 21, 1860.
11. Hattie J. Roach, *A History of Cherokee County,* p. 61; Marshall

Texas Republican, August 11, 1860; New York *Day Book,* September 8, 1860, quoted in Austin (Tex.) *Southern Intelligencer,* October 10, 1860.

12. H. N. P. Gammel, comp., *The Laws of Texas, 1822–1898,* I, 1265–1266.

13. Rusk *Enquirer,* quoted in the San Augustine (Tex.) *Red Land Express,* August 18, 1860; Tyler *Reporter,* August 8, 1860.

14. Anonymous letter, posted "Texas, August 7," New York *Daily Tribune,* August 22, 1860; Corsicana (Tex.) *Navarro Express,* August 25, 1860; Austin (Tex.) *Southern Intelligencer,* October 10, 1860.

15. Dallas (Tex.) *Morning News,* July 10, 1892; S. B. Barron, *The Lone Star Defenders,* p. 17.

16. Wellsburg *Herald,* September 14, 1860.

17. New Orleans *Daily Picayune,* August 25, 1860; Marshall *Texas Republican,* August 25, 1860; Houston *Petrel,* August 24, 1860, quoted in Cincinnati *Daily Commercial,* September 1, 1860.

18. Corsicana (Tex.) *Navarro Express,* August 25, 1860; Anderson *Texas Baptist,* August 16, 1860.

19. For references to some of the hangings, see the Marshall *Texas Republican,* August 11, 18, September 1, 1860; Austin (Tex.) *State Gazette,* September 15, 29, 1860; Henderson (Tex.) *Times,* August 27, 1860, November 25, 1937; Palestine (Tex.) *Trinity Advocate,* August 8, 1860; San Augustine (Tex.) *Red Land Express,* August 11, 18, 25, 1860; Galveston (Tex.) *Weekly News,* August 4, 1860; Galveston *Texas Christian Advocate,* August 2, 9, 16, 1860; Galveston *Weekly Civilian and Gazette,* August 14, 1860; Washington (D.C.) *Constitution,* August 9, 1860; Fort Worth *Chief,* quoted in Washington (D.C.) *Constitution,* August 15, 1860; Washington (D.C.) *Daily National Intelligencer,* August 11, 1860; Clarksville (Tex.) *Standard,* September 22, 1860; Weatherford (Tex.) *White Man,* September 15, 1860; Charleston *Mercury,* September 8, 1860.

20. Galveston (Tex.) *Weekly News,* July 28, 1860, quoted in New Orleans *Daily Delta,* July 30, 1860; Belton (Tex.) *Democrat,* quoted in Cincinnati *Daily Commercial,* August 30, 1860; Weatherford (Tex.) *White Man,* September 15, 1860.

21. Marshall *Texas Republican,* August 11, 18, 1860; New York *Day Book,* September 8, 1860, quoted in Austin (Tex.) *Southern Intelligencer,* October 12, 1860.

22. For several examples of forced evictions from the state, see Palestine (Tex.) *Trinity Advocate,* August 22, 1860, quoted in Galveston (Tex.) *Civilian and Gazette* (weekly ed.) , August 28, 1860; Rusk (Tex.) *Enquirer,* quoted in San Antonio *Ledger and Texan,* September 5, 1860.

23. Cameron (Tex.) *Sentinel,* August 11, 1860, quoted in New York *Times,* August 30, 1860.

24. Corsicana *Navarro Express,* August 25, 1860.

25. San Augustine (Tex.) *Red Land Express,* October 20, 1860.
26. New York *Daily Tribune,* August 22, 1860.
27. Paris *Press,* quoted in Austin *Southern Intelligencer,* September 5, 1860; Marshall *Texas Republican,* July 28, 1860; Mt. Pleasant *Union,* quoted in Marshall *Texas Republican,* September 1, 1860.
28. La Grange (Tex.) *True Issue,* August 2, 1860.
29. Austin Southern (Tex.) *Intelligencer,* August 15, 1860.
30. Galveston *Civilian and Gazette* (weekly ed.), September 18, 1860.
31. La Grange (Tex.) *True Issue,* August 2, 1860.
32. Clarksville (Tex.) *Northern Standard,* July 14, 1860.
33. "Reminiscences of Rev. R. M. White," *A Memorial and Biographical History of Ellis County, Texas,* pp. 95–96.
34. Bates, *History of Denton County,* pp. 348–349.
35. Palestine (Tex.) *Trinity Advocate,* quoted in the Galveston *Civilian and Gazette* (weekly ed.), September 4, 1860.
36. Dallas *Morning News,* July 10, 1892.
37. La Grange *True Issue,* October 18, 1860; Paris *Press,* August 18, 1860.
38. Louis J. Wortham, *A History of Texas, from Wilderness to Commonwealth,* III, 320–321.
39. Austin *Southern Intelligencer,* August 15, 1860.
40. Lucadia Pease to Juliet Niles, September 20, 1860, Pease Papers, Austin Public Library, Austin, Texas.
41. Hayneville *Watchman,* August 3, 1860.
42. Richmond *Whig,* September 13, 1860; Newbern *Weekly Progress,* October 23, 1860; Raymond *Hinds County Gazette,* November 7, 1860. See also Salisbury (N.C.) *Carolina Watchman,* November 13, 1860; San Antonio *Alamo Express,* August 25, 1860; Nashville *Republican Banner,* August 4, 1860; Lynchburg *Virginian,* July 28, 1860; Wheeling (Va.) *Daily Intelligencer,* August 17, 1860; Wellsburg (Va.) *Herald,* September 21, 1860.
43. Athens *Southern Banner,* September 13, 1860; Houston *Telegraph,* quoted in Galveston *Crisis,* September 3, 1860; Austin *State Gazette,* September 22, 1860. See also Milledgeville (Ga.) *Federal Union,* September 11, 1860; Montgomery (Ala.) *Weekly Mail,* August 30, 1860; Corsicana (Tex.) *Navarro Express,* August 25, 1860; Weatherford (Tex.) *White Man,* September 15, 1860; Montgomery (Ala.) *Weekly Advertiser,* August 15, 1860.
44. John E. Campbell to his brother, August 23, 1860, Campbell Papers, University of Texas Archives, Austin, Texas.
45. Austin (Tex.) *State Gazette,* September 15, 1860; San Augustine (Tex.) *Red Land Express,* September 15, 29, 1860; Galveston (Tex.) *Civilian and Gazette,* September 25, 1860.
46. Raleigh *Register,* September 12, 1860; Alexandria *Gazette,* July 27, 1860; Knoxville *Whig,* September 1, 1860; New Orleans *Daily Picayune,* August 2, 19, September 8, 1860; Montgomery *Weekly Post,* August 1, 1860. See also Talladega *Alabama Reporter,* August 2,

1860; Charlotte *North Carolina Whig,* August 3, 1860; New Orleans *Bee* (French ed.), August 8, 1860; Milledgeville (Ga.) *Southern Recorder,* August 7, 1860; Augusta (Ga.) *Chronicle and Sentinel,* August 1, 1860; Rome (Ga.) *Weekly Courier,* September 7, 1860; Wadesborough *North Carolina Argus,* September 13, 1860.

47. New Orleans *Daily Delta,* July 31, 1860; Fayetteville *Arkansian,* August 17, 1860; Montgomery *Weekly Mail,* August 3, 1860; Galveston *Christian Advocate,* quoted in Austin *State Gazette,* October 6, 1860. See also San Antonio *Daily Herald,* July 25, 1860; Tallahassee *East Floridian,* August 16, 1860; Galveston (Tex.) *Weekly News,* August 11, 1860; Marshall *Texas Republican,* August 25, 1860; Opelousas (La.) *Courier* (French ed.), August 25, 1860; Wilmington (N.C.) *Daily Journal,* July 31, 1860; Savannah (Ga.) *News,* quoted in Tallahassee *Floridian and Journal,* August 11, 1860; Norfolk (Va.) *Southern Argus,* July 27, 1860; Austin (Tex.) *State Gazette,* September 8, 1860; Athens (Ga.) *Southern Banner,* November 1, 1860.

Notes to Chapter VI

1. Albany *Patriot,* September 20, 1860; Little Rock *Arkansas State Gazette,* October 6, 1860.

2. New Orleans *Daily Picayune,* July 14, 1860.

3. Nichols, *The Disruption of American Democracy,* pp. 338, 339; Craven, *The Growth of Southern Nationalism,* pp. 346–347; Dumond, *The Secession Movement,* pp. 109–110.

4. Rome *Weekly Courier,* August 31, 1860; New Orleans *Daily Picayune,* September 19, 1860. See also New Orleans *Bee,* October 3, 1860; Fayetteville (N.C.) *Observer,* September 24, 1860; Macon (Ga.) *Daily Telegraph,* August 25, 1860; Augusta (Ga.) *Chronicle and Sentinel,* October 27, 1860; Lynchburg (Va.) *Republican,* August 8, 1860; Lynchburg *Virginian,* September 3, 1860; Norfolk (Va.) *Southern Argus,* September 12, 21, 1860; Marshall *Texas Republican,* September 15, 1860; Tuscumbia (Ala.) *States' Rights Democrat,* September 24, 28, 1860; Greenville *South Alabamian,* September 22, 1860; McKinney (Tex.) *Messenger,* September 14, 1860; Greensboro (N.C.) *Times,* October 20, 1860; Fayetteville *North Carolinian,* August 25, 1860; Athens (Ga.) *Southern Banner,* October 4, 1860; Columbus (Ga.) *Enquirer,* July 24, 1860; San Antonio *Daily Herald,* September 12, 1860.

5. Montgomery *Weekly Confederation,* August 17, 1860; Camden *Weekly Journal,* October 9, 1860. See also Fayetteville (Tenn.) *Lincoln Journal,* September 27, 1860; Memphis *Daily Appeal,* September 27, 1860.

6. Nichols, *The Disruption of American Democracy,* pp. 338–339; Craven, *The Growth of Southern Nationalism,* pp. 346–347; Dumond, *The Secession Movement,* pp. 109–110.

7. Hayneville *Chronicles,* October 18, 1860; Dallas *Herald,* October 31, 1860; Macon *Daily Telegraph,* October 16, 1860; Albany *Patriot,* October 18, 1860. See also Wilmington (N.C.) *Daily Journal,* October 12, 1860; Little Rock *Old-Line Democrat,* October 25, 1860; Spartanburg (S.C.) *Carolina Spartan,* October 18, 1860; Columbia *Daily South Carolinian,* October 7, 1860; Sandersville *Central Georgian,* October 17, 1860; Florence (Ala.) *Gazette,* October 17, 1860; Baton Rouge (La.) *Daily Advocate,* October 12, 1860; Nashville *Union and American,* October 12, 1860; Clarksville (Tenn.) *Jeffersonian,* October 17, 1860; Clarksville (Va.) *Tobacco Plant,* October 19, 1860; Jacksonville (Ala.) *Republican,* October 18, 1860; Jackson *Weekly Mississippian,* October 17, 1860; Raleigh *North Carolina Standard* (semiweekly ed.) , October 13, 1860; Milledgeville (Ga.) *Federal Union,* October 16, 1860; Benton (Ala.) *Weekly Herald,* October 18, 1860.

8. Montgomery *Weekly Advertiser,* October 17, 1860. See also Newberry (S.C.) *Conservatist,* October 30, 1860.

9. Milledgeville *Southern Recorder,* October 16, 1860; Nashville *Republican Banner,* October 11, 1860. See also Alexandria (Va.) *Gazette,* October 11, 1860; Hayneville (Ala.) *Watchman,* October 19, 1860; Clarksville (Tenn.) *Chronicle,* October 19, 1860; Knoxville *Whig,* October 13, 1860; Wadesborough *North Carolina Argus,* October 25, 1860.

10. San Antonio *Alamo Express,* October 15, 23, 1860; Augusta *Chronicle and Sentinel,* October 13, 1860. See also Charlotte *North Carolina Whig,* October 23, 1860; Lynchburg *Virginian,* October 12, 1860; Newbern (N.C.) *Weekly Progress,* October 16, 1860.

11. For some exceptions to this generalization, see Newberry (S.C.) *Rising Sun,* August 22, 1860; Anderson (S.C.) *Intelligencer,* August 21, 1860; Hayneville (Ala.) *Chronicle,* August 16, 23, 1860; Edgefield (S.C.) *Advertiser,* September 5, 1860; Abbeville (S.C.) *Independent Press,* August 17, 1860; Camden (S.C.) *Weekly Journal,* July 31, 1860; Spartanburg (S.C.) *Carolina Spartan,* July 5, 1860.

12. Macon *Daily Telegraph,* August 14, October 25, 1860; Knoxville *Register,* October 25, 1860.

13. Columbus *Corner Stone,* quoted in Claiborne (Ala.) *Southern Champion,* September 28, 1860. See also Newberry (S.C.) *Rising Sun,* October 3, 1860.

14. Camden *Weekly Journal,* November 6, 1860; Columbus *Enquirer,* September 25, 1860. See also Nashville *Republican Banner,* October 30, 1860; Montgomery (Ala.) *Daily Confederation,* October 7, 1860; Selma *Alabama State Sentinel,* October 24, 1860; Baton Rouge (La.) *Weekly Gazette and Comet,* October 13, 1860; Charlotte *North Carolina Whig,* November 5, 1860.

15. Montgomery *Mail,* quoted in Nashville *Republican Banner,* September 28, 1860; Auburn *Sketch Book,* quoted in Richmond *Whig,* October 17, 1860; Albany *Patriot,* September 27, 1860. See also

Fernandina *East Floridian,* October 31, 1860; Weatherford (Tex.) *White Man,* September 15, 1860; Milledgeville (Ga.) *Federal Union,* October 9, 1860; Prattville (Ala.) *Southern Statesman,* October 27, 1860; Opelousas (La.) *Courier,* November 3, 1860; Opelika (Ala.) *Weekly Southern Era,* September 29, 1860; Benton (Ala.) *Weekly Herald,* September 20, 1860; Natchez *Mississippi Free Trader,* October 29, November 5, 1860; Alexandria *Louisiana Democrat,* November 5, 1860; Atlanta *Daily Intelligencer,* October 18, November 3, 1860; Richmond (Tex.) *Reporter,* quoted in La Grange (Tex.) *True Issue,* October 25, 1860; Jefferson (Tex.) *Herald,* quoted in New Orleans *Daily Delta,* October 17, 1860; Tuscumbia (Ala.) *Constitution,* October 24, November 7, 1860; Beaufort (S.C.) *Enterprise,* October 10, 1860; Marshall *Texas Republican,* September 22, 1860; Dallas *Herald,* October 11, November 7, 1860; Lavaca (Tex.) *Gulf Key,* quoted in San Antonio *Ledger and Texan,* August 25, 1860; Austin (Tex.) *State Gazette,* October 20, 1860; Jackson *Weekly Mississippian,* October 3, 1860; Charleston *Daily Courier,* October 22, 1860; Montgomery (Ala.) *Weekly Advertiser,* August 15, 1860; Marin (S.C.) *Star,* quoted in Selma *Alabama State Sentinel* (weekly ed.), November 7, 1860; Camden (Ala.) *Republic,* October 25, 1860; Newberry (S.C.) *Rising Sun,* October 17, 1860.

16. Baton Rouge *Daily Advocate,* September 21, 1860; Richmond *Enquirer,* August 17, 1860. See also Waco (Tex.) *South West,* October 17, 1860; Dallas *Herald,* November 7, 1860; Austin (Tex.) *State Gazette,* October 20, 1860; Newberry (S.C.) *Rising Sun,* October 24, 1860; New Orleans *Daily Delta,* October 18, 1860; Nashville *Union and American,* October 24, 1860; Natchez *Mississippi Free Trader,* November 5, 1860; Fernandina *East Floridian,* October 24, 1860.

17. Montgomery *Weekly Mail,* October 26, 1860.

18. Clarke County *Journal,* quoted in Richmond *Examiner,* November 13, 1860; Norfolk *Southern Argus,* October 22, 1860; Alexandria *Sentinel,* quoted in Lynchburg *Virginian,* October 13, 1860; Lynchburg *Republican,* quoted in Alexandria (Va.) *Gazette,* August 20, 1860. See also Nashville *Union and American,* October 23, 1860; Richmond *Enquirer,* October 16, 1860; Asheville (N.C.) *News,* November 1, 1860; Kanawha (Va.) *Valley Star,* October 30, 1860; Wilmington (N.C.) *Daily Journal,* October 23, 1860.

19. St. Augustine *Examiner,* September 15, October 13, 1860; Athens *Southern Banner,* October 25, November 1, 1860.

20. Fayetteville *Arkansian,* September 21, 1860; Clarksville *Northern Standard,* September 22, 1860. See also San Antonio *Daily Herald,* November 7, 1860; Fayetteville *North Carolinian,* November 3, 1860; Clarksville (Tenn.) *Jeffersonian,* October 31, 1860.

21. Marietta *Southern Statesman,* quoted in Richmond *Whig,* November 5, 1860; Milton (N.C.) *Chronicle,* quoted in Raleigh *Democratic Press,* October 3, 1860; Macon *Daily Telegraph,* October

25, 1860. See also Raleigh *North Carolina Standard,* November 7, 1860.

22. Little Rock *Arkansas State Gazette,* September 15, 1860; Rome *Weekly Courier,* October 12, 1860. See also Alexandria (La.) *Constitutional,* September 8, 1860; New Orleans *Bee,* October 27, 1860; Alexandria (Va.) *Gazette,* September 1, 1860; Clarksville (Tenn.) *Chronicle,* October 12, 1860.

23. La Grange *True Issue,* May 25, 1860.

24. Wadesborough *North Carolina Argus,* November 8, 1860; Raleigh *National Democrat,* October 17, 1860. See also Baton Rouge (La.) *Weekly Gazette and Comet,* November 3, 1860; New Orleans *Daily Picayune,* October 4, 1860; McKinney (Tex.) *Messenger,* September 14, 1860; Alexandria (Va.) *Gazette,* October 12, 1860; Staunton (Va.) *Vindicator,* October 5, 1860; Hayneville (Ala.) *Watchman,* September 21, 1860; Clarksville (Tenn.) *Chronicle,* October 5, 1860; Murfreesboro (N.C.) *Citizen,* quoted in Richmond *Examiner,* November 3, 1860; Columbus (Ga.) *Enquirer,* September 4, 1860; Newbern (N.C.) *Weekly Progress,* August 28, 1860; Salisbury *North Carolina Watchman,* September 11, 1860; Augusta (Ga.) *Chronicle and Sentinel,* September 20, 1860; Raleigh *North Carolina Presbyterian,* June 2, 1860; Raleigh *Register,* September 15, 1860; New Orleans *Bee,* October 15, 1860; Nashville *Republican Banner,* September 20, October 23, 1860; Fayetteville (N.C.) *Observer,* quoted in Salisbury (N.C.) *Watchman,* September 25, 1860.

25. Montgomery (Ala.) *Weekly Post,* October 3, 1860; Augusta (Ga.) *Daily Constitutionalist,* November 3, 1860; Lynchburg *Virginian,* October 27, 1860; Columbus (Ga.) *Enquirer,* July 31, 1860; New Orleans *Daily Picayune,* October 31, 1860; Selma *Alabama State Sentinel,* October 17, 1860.

26. La Grange (Tex.) *True Issue,* October 4, 1860; Knoxville *Whig,* October 6, 1860; Columbus (Ga.) *Enquirer,* October 30, 1860; Asheville (N.C.) *Spectator,* quoted in Salisbury (N.C.) *Carolina Watchman,* October 16, 1860.

27. Greensboro *Times,* October 6, 1860.

28. Hayneville *Watchman,* October 26, 1860. See also Montgomery (Ala.) *Weekly Montgomery Confederation,* November 2, 1860; New Orleans *Bee,* October 18, 1860; Lynchburg *Virginian,* October 31, 1860; New Orleans *Daily Picayune,* October 24, 26, 1860; Charlestown *Virginia Free Press,* November 1, 1860.

29. New Orleans *Bee,* October 5, 1860. See also Montgomery (Ala.) *Weekly Montgomery Confederation,* October 19, 1860.

30. Alexandria *Constitutional,* September 29, 1860; Knoxville *Whig,* October 20, 1860. See also Memphis *Daily Appeal,* October 31, 1860; Jackson (Miss.) *News,* quoted in Canton (Miss.) *American Citizen,* September 22, 1860; Lynchburg *Virginian,* October 13, 1860; Little Rock *Arkansas State Gazette,* November 10, 1860; Columbus (Ga.) *Enquirer,* August 28, 1860.

31. Anderson *Intelligencer*, September 4, 1860; Florence (Ala.) *Gazette*, October 31, 1860; Hayneville *Chronicle*, November 1, 1860. See also Richmond *Enquirer*, October 19, 1860; Tarboro (N.C.) *Southerner*, quoted in Salisbury (N.C.) *Carolina Watchman*, September 18, 1860; Camden (S.C.) *Weekly Journal*, September 18, 1860; Corsicana (Tex.) *Navarro Express*, October 26, 1860; Columbus (Ga.) *Times*, quoted in Nashville *Republican Banner*, September 4, 1860; Albany (Ga.) *Patriot*, October 18, 1860.

32. New Orleans *Daily Delta*, September 21, October 6, 1860; Atlanta *Daily Intelligencer*, October 29, 1860; Jackson *Weekly Mississippian*, October 30, 1860; Montgomery *Weekly Mail*, November 2, 1860. See also Opelika (Ala.) *Weekly Southern Era*, September 8, 1860; Norfolk (Va.) *Southern Argus*, October 30, 1860; Baton Rouge (La.) *Daily Advocate*, October 27, 1860; Montgomery (Ala.) *Weekly Advertiser*, September 19, 1860.

33. Selma *Alabama State Sentinel*, October 24, 1860.

34. Oliver Knight, *Fort Worth: Outpost on the Trinity*, pp. 48–50; Fernandina *East Floridian*, October 24, 1860.

35. Macon *Daily Telegraph*, October 31, 1860.

36. Bellville *Countryman*, quoted in Cincinnati *Commercial*, August 20, 1860; Bellville *Countryman*, August 25, 1860; New York *Daily Tribune*, July 30, 1860.

37. New York *Daily Tribune*, September 12, 1860; Memphis *Avalanche*, September 8, 1860.

38. Jackson *Weekly Mississippian*, October 3, 17, 1860; Milledgeville *Federal Union*, September 25, 1860; Newberry *Conservatist*, September 4, 1860. See also Athens (Ga.) *Southern Banner*, October 11, 1860; Hayneville (Ala.) *Chronicle*, September 6, 1860; Alexandria *Louisiana Democrat*, October 24, 1860; Raleigh *Democratic Press*, September 12, 1860; Macon (Ga.) *Daily Telegraph*, September 18, 1860; Hayneville (Ala.) *Chronicle*, November 1, 1860; Fayetteville *North Carolinian*, September 22, 1860; Fite, *The Presidential Campaign of 1860*, p. 181; Nichols, *The Disruption of American Democracy*, p. 343; Capers, *Stephen A. Douglas*, p. 212.

39. New Orleans *Bee*, September 3, 11, 1860; Salisbury *Carolina Watchman*, November 6, 1860; Shreveport *South-Western*, August 22, 1860. See also Fayetteville (N.C.) *Observer*, October 8, 1860; Baton Rouge (La.) *Weekly Gazette and Comet*, June 24, 1860.

40. Memphis *Daily Appeal*, October 3, 1860; Montgomery *Confederation*, September 28, 1860.

41. New Orleans *Bee* (French ed.), November 1, 1860; Van Buren *Press*, December 7, 1860; Greensboro *Times*, September 8, 1860. See also Columbus (Ga.) *Enquirer*, September 4, 1860.

42. Augusta *Daily Constitutionalist*, September 21, 1860; Newbern *Weekly Progress*, September 25, 1860. See also Augusta (Ga.) *Chronicle and Sentinel*, October 7, 19, 1860.

43. La Grange *True Issue*, September 6, 1860.

Notes to Chapter VII

1. Rome *Weekly Courier,* November 16, 1860.
2. San Antonio *Daily Herald,* November 14, 1860; False River *Pointe Coupée Democrat,* November 10, 1860; Fairmont *True Virginian,* November 10, 1860; Montgomery *Weekly Confederation,* November 23, 1860. See also Montgomery (Ala.) *Post,* quoted in Hillsborough (N.C.) *Recorder,* November 21, 1860; Raleigh *Spirit of the Age,* November 14, 1860; Athens (Ga.) *Post,* quoted in Nashville *Republican Banner,* November 18, 1860; Alexandria (Va.) *Gazette,* November 8, 1860; Richmond *Dispatch,* November 8, 1860; Augusta (Ga.) *Chronicle and Sentinel,* November 8, 1860; Augusta (Ga.) *Daily Constitutionalist,* November 13, 1860; Florence (Ala.) *Gazette,* November 14, 1860; Martinsburg (Va.) *Republican,* quoted in Richmond *Examiner,* November 3, 1860; Van Buren (Ark.) *Press,* November 23, 1860; Fayetteville *Arkansian,* November 17, 1860; Des Arc (Ark.) *Constitutional Union,* November 16, 1860; Greensboro (N.C.) *Times,* November 17, 1860.
3. Fayetteville *North Carolinian,* November 17, 1860. See also Carrollton *West Alabamian,* December 12, 1860; Montgomery (Ala.) *Weekly Advertiser,* November 14, 1860; Sulphur Springs (Tex.) *Independent Monitor,* December 1, 1860; Dallas *Herald,* December 5, 1860; Corsicana (Tex.) *Navarro Express,* November 16, 1860; Grove Hill (Ala.) *Clarke County Democrat,* November 29, 1860; Jackson *Weekly Mississippian,* November 14, 1860; Florence (Ala.) *Gazette,* November 21, 1860; Athens (Ga.) *Southern Banner,* November 29, December 3, 1860; Hayneville (Ala.) *Chronicle,* November 8, 22, 1860; Paulding (Miss.) *Eastern Clarion,* quoted in Jackson *Weekly Mississippian,* November 21, 1860; Wilmington (N.C.) *Daily Journal,* November 13, 1860; Norfolk (Va.) *Southern Argus,* November 8, 1860; New Orleans *Daily Delta,* November 23, 1860; Troy (Ala.) *Advertiser,* quoted in Florence (Ala.) *Gazette,* November 21, 1860; Spartanburg (S.C.) *Carolina Spartan,* December 6, 1860; Barbour (Va.) *Jeffersonian Democrat,* quoted in Richmond *Examiner,* November 13, 1860.
4. Montgomery *Weekly Mail,* December 11, 1860.
5. False River *Pointe Coupée Democrat,* November 24, 1860; Atlanta *Daily Intelligencer,* November 15, 1860. See also Montgomery (Ala.) *Weekly Advertiser,* November 21, 1860; Charleston *Mercury,* December 18, 1860; Newberry (S.C.) *Rising Sun,* December 26, 1860; Dallas *Herald,* November 14, 1860; New Orleans *Daily Delta,* November 30, 1860; Grove Hill (Ala.) *Clarke County Democrat,* November 15, 1860.
6. Newberry *Conservatist,* November 13, 20, 1860. See also Jackson *Weekly Mississippian,* December 19, 1860; Charleston *Mercury,*

December 4, 1860; Benton (Ala.) *Weekly Herald,* November 15, 1860; Camden (S.C.) *Weekly Journal,* November 13, 1860; Oxford (Miss.) *Mercury,* quoted in Jackson *Weekly Mississippian,* November 21, 1860; Baton Rouge (La.) *Daily Advocate,* November 8, 1860; Opelika (Ala.) *Weekly Southern Era,* November 17, 1860; Newmansville (Fla.) *Dispatch,* quoted in Fernandina *Weekly East Floridian,* November 21, 1860; Columbia *South Carolinian,* quoted in Spartanburg (S.C.) *Carolina Spartan,* November 15, 1860; Marianna (Fla.) *Patriot,* quoted in Fernandina *Weekly East Floridian,* December 5, 1860; Bainbridge *Southern Georgian,* quoted in Albany (Ga.) *Patriot,* December 6, 1860; Natchez *Mississippi Free Trader,* November 12, 1860; Columbus (Miss.) *Democrat,* quoted in Jackson *Weekly Mississippian,* November 21, 1860; Fernandina *Weekly East Floridian,* November 14, 1860; Atlanta *Daily Intelligencer,* November 14, 21, 1860; Montgomery *Weekly Mail,* November 16, 1860.

7. Austin *State Gazette,* November 10, 1860; Athens *Southern Banner,* December 6, 1860; Wetumpka *Enquirer,* quoted in Florence (Ala.) *Gazette,* November 14, 1860. See also Hayneville (Ala.) *Watchman,* November 16, 1860; Newberry (S.C.) *Rising Sun,* December 12, 1860; Montgomery (Ala.) *Weekly Advertiser,* November 21, 1860; Natchez *Mississippi Free Trader,* December 3, 1860; Dallas *Herald,* November 21, 1860; Grove Hill (Ala.) *Clarke County Democrat,* November 22, 1860; Raleigh *Democratic Press,* November 21, 1860; New Orleans *Daily Delta,* November 6, 1860; Atlanta *Daily Intelligencer,* November 23, 1860.

8. Opelousas *Courier,* November 17, 1860; Key West *Key of the Gulf,* quoted in Fernandina *Weekly East Floridian,* November 21, 1860; Charleston *Mercury,* November 19, 1860. See also Raleigh *State Journal,* December 8, 1860; Carrollton *West Alabamian,* December 12, 1860; Marshall *Texas Republican,* December 1, 1860; Newberry (S.C.) *Rising Sun,* November 28, 1860; Columbia *Daily South Carolinian,* December 12, 1860; St. Augustine (Fla.) *Examiner,* December 15, 1860; False River (La.) *Pointe Coupée Democrat,* December 8, 1860; New Orleans *Daily Delta,* November 22, 1860; Norfolk (Va.) *Southern Argus,* November 24, 1860.

9. Montgomery *Weekly Mail,* November 30, 1860; New Orleans *Daily Delta,* November 8, 1860. See also Wilmington (N.C.) *Daily Journal,* November 17, 1860; Newberry (S.C.) *Rising Sun,* November 14, 1860; Hayneville (Ala.) *Watchman,* November 23, 1860; Anderson (S.C.) *Intelligencer,* November 22, 1860; Tuscumbia (Ala.) *States' Rights Democrat,* December 7, 20, 1860; Benton (Ala.) *Weekly Herald,* November 29, 1860; St. Augustine (Fla.) *Examiner,* December 8, 1860; Hayneville (Ala.) *Chronicle,* November 22, 29, 1860; Auburn (Ala.) *Sketch Book,* November 30, 1860; Plaquemine (La.) *Gazette and Sentinel,* December 15, 1860; Greenville (Ala.) *Southern Messenger,* November 28, 1860.

10. Norfolk *Southern Argus,* November 14, December 11, 1860; Plaquemine *Gazette and Sentinel,* December 1, 1860.
11. Florence (Ala.) *Gazette,* December 5, 1860; Spartanburg (S.C.) *Carolina Spartan,* November 22, 1860; Natchez *Mississippi Free Trader,* November 26, 1860; Jacksonville (Fla.) *Standard,* quoted in Fernandina *Weekly East Floridian,* November 21, 1860; Norfolk (Va.) *Southern Argus,* December 15, 1860.
12. Little Rock *Old-Line Democrat,* December 20, 1860; San Antonio *Daily Herald,* December 14, 1860. See also Auburn (Ala.) *Sketch Book,* November 9, 1860; Albany (Ga.) *Patriot,* November 15, 1860; Nashville *Union and American,* November 17, 22, December 9, 1860; Clarksville (Tenn.) *Jeffersonian,* November 21, 1860; Corsicana (Tex.) *Navarro Express,* December 7, 19, 1860; Alexandria *Louisiana Democrat,* December 15, 1860; Columbus (Ga.) *Enquirer,* December 4, 1860; Plaquemine (La.) *Gazette and Sentinel,* November 17, 1860; Edgefield (S.C.) *Advertiser,* November 14, 1860.
13. Tappahannock *Southerner,* quoted in Richmond *Examiner,* November 13, 1860; Raleigh *Register,* November 17, 1860. See also Greensboro *Alabama Beacon,* November 9, 1860; Raleigh *North Carolina Standard* (semiweekly ed.), December 11, 1860; Vicksburg (Miss.) *Whig,* quoted in Richmond *Whig,* November 14, 1860; Albemarle (N.C.) *Southron,* quoted in Greensboro (N.C.) *Times,* December 1, 1860; Richmond *Virginia Index,* quoted in Alexandria (Va.) *Gazette,* November 26, 1860; Shenandoah (Va.) *Spirit of Democracy,* quoted in Fairmont *True Virginian,* November 17, 1860; Brandon (Miss.) *Republican,* quoted in Vicksburg (Miss.) *Weekly Vicksburg Whig,* November 28, 1860; Newbern (N.C.) *Weekly Progress,* November 13, 1860; Nashville *Republican Banner,* December 4, 1860; Hamilton (Ga.) *Enterprise,* quoted in Milledgeville (Ga.) *Southern Recorder,* December 4, 1860; West Baton Rouge (La.) *Sugar Planter,* December 1, 1860; Wadesborough *North Carolina Argus,* November 15, 1860; Newbern (N.C.) *Weekly Progress,* November 20, 1860; Baton Rouge (La.) *Weekly Gazette and Comet,* December 15, 1860.
14. Milledgeville *Southern Recorder,* November 20, 1860; Clarksville *Chronicle,* November 16, December 14, 1860; Wilmington *Herald,* quoted in Wadesborough *North Carolina Argus,* November 15, 1860. See also Staunton (Va.) *Spectator,* December 4, 1860; Lynchburg *Virginian,* November 15, 1860; Vicksburg (Miss.) *Whig,* quoted in Hillsborough (N.C.) *Recorder,* November 14, 1860; Selma *Alabama State Sentinel,* November 21, 1860; Greensboro (N.C.) *Times,* November 10, 1860; Galveston (Tex.) *Civilian and Gazette,* November 20, 1860; Little Rock *Arkansas State Gazette,* November 10, 1860; Raleigh *Spirit of the Age,* December 5, 1860; Fayetteville (Tenn.) *Lincoln Journal,* November 29, 1860.
15. Knoxville *Whig,* November 24, 1860; Norfolk *Herald,* quoted in Lynchburg *Virginian,* November 14, 1860; Clarksville *Jeffersonian,*

December 11, 1860; Kosciusko *Chronicle,* December 14, 1860. See also Clarksville (Tenn.) *Chronicle,* November 9, 1860; Nashville *Republican Banner,* November 10, 1860; Des Arc (Ark.) *Constitutional Union,* November 23, 1860; Lynchburg *Virginian,* November 12, 1860; Greensboro (N.C.) *Patriot,* quoted in Wadesborough *North Carolina Argus,* November 15, 1860; Petersburg (Va.) *Intelligencer,* quoted in Richmond *Examiner,* November 13, 1860; San Antonio *Ledger and Texan,* November 17, 1860; Fayetteville *Arkansian,* November 24, 1860; Des Arc (Ark.) *Constitutional Union,* November 30, 1860; Washington (N.C.) *Dispatch,* quoted in Salisbury (N.C.) *Carolina Watchman,* November 13, 1860; Chattanooga *Gazette,* quoted in Fayetteville (N.C.) *Observer,* December 3, 1860; Galveston (Tex.) *Civilian and Gazette,* November 27, 1860.

16. Hillsborough *Recorder,* November 14, 1860. See also Fayetteville *Arkansian,* December 1, 1860; Alexandria (La.) *Constitutional,* November 17, 1860; New Orleans *Bee,* November 12, 1860; Newbern (N.C.) *Weekly Progress,* November 20, 1860; Little Rock *Arkansas State Gazette,* November 24, 1860; Richmond *Whig,* November 9, 1860; Fayetteville (Tenn.) *Lincoln Journal,* November 15, 1860; Athens (Tenn.) *Post,* November 23, 1860; Petersburg (Va.) *Intelligencer,* quoted in Hillsborough (N.C.) *Recorder,* November 14, 1860; Canton (Miss.) *American Citizen,* November 21, 1860; Charlestown *Virginia Free Press,* December 13, 1860; Fayetteville (N.C.) *Observer,* November 12, 1860; Natchez (Miss.) *Courier,* quoted in Alexandria (Va.) *Gazette,* November 24, 1860; San Antonio *Ledger and Texan,* November 24, 1860; Montgomery (Ala.) *Univeralist Herald,* November 30, 1860; Marietta (Ga.) *Southern Statesman,* quoted in Salisbury (N.C.) *Carolina Watchman,* November 13, 1860; Van Buren (Ark.) *Press,* November 9, 16, 23, 1860.

17. Clarksville *Chronicle,* November 9, 1860; Nichols, *The Disruption of American Democracy,* pp. 367–374; Dumond, *The Secession Movement,* pp. 136–145; Craven, *The Growth of Southern Nationalism,* pp. 359–377; Nevins, *The Emergence of Lincoln,* II, 318–320.

18. Charleston *Daily Courier,* November 16, 1860; Jackson *Weekly Mississippian,* November 14, 1860; Jacksonville (Ala.) *Republican,* November 22, December 13, 1860; New Orleans *Daily Delta,* December 15, 1860; Corsicana (Tex.) *Navarro Express,* November 23, 1860.

19. Albany *Patriot,* November 22, 1860; St. Augustine *Examiner,* November 24, 1860. See also Charleston *Mercury,* November 20, 1860; New Orleans *Daily Delta,* November 14, 1860; Corsicana (Tex.) *Navarro Express,* November 16, 1860; Milledgeville (Ga.) *Federal Union,* November 27, 1860; Benton (Ala.) *Weekly Herald,* December 6, 1860.

20. Vicksburg *Weekly Vicksburg Whig,* November 14, 1860; Charles-town *Virginia Free Press,* November 15, 1860; Clarksville *Chronicle,* December 21, 1860. See also Raleigh *Register,* November 17, 1860; Nashville *Republican Banner,* November 13, 1860; Staunton (Va.) *Vindicator,* November 16, 27, 1860; Charlottesville (Va.) *Review,* quoted in Richmond *Enquirer,* November 23, 1860; Raleigh *Register,* quoted in Salisbury (N.C.) *Carolina Watchman,* December 11, 1860; Des Arc (Ark.) *Constitutional Union,* December 21, 1860; Lynchburg *Virginian,* November 9, 1860; Alexandria (Va.) *Gazette,* November 13, 1860.

21. New Orleans *Bee,* November 21, 1860; Newbern *Weekly Progress,* December 11, 1860.

22. Richmond *Whig,* December 17, 1860; West Baton Rouge *Sugar Planter,* November 24, 1860. See also Richmond *Dispatch,* December 3, 1860; Clarksville (Tenn.) *Jeffersonian,* November 21, 1860; Fairmont *True Virginian,* November 17, 1860; Athens (Tenn.) *Post,* November 23, 1860; New Orleans *Bee,* November 17, 1860; Nashville *Union and American,* November 8, 1860; Mur-freesboro (N.C.) *Citizen,* quoted in Lynchburg *Virginian,* November 14, 1860; Petersburg (Va.) *Express,* quoted in Fairmont *True Virginian,* November 24, 1860. Two papers which supported co-ercion even after Lincoln's election were Knoxville (Tenn.) *Whig,* December 15, 1860 and Nashville *Republican Banner,* November 16, 1860.

23. Memphis *Daily Appeal,* November 29, 1860. See also Rome (Ga.) *Weekly Courier,* November 23, 1860; Richmond *Whig,* November 22, December 20, 1860; Milledgeville (Ga.) *Southern Recorder,* November 20, 1860; Sandersville *Central Georgian,* December 5, 1860; Newbern (N.C.) *Weekly Progress,* November 27, 1860; Staunton (Va.) *Vindicator,* December 7, 1860; New Orleans *Bee,* November 19, 1860; Indianola (Tex.) *Courier,* December 1, 1860; Van Buren (Ark.) *Press,* December 14, 1860; Fredericksburg (Va.) *Recorder,* quoted in Richmond *Examiner,* November 13, 1860; Fredericksburg (Va.) *Herald,* quoted in Richmond *Whig,* November 21, 1860; Augusta (Ga.) *Chronicle and Sentinel,* December 15, 1860; Baton Rouge (La.) *Weekly Gazette and Comet,* November 17, 1860; Clarksville (Tenn.) *Chronicle,* November 16, 1860; Alexandria (Va.) *Gazette,* December 1, 1860; Petersburg (Va.) *Express,* quoted in Greensboro (N.C.) *Times,* December 1, 1860.

24. Columbus *Enquirer,* December 25, 1860.

25. Alexandria *Louisiana Democrat,* November 28, 1860; Richmond *Whig,* November 28, 1860; Newberry *Rising Sun,* November 28, 1860.

26. Atlanta *Daily Intelligencer,* November 9, 1860.

27. Hayneville *Chronicle,* November 22, 1860; Richmond *Whig,* November 28, 1860; Grove Hill *Clarke County Democrat,* December 6, 1860.

28. Montgomery *Weekly Confederation*, November 30, 1860; Tuscumbia *States' Rights Democrat*, December 21, 1860; Selma *Alabama State Sentinel*, November 10, 1860; Prattville *Autauga Citizen*, November 22, 1860; Montgomery *Weekly Post*, December 12, 1860.

29. Greensboro *Alabama Beacon*, November 30, December 7, 1860. See also Grove Hill *Clarke County Democrat*, December 6, 1860.

30. Montgomery *Weekly Confederation*, July 27, October 7, 19, November 2, 23, December 7, 1860; Montgomery *Weekly Post*, October 3, 31, November 21, 1860; Augusta *Daily Constitutionalist*, November 3, 30, 1860.

31. Memphis *Daily Appeal*, November 10, December 11, 1860.

32. New Orleans *Bee*, October 5, December 14, 1860.

33. *Ibid.*, November 8, 10, 12, 13, 1860.

34. *Ibid.*, November 21, 28, December 4, 1860.

35. Vicksburg *Weekly Vicksburg Whig*, November 14, December 12, 1860; Harrisonburg *Rockingham Register and Advertiser*, November 16, 30, December 7, 1860; Little Rock *Arkansas State Gazette*, November 24, December 22, 1860. See also Van Buren (Ark.) *Press*, November 16, 23, December 21, 1860.

36. Augusta *Chronicle and Sentinel*, November 13, 25, December 12, 1860; New Orleans *Bee*, December 5, 14, 1860.

37. Nevins, *The Emergence of Lincoln*, II, 335–340, David M. Potter, *Lincoln and His Party in the Secession Crisis*, pp. 69–74. For examples of Northern editorials that offended Southerners see Howard C. Perkins, ed., *Northern Editorials on Secession*, I, 88–92.

38. Augusta *Daily Constitutionalist*, December 7, 1860; New Orleans *Bee*, November 29, 1860. See also Vicksburg (Miss.) *Weekly Vicksburg Whig*, December 12, 1860; Van Buren (Ark.) *Press*, December 21, 1860; Alexandria (Va.) *Gazette*, November 10, 1860.

39. Most secessionist journals ridiculed the President's message. They especially stressed Buchanan's weak logic. See Natchez *Mississippi Free Trader*, December 17, 1860; Hayneville (Ala.) *Chronicle*, December 13, 1860; Montgomery (Ala.) *Weekly Advertiser*, December 12, 1860; Macon (Ga.) *Daily Telegraph*, December 7, 1860; Corsicana (Tex.) *Navarro Express*, December 21, 1860; Charleston *Courier*, December 14, 1860; Newberry (S.C.) *Conservatist*, December 11, 1860; New Orleans *Sunday Delta*, December 9, 1860; Norfolk *Southern Argus*, December 8, 1860. For critical Unionist papers see Knoxville *Whig*, December 15, 1860; Clarksville (Tenn.) *Chronicle*, December 7, 1860; Staunton (Va.) *Spectator*, December 11, 1860; Raleigh *Spirit of the Age*, December 12, 1860. Many other Unionist journals approved the President's message. See Des Arc (Ark.) *Constitutional Union*, December 14, 1860; Alexandria (Va.) *Gazette*, December 5, 1860; Augusta *Chronicle and Sentinel*, December 9, 1860; Fayetteville (N.C.) *Observer*, December 10, 1860; Nashville *Republican Banner*, December 8, 1860.

40. Baton Rouge *Weekly Gazette and Comet,* December 8, 1860; Harrisonburg *Valley Democrat,* December 7, 1860; "Diary of John Brown," photocopy of original manuscript, University of Texas Archives, Austin, Texas.
41. Hillsborough *Recorder,* December 12, 1860.

Notes to Chapter VIII

1. Nevins, *The Emergence of Lincoln,* II, 318–319, 359–365; Charles P. Roland, *The Confederacy,* pp. 1–2; Harold S. Schultz, *Nationalism and Sectionalism in South Carolina, 1852–1860,* pp. 225–230.
2. Anderson *Intelligencer,* January 6, 1861; Columbia *Daily Southern Guardian,* December 21, 1860; Charleston *Mercury,* December 21, 1860; Camden *Weekly Journal,* January 1, 1861; Charleston *Daily Courier,* December 21, 1860.
3. Natchez *Mississippi Free Trader,* December 24, 1860; Indianola *Courier,* January 5, 1861; St. Augustine *Examiner,* December 29, 1860. See also Corsicana (Tex.) *Navarro Express,* January 2, 1861; Greenville *South Alabamian,* December 22, 1860; Augusta (Ga.) *Daily Constitutionalist,* December 21, 1860; Albany (Ga.) *Patriot,* December 27, 1860; New Orleans *Bee,* December 22, 28, 1860; Jacksonville (Ala.) *Republican,* January 3, 1861; Athens (Ga.) *Southern Banner,* December 27, 1860.
4. Raleigh *State Journal,* December 22, 1860. See also Nashville *Union and American,* December 22, 1860; Fayetteville *Arkansian,* January 5, 1861; Richmond *Dispatch,* December 22, 1860; Richmond *Enquirer,* December 21, 1860.
5. Charlestown *Virginia Free Press,* January 3, 1861; Clarksville *Jeffersonian,* January 16, 1861. See also Des Arc (Ark.) *Constitutional Union,* January 4, 1861; Austin (Tex.) *Southern Intelligencer,* January 2, 1861; Nashville *Republican Banner,* December 22, 1860; Fayetteville (N.C.) *Observer,* December 24, 1860; Staunton (Va.) *Spectator,* January 15, 1861; Alexandria (Va.) *Gazette,* December 22, 1860; Van Buren (Ark.) *Press,* January 4, 1861; Baton Rouge (La.) *Weekly Gazette and Comet,* December 29, 1860.
6. Dumond, *The Secession Movement,* p. 148; Nichols, *The Disruption of American Democracy,* pp. 372, 373, 429, 435; Craven, *The Growth of Southern Nationalism,* pp. 363–377.
7. Dumond, *The Secession Movement,* pp. 175–178; Nichols, *The Disruption of American Democracy,* pp. 417–431; Milton, *The Eve of Conflict,* pp. 512–515.
8. Richmond *Dispatch,* December 31, 1860; Raleigh *State Journal,* January 2, 1861; Nashville *Union and American,* January 6, 1861; Fayetteville *North Carolinian,* January 12, 1861; New Orleans *Bee,* January 10, 1861.
9. Richmond *Whig,* January 1, 1861. See also Salisbury (N.C.)

Carolina Watchman, January 29, 1861; Fayetteville (N.C.) *Observer,* quoted in Hillsborough (N.C.) *Recorder,* February 20, 1861; Lynchburg *Virginian,* December 28, 1860.

10. Raleigh *North Carolina Standard* (semiweekly ed.), January 19, 1861; Staunton (Va.) *Spectator,* January 1, 1861; Fayetteville (N.C.) *Observer,* December 31, 1860. See also Raleigh *Register,* December 26, 1860; Nashville *Republican Banner,* December 29, 1860; Knoxville *Whig,* January 5, 1861.

11. Raleigh *Register,* December 26, 1860; Lynchburg *Virginian,* December 28, 1860. On January 19, 1861, the Raleigh *Register* came out strongly against coercion and promised to advocate secession, should the federal government attempt to restore the Union by force.

12. Nashville *Republican Banner,* January 20, 1861; Little Rock *Arkansas State Gazette,* December 29, 1860. See also Alexandria (Va.) *Gazette,* January 12, 1861; Richmond *Central Presbyterian,* December 29, 1860; Athens (Tenn.) *Post,* March 1, 1861; Lynchburg *Virginian,* February 10, 1861; Clarksville (Tenn.) *Chronicle,* January 4, 1861; Greensboro (N.C.) *Times,* January 12, 1861; Staunton (Va.) *Vindicator,* March 1, 1861; Salisbury (N.C.) *Carolina Watchman,* January 8, 1861; Vicksburg (Miss.) *Weekly Whig,* January 23, 1861; Des Arc (Ark.) *Constitutional Union,* January 4, 1861; Galveston (Tex.) *Civilian and Gazette,* December 20, 1860; Raleigh *North Carolina Standard* (semiweekly ed.), January 19, 1861.

13. Knoxville *Whig,* January 12, 1861; Wellsburg (Va.) *Herald,* January 11, 1861; San Antonio (Tex.) *Alamo Express,* February 6, 1861; Lynchburg *Virginian,* January 21, 1861.

14. Little Rock *Arkansas State Gazette,* January 5, 1861; Raleigh *North Carolina Standard* (semiweekly ed.), February 5, 1861; Richmond *Whig,* January 9, 1861; Des Arc *Constitutional Union,* January 18, 1861. See also Baton Rouge (La.) *Weekly Gazette and Comet,* January 12, 1861; Knoxville (Tenn.) *Whig,* February 16, 1861; Alexandria (La.) *Constitutional,* December 22, 1860, January 12, 1861; San Antonio (Tex.) *Alamo Express,* February 6, 1861; Salisbury (N.C.) *Carolina Watchman,* January 8, 1861.

15. Salisbury *Daily Banner,* quoted in Salisbury *Carolina Watchman,* February 5, 1861. See also Salisbury *Carolina Watchman,* January 15, 1861; Charlotte *North Carolina Whig,* January 22, 1861; Alexandria (Va.) *Gazette,* December 28, 1860; Athens (Tenn.) *Post,* February 15, 1861.

16. Raleigh *North Carolina Standard,* February 8, 1861. See also Salisbury *Carolina Watchman,* January 29, 1861; Newbern *Weekly Progress,* January 1, 1861.

17. Lincoln to William Kellogg, December 11, 1860. Roy P. Basler, ed., *The Collected Works of Abraham Lincoln,* IV, 150; Potter, *Lincoln and His Party in the Secession Crisis,* pp. 156–187.

18. Charlotte *North Carolina Whig,* January 29, 1861; Jonesborough (Tenn.) *Express,* January 25, 1861; Nashville *Republican Banner,* January 19, 1861; Raleigh *Spirit of the Age,* January 30, 1861; Harrisonburg (Va.) *Valley Democrat,* February 8, 1861; Fayetteville (Tenn.) *Lincoln Journal,* February 7, 1861; Richmond *Whig,* January 12, 1861; Wadesborough *North Carolina Argus,* January 17, 1861; Greensboro (N.C.) *Times,* January 19, 1861; Wheeling (Va.) *Daily Intelligencer,* January 1, 1861; Raleigh *North Carolina Standard* (semiweekly ed.), January 19, 1861; Somerville (Tenn.) *Times,* quoted in Nashville *Republican Banner,* February 16, 1861.

19. Wadesborough *North Carolina Argus,* January 31, 1861; Nashville *National Democrat,* quoted in Van Buren (Ark.) *Press,* March 1, 1861; Harrisonburg (Va.) *Rockingham Register and Advertiser,* March 1, 1861; Richmond *Whig,* March 2, 1861; Clarksville (Tenn.) *Jeffersonian,* February 27, 1861; Raleigh *Spirit of the Age,* February 20, 1861; Nashville *Republican Banner,* March 1, 1861. The eight Southern states which sent no representatives to the Convention were: South Carolina, Georgia, Florida, Alabama, Mississippi, Louisiana, Texas, and Arkansas.

20. Wellsburg *Herald,* February 22, 1861. See also Greensboro (N.C.) *Times,* February 2, 1861.

21. Charlotte (N.C.) *Bulletin,* quoted in Wadesborough *North Carolina Argus,* February 14, 1861. See also Raleigh *State Journal,* February 13, 1861; Nashville *Union and American,* December 26, 1860; New Orleans *Bee,* January 16, 1861; Baton Rouge (La.) *Daily Advocate,* January 1, 1861; Memphis *Daily Appeal,* January 5, 19, 1861; Waco (Tex.) *South West,* January 16, 1861; Macon (Ga.) *Daily Telegraph,* December 29, 1860, January 9, 1861; Galveston (Tex.) *Weekly News,* February 19, 1861; Richmond *Dispatch,* February 11, 1861; Clarksville (Va.) *Tobacco Plant,* February 1, 1861; Richmond *Daily Enquirer,* January 19, 1861; Memphis *Avalanche,* January 21, March 1, 3, 1861; Nashville *Union and American,* January 20, February 22, 1861; Richmond *Examiner,* March 2, 1861; Atlanta *Gate-City Guardian,* February 18, 1861.

22. Wilmington *Daily Journal,* April 1, 1861; Fayetteville *Arkansian,* March 8, 1861; Augusta *Daily Constitutionalist,* January 1, 1861.

23. Atlanta *Daily Intelligencer,* January 4, 1861; Augusta *Daily Constitutionalist,* December 22, 1860; Marshall *Texas Republican,* January 26, 1861.

24. Atlanta *Southern Confederacy,* March 4, 1861; Montgomery *Weekly Mail,* December 21, 1860.

25. New Orleans *Daily True Delta,* February 19, 1861; San Antonio *Alamo Express,* February 8, 1861; Knoxville *Whig,* January 19, 1861; Nashville *Republican Banner,* February 21, 1861. See also La Grange (Ga.) *Reporter,* quoted in Alexandria (Va.) *Gazette,* February 28, 1861; Augusta (Ga.) *Chronicle and Sentinel,* February 13,

1861; Raleigh *Register,* January 26, 1861; La Grange (Tex.) *True Issue,* January 24, 1861; Clarksville (Tenn.) *Jeffersonian,* February 13, 1861; Staunton (Va.) *Spectator,* February 12, 1861.

26. Raleigh *State Journal,* January 30, 1861.

27. Raleigh *Banner,* quoted in Van Buren (Ark.) *Press,* March 20, 1861.

28. Galveston *Union,* January 10, 1861; La Grange *True Issue,* January 24, February 21, 1861; San Antonio *Weekly Herald,* February 2, 1861.

29. A. B. Hendren to Governor John Letcher, February 18, 1861, quoted in Clement Eaton, *The Freedom-of-Thought Struggle in the Old South,* p. 398.

30. Grove Hill *Clarke County Democrat,* January 10, 1861; Atlanta *Daily Intelligencer,* January 28, 1861; Memphis *Daily Appeal,* January 11, 1861; Albany *Patriot,* November 15, 1860. See also Memphis *Avalanche,* January 21, 1861; Clarksville (Va.) *Tobacco Plant,* February 1, 1861; Columbia (S.C.) *Daily Southern Guardian,* quoted in Anderson (S.C.) *Intelligencer,* December 13, 1860.

31. New Orleans *Daily Delta,* November 29, 1860; Richmond *Dispatch,* December 15, 1860. See also Savannah *Daily Morning News,* January 10, 1861; Macon (Ga.) *Daily Telegraph,* January 2, 1861; Greensburg (La.) *Imperial,* February 2, 1861; Newberry (S.C.) *Rising Sun,* December 5, 1860; Augusta (Ga.) *Daily Constitutionalist,* January 10, 1861; Edgefield (S.C.) *Advertiser,* January 16, 1861; Richmond *Examiner,* March 2, 1861.

32. Dumond, *The Secession Movement,* pp. 189–212; James G. Randall and David Donald, *The Civil War and Reconstruction,* 2d ed., pp. 135–141.

33. Athens *Southern Banner,* January 23, 1861; New Orleans *Sunday Delta,* January 27, 1861; Milledgeville *Federal Union,* January 15, 1861; Atlanta *Daily Intelligencer,* February 2, 1861. See also St. Augustine (Fla.) *Examiner,* January 19, 1861; Alexandria *Louisiana Democrat,* January 30, 1861; Marshall *Texas Republican,* March 2, 1861; Dallas *Herald,* February 6, 1861; Corsicana (Tex.) *Navarro Express,* February 13, 1861; Baton Rouge (La.) *Daily Advocate,* January 27, 1861; Waco (Tex.) *South West,* January 16, 1861; Jackson *Weekly Mississippian,* January 16, 1861; Florence (Ala.) *Gazette,* January 16, 1861; Austin (Tex.) *State Gazette,* March 2, 1861; Savannah (Ga.) *Daily Morning News,* January 22, 1861; New Orleans *Bee,* January 28, 1861; Talledega (Ala.) *Democratic Watchtower,* January 16, 1861.

34. Augusta *Daily Constitutionalist,* January 29, February 14, 1861. See also Prattville (Ala.) *Autauga Citizen,* January 17, 1861; Montgomery (Ala.) *Weekly Confederation,* January 11, 18, 1861.

35. Clarksville *Northern Standard,* January 26, 1861; Camden *Republic,* January 31, 1861; Atlanta *Daily Intelligencer,* January 30, 1861; Plaquemine *Gazette and Sentinel,* February 16, 1861. See also Macon (Ga.) *Daily Telegraph,* January 19, 1861; Albany (Ga.)

Patriot, January 24, 1861; Atlanta *Gate-City Guardian,* February 12, 1861; Athens (Ga.) *Southern Recorder,* February 6, 1861.

36. Clarksville *Northern Standard,* March 23, 1861; Memphis *Daily Appeal,* February 26, 1861; Atlanta *Gate-City Guardian,* February 12, 1861; Jacksonville *Republican,* January 17, 1861; Richmond *Enquirer,* March 23, 1861.

37. Marshall *Texas Republican,* March 23, 1861; Wilson *Ledger,* December 25, 1860. See also Augusta (Ga.) *Chronicle and Sentinel,* February 17, 1861.

38. Vicksburg *Weekly Vicksburg Whig,* January 2, 1861; Rome *Weekly Courier,* January 4, 1861; Baton Rouge *Weekly Gazette and Comet,* December 29, 1860; January 5, 1861; Shreveport *South-Western,* January 9, 1861. See also Augusta (Ga.) *Chronicle and Sentinel,* January 1, 1861; Milledgeville (Ga.) *Southern Recorder,* January 15, 1861; West Baton Rouge (La.) *Sugar Planter,* December 22, 1860, January 5, 1861; Mount Pleasant (Tex.) *Union,* quoted in Marshall *Texas Republican,* January 12, 1861; Sandersville *Central Georgian,* January 2, 1861.

39. Augusta *Chronicle and Sentinel,* January 20, 1861; Alexandria *Constitutional,* February 2, 1861; Natchez *Courier,* January 11, 1861, quoted in Hillsborough (N.C.) *Recorder,* February 6, 1861. See also Baton Rouge (La.) *Weekly Gazette and Comet,* February 2, 1861; Rome (Ga.) *Weekly Courier,* January 25, 1861; McKinney (Tex.) *Messenger,* March 1, 1861; San Antonio (Tex.) *Alamo Express,* February 15, 1861.

40. West Baton Rouge *Sugar Planter,* February 16, 1861. See also Rome (Ga.) *Weekly Courier,* January 25, 1861; Milledgeville (Ga.) *Southern Recorder,* January 22, 1861; Vicksburg (Miss.) *Weekly Vicksburg Whig,* January 23, 1861; Sandersville *Central Georgian,* January 23, 1861; La Grange (Tex.) *True Issue,* February 21, 1861; Shreveport (La.) *South-Western,* January 30, February 6, 1861; Alexandria (La.) *Constitutional,* February 16, 1861.

41. Augusta *Chronicle and Sentinel,* January 26, 29, February 5, 13, 1861. The proposal that the South adopt a constitutional monarchy had little support in the Southern press. For criticism of the idea, see Sandersville *Central Georgian,* February 6, 1861 and Newbern (N.C.) *Weekly Progress,* January 21, 1861.

42. Tuscumbia *North Alabamian,* quoted in Alexandria (Va.) *Gazette,* March 14, 1861; Tuscumbia *North Alabamian,* March 8, 1861, quoted in Lynchburg *Virginian,* March 19, 1861; Corinth *Advertiser,* February 9, 1861, quoted in Wheeling (Va.) *Daily Intelligencer,* February 28, 1861; McKinney *Messenger,* March 1, 1861. See also Tuscaloosa (Ala.) *Monitor,* quoted in Wadesborough *North Carolina Argus,* March 7, 1861; San Antonio *Alamo Express,* March 1, 6, 15, 22, 29, April 3, 5, 10, 1861.

43. New Orleans *Daily True Delta,* February 6, 13, March 6, 7, 23, 27, 1861.

44. Potter, *Lincoln and His Party in the Secession Crisis*, pp. 312, 313; Dumond, *The Secession Movement*, pp. 217, 218, 244–246, 257, 258.

45. Trenton *Southern Standard*, February 16, 1861; Charlottesville *Review*, February 15, 1861; Charlestown *Virginia Free Press*, February 7, 1861; Wellsburg *Herald*, February 15, 1861. See also Richmond *Whig*, February 8, 1861; Richmond *Dispatch*, February 6, 1861; Raleigh *North Carolina Standard* (semiweekly ed.), March 2, 1861; Van Buren (Ark.) *Press*, February 22, 1861.

46. Alexandria *Gazette*, February 8, 1861; Little Rock *Arkansas State Gazette*, February 28, 1861; Van Buren *Press*, January 25, 1861. See also Richmond *Whig*, January 26, February 8, 1861; Charlotte *North Carolina Whig*, January 15, 1861; Wadesborough *North Carolina Argus*, January 17, 1861; Lynchburg *Virginian*, January 7, 1861; Greensboro (N.C.) *Times*, February 16, 1861; Staunton (Va.) *Vindicator*, February 8, 22, 1861; Batesville (Ark.) *Balance*, quoted in Fayetteville *Arkansian*, February 15, 1861.

47. Newbern *Weekly Progress*, January 8, 1861; Fayetteville *Arkansian*, February 22, 1861; Des Arc *Constitutional Union*, January 18, 1861.

48. Newbern *Weekly Progress*, January 8, 1861; Jonesborough *Union*, quoted in Jonesborough *Express*, January 25, 1861.

49. Fayetteville *Arkansian*, December 8, 1860; Knoxville *Whig*, January 26, 1861. See also Jonesborough (Tenn.) *Express*, January 25, 1861.

50. Harrisonburg (Va.) *Valley Democrat*, quoted in Hillsborough (N.C.) *Recorder*, January 9, 1861; Fayetteville (N.C.) *Observer*, December 10, 1860; Lynchburg *Virginian*, January 9, 1861; Richmond *Whig*, December 15, 1860; Raleigh *Register*, February 6, 1861; Charlottesville (Va.) *Review*, February 15, 1861; Raleigh *Daily Ad Valorem Banner*, February 23, 1861; Greensboro (N.C.) *Times*, December 22, 1860.

51. Raleigh *North Carolina Standard* (semiweekly ed.), February 2, 1861; Richmond *Whig*, March 1, 1861. See also Nashville *Republican Banner*, January 16, 1861; Harrisonburg *Virginia Citizen*, February 1, 1861; Clarksville (Tenn.) *Jeffersonian*, January 23, 1861; Little Rock *Arkansas State Gazette*, February 16, 1861; Lynchburg *Virginian*, February 6, 1861; Raleigh *North Carolina Christian Advocate*, February 4, 1861; Hillsborough (N.C.) *Recorder*, February 27, 1861.

52. Dumond, *The Secession Movement*, pp. 230–232; Potter, *Lincoln and His Party in the Secession Crisis*, pp. 156–187; Nichols, *The Disruption of American Democracy*, pp. 466–482; Milton, *The Eve of Conflict*, pp. 519–551.

53. Lynchburg *Virginian*, December 13, 1860; Alexandria *Gazette*, December 22, 1860.

54. Dumond, *The Secession Movement*, pp. 258, 259; Potter, *Lincoln and His Party in the Secession Crisis*, pp. 315–318.

55. Richmond *Examiner,* March 4, 1861.
56. Charlotte *North Carolina Whig,* February 26, 1861; Clarksville *Chronicle,* February 22, 1861; Staunton *Vindicator,* February 22, 1861. See also Little Rock *Arkansas State Gazette,* February 28, 1861; Nashville *Daily Patriot,* February 15, 24, 1861; Richmond *Dispatch,* February 21, 1861; Clarksville (Tenn.) *Jeffersonian,* February 20, 1861; Wilmington (N.C.) *Journal,* February 16, 1861; Alexandria (Va.) *Gazette.* March 2, 1861.
57. Greensboro *Times,* February 23, 1861.
58. Raleigh *Register,* March 3, 1861.

Notes to Chapter IX

1. Basler, ed., *The Collected Works of Abraham Lincoln,* IV, 265–266.
2. *Ibid.,* pp. 269–271.
3. Atlanta *Southern Confederacy,* March 5, 1861; New Orleans *Daily Delta,* March 6, 1861. See also Corsicana (Tex.) *Navarro Express,* March 20, 1861; San Antonio *Ledger and Texan,* March 16, 1861; Charleston *Mercury,* quoted in New Orleans *Daily True Delta,* March 13, 1861; La Grange (Tex.) *True Issue,* March 14, 1861; Augusta (Ga.) *Chronicle and Sentinel,* March 6, 1861; Clarksville (Tex.) *Northern Standard,* March 16, 1861.
4. Nashville *Union and American,* March 5, 1861; Richmond *Dispatch,* March 5, 1861; Wilmington *Daily Herald,* quoted in Wadesborough *North Carolina Argus,* March 14, 1861. See also Memphis *Avalanche,* March 5, 1861; Richmond *Examiner,* March 11, 1861.
5. Wilmington *Daily Journal,* March 7, 1861; Raleigh *State Journal,* March 9, 1861.
6. Harrisonburg *Rockingham Register and Advertiser,* March 8, 1861. See also Newbern (N.C.) *Weekly Progress,* March 12, 1861; Des Arc (Ark.) *Constitutional Union,* March 15, 1861; Staunton (Va.) *Vindicator,* March 8, 1861; Fayetteville *Arkansian,* March 15, 1861; Paris (Tenn.) *Sentinel,* March 6, 1861; Richmond *Examiner,* March 5, 1861; Little Rock *True Democrat,* March 9, 1861.
7. Salisbury *Carolina Watchman,* March 12, 1861; Harrisonburg *Virginia Citizen,* March 22, 1861. See also Hillsborough (N.C.) *Recorder,* March 13, 1861; Fayetteville (N.C.) *Observer,* quoted in Wadesborough *North Carolina Argus,* March 14, 1861.
8. Knoxville *Whig,* March 9, 1861; Nashville *Republican Banner,* March 6, 1861; Raleigh *North Carolina Standard,* March 9, 1861. See also Charlestown *Virginia Free Press,* March 7, 1861; Wellsburg (Va.) *Herald,* March 8, 1861; Wheeling (Va.) *Daily Intelligencer,* March 6, 1861; Lynchburg *Virginian,* March 11, 1861; Petersburg (Va.) *Express,* quoted in Wadesborough *North Carolina Argus,* March 14, 1861.
9. Van Buren *Press,* March 8, 1861; Clarksville *Jeffersonian,* March 13, 1861. See also Little Rock *Arkansas State Gazette,* March 9, 1861;

Fayetteville (Tenn.) *Lincoln Journal,* March 14, 1861. Virginia's two Republican papers, the Wellsburg *Herald* and the Wheeling *Daily Intelligencer,* implied a coercive policy after Lincoln's inaugural. See Wellsburg *Herald,* March 22, 1861, and Wheeling *Daily Intelligencer,* March 12, 1861.

10. Charlotte *North Carolina Whig,* March 12, 1861; Richmond *Whig,* March 6, 1861. See also Raleigh *Register,* March 9, 1861; Alexandria (Va.) *Gazette,* March 5, 13, 1861; Clarksville (Tenn.) *Chronicle,* March 8, 15, 1861.

11. Potter, *Lincoln and His Party in the Secession Crisis,* pp. 336–363; Nichols, *The Disruption of American Democracy,* pp. 492–500.

12. Milledgeville *Southern Federal Union,* April 2, 1861.

13. Memphis *Avalanche,* March 16, 1861; Clarksville *Tobacco Plant,* March 29, 1861. See also Nashville *Union and American,* March 6, 1861; Wilmington (N.C.) *Daily Journal,* March 14, 1861.

14. Fort Smith *Daily Times and Herald,* April 5, 1861; Richmond *Examiner,* April 5, 1861. See also Raleigh *State Journal,* March 13, 1861; Des Arc (Ark.) *Constitutional Union,* March 22, 1861; Paris (Tenn.) *Sentinel,* March 30, April 3, 1861; Richmond *Daily Enquirer,* March 12, 26, 28, April 9, 1861; Richmond *Dispatch,* March 26, 1861; Fayetteville *North Carolinian,* March 16, 1861; Harrisonburg (Va.) *Rockingham Register and Advertiser,* March 29, April 5, 1861; Little Rock *True Democrat,* March 12–16, 1861.

15. Wilmington *Daily Journal,* March 14, 21, 1861.

16. Staunton *Vindicator,* March 22, 1861; Memphis *Daily Appeal,* March 21, 1861; Richmond *Examiner,* March 6, 1861. See also Newbern (N.C.) *Weekly Progress,* April 2, 1861.

17. Memphis *Avalanche,* March 16, 1861; Memphis *Daily Appeal,* March 26, 1861. See also Little Rock *True Democrat,* March 13, 1861; Richmond *Examiner,* March 28, 1861.

18. Nashville *Republican Banner,* April 5, 1861; Lynchburg *Virginian,* April 5, 1861; Memphis *Avalanche,* March 9, 1861; Charlestown *Virginia Free Press,* April 4, 1861.

19. Charlotte *North Carolina Whig,* March 26, 1861; Raleigh *State Journal,* April 3, 6, 10, 1861.

20. Van Buren *Press,* March 13, 1861; Petersburg *Daily Express,* March 12, 1861; Hillsborough *Recoder,* March 20, April 3, 1861; Gallatin *Courier,* March 27, 1861. See also Greensboro (N.C.) *Times,* March 30, 1861; Richmond *Whig,* March 14, 1861.

21. Little Rock *Arkansas State Gazette,* March 23, 1861; Raleigh *North Carolina Standard* (semiweekly ed.), April 3, 1861; Clarksville *Jeffersonian,* March 27, 1861. See also Raleigh *Register,* March 30, 1861; Nashville *Republican Banner,* April 3, 1861; Lynchburg *Virginian,* April 1, 1861; Van Buren (Ark.) *Press,* March 20, 1861; Clarksville (Tenn.) *Chronicle,* March 29, 1861.

22. Harrisonburg *Virginia Citizen,* March 22, 1861. See also Staunton (Va.) *Spectator,* April 2, 1861; Salem (N.C.) *People's Press,* March 29, 1861; Wadesborough *North Carolina Argus,* April 4, 1861; Rich-

mond *Whig,* March 25, 1861; Nashville *Republican Banner,* April 12, 1861.

23. Alexandria (Va.) *Gazette,* April 5, 1861; Van Buren *Press,* April 3, 1861; Clarksville (Tenn.) *Chronicle,* March 22, 1861; Greensboro (N.C.) *Times,* March 23, 1861.

24. Potter, *Lincoln and His Party in the Secession Crisis,* pp. 336–375; Randall and Donald, *The Civil War and Reconstruction,* pp. 169–175; Nichols, *The Disruption of American Democracy,* pp. 495–500.

25. Memphis *Avalanche,* April 8, 10, 1861; Wilmington *Daily Journal,* April 11, 1861; Clarksville *Tobacco Plant,* April 12, 1861. See also Raleigh *Register,* April 13, 1861; Alexandria (Va.) *Gazette,* April 10, 1861; Richmond *Examiner,* April 6, 1861; Clarksville (Tenn.) *Chronicle,* April 12, 1861.

26. Clement Eaton, *A History of the Southern Confederacy,* pp. 36–37; Randall and Donald, *The Civil War and Reconstruction,* pp. 176–177; W. A. Swanberg, *First Blood: The Story of Fort Sumter,* pp. 291–339.

27. Memphis *Avalanche,* April 10, 1861; Raleigh *State Journal,* April 17, 1861. See also Wilmington (N.C.) *Daily Journal,* April 18, 1861; Richmond *Dispatch,* April 19, 1861; Kanawha (Va.) *Valley Star,* April 23, 1861; Newbern (N.C.) *Weekly Progress,* April 23, 1861; Richmond *Examiner,* April 19, 1861.

28. Richmond *Examiner,* April 15, 1861; Nashville *Union and American,* April 16, 1861; Memphis *Avalanche,* April 15, May 1, 1861. See also Little Rock *True Democrat,* April 18, 1861; Clarksville (Va.) *Tobacco Plant,* April 19, 1861; Fayetteville *North Carolinian,* April 20, 1861; Wilmington (N.C.) *Daily Journal,* April 18, 1861.

29. Nashville *Republican Banner,* April 13, 1861; Knoxville *Whig,* April 27, 1861.

30. Fayetteville *Observer,* April 15, 1861; Raleigh *North Carolina Standard* (semiweekly ed.), April 17, 1861; Lynchburg *Virginian,* April 15, 1861. See also Alexandria (Va.) *Gazette,* April 17, 1861; Hillsborough (N.C.) *Recorder,* April 17, 1861; Athens (Tenn.) *Post,* April 19, 1861; Gallatin (Tenn.) *Courier,* April 17, 1861; Clarksville (Tenn.) *Jeffersonian,* May 1, 1861.

31. Randall and Donald, *The Civil War and Reconstruction,* p. 177.

32. Richmond *Whig,* April 15, 16, 1861; Lynchburg *Virginian,* April 16, 1861; Raleigh *North Carolina Standard* (semiweekly ed.), April 24, 1861. See also Hillsborough (N.C.) *Recorder,* April 24, 1861; Greensboro (N.C.) *Times,* April 20, 1861; Salisbury (N.C.) *Carolina Watchman,* April 16, 1861; Alexandria (Va.) *Gazette,* April 16, 1861; Nashville *Republican Banner,* April 16, 18, 1861; Wadesborough *North Carolina Argus,* April 18, 1861; Fayetteville (N.C.) *Observer,* May 20, 1861; Gallatin (Tenn.) *Courier,* April 17, 1861.

33. Athens *Post,* April 15, 26, May 3, 1861; Raleigh *Register,* April 17,

20, 27, 1861; Richmond *Enquirer,* April 18, 1861. See also Nashville *Republican Banner,* April 24, 25, May 9, 1861; Van Buren (Ark.) *Press,* April 17, 24, 1861; Wadesborough *North Carolina Argus,* April 18, 25, 1861; Clarksville (Tenn.) *Chronicle,* April 19, 26, 1861; Alexandria (Va.) *Gazette,* April 19, 1861; Salisbury (N.C.) *Carolina Watchman,* April 23, 1861.

34. Raleigh *North Carolina Standard* (semiweekly ed.) , April 17, 1861; Little Rock *Arkansas State Gazette,* April 20, May 4, 1861; Raleigh *Weekly Ad Valorem Banner,* April 25, 1861; Austin (Tex.) *Intelligencer,* May 8, 1861.

35. De Witt C. Roberts, *Southern Sketches, Or, Eleven Years Down South, Including Three in Dixie,* pp. 30, 31.

36. San Antonio *Alamo Express,* April 15, 17, May 3, 1861; Pearson Newcomb, "That Man From Texas, A Minority of One: The Story of James P. Newcomb," microfilm of typescript in possession of Dale Somers, Department of History, Georgia State College; original in possession of Pearson Newcomb, San Antonio, Texas, pp. 126-128.

37. Wellsburg *Herald,* May 3, 10, 24, 1861; Wheeling *Daily Intelligencer,* April 15, 16, 25, May 18, 1861.

38. Knoxville *Whig,* April 20, 27, May 4, 18, 25, June 15, October 26, 1861. See also Jonesborough (Tenn.) *Express,* August 15, 1862. When the Federal government recaptured Tennessee in the fall of 1863, Brownlow resumed the editorship of his paper, which he then called *Brownlow's Knoxville Whig and Rebel Ventilator.* In his first issue after returning (November 11, 1863) the Parson said: "We are not here to *excuse* this or that act of the Washington Government; nor yet to censure President Lincoln for what he has done, or to wish that he had done otherwise. We endorse all he has done, and we find fault with him for not having done more of the same sort! The Federal Government has been too lenient, and too slow to punish rebels, and to crush out this most abominable, wicked and uncalled for rebellion, from its very commencement."

39. Richmond *Whig,* April 19, 1861; Charlottesville (Va.) *Review,* May 24, 1861; Little Rock *Arkansas State Gazette,* May 11, 1861; Clarksville (Tenn.) *Jeffersonian,* May 8, 1861; Fayetteville (Tenn.) *Lincoln Journal,* June 27, 1861; Nashville *Republican Banner,* May 9, 1861.

40. Wadesborough *North Carolina Argus,* May 2, 1861; Harrisonburg *Rockingham Register and Advertiser,* April 26, 1861.

41. Hillsborough *Recorder,* May 29, 1861.

42. Petersburg *Daily Express,* April 17, 1861; Clarksville *Jeffersonian,* May 15, 1861; Charlotte *North Carolina Whig,* April 23, 1861. See also Clarksville (Tenn.) *Chronicle,* May 10, 1861; Charlottesville (Va.) *Review,* May 24, 1861; Newbern *Weekly Progress,* April 23, 1861.

43. Milledgeville *Southern Federal Union,* April 23, 1861. See also Richmond *Dispatch,* April 13, 19, 1861; Knoxville *Register,* quoted in Nashville *Republican Banner,* April 30, 1861; Memphis *Daily Appeal,* April 13, 1861; Alexandria (La.) *Constitutional,* April 13, 1861; Greensboro (N.C.) *Times,* March 9, 1861; Memphis *Avalanche,* May 6, 1861.

44. Raleigh *Democratic Press,* May 8, 1861; Raleigh *Church Intelligencer,* May 9, 1861; Fayetteville *North Carolina Presbyterian,* April 27, 1861; Memphis, Arkansas and Ouachita *Christian Advocate,* July 11, 1861. See also Richmond *Christian Advocate,* May 2, 1861; Raleigh *Spirit of the Age,* April 24, 1861; Raleigh *North Carolina Christian Advocate,* April 29, 1861; Richmond *Religious Herald,* April 25, 1861.

45. Memphis *Daily Appeal,* May 8, 1861.

Notes to Chapter X

1. Floyd County *Southern Era,* quoted in Wheeling *Daily Intelligencer,* April 11, 1861.

2. Quoted in Eaton, *The Freedom-of-Thought Struggle in the Old South,* p. 399.

3. Atlanta *Gate-City Guardian,* February 23, 1861; New Orleans *Daily Picayune,* September 8, 1860.

4. Van Buren *Press,* November 30, 1860; Athens *Post,* March 1, 1861.

5. Craven, *The Growth of Southern Nationalism,* p. 400.

6. Fredericksburg *Herald,* quoted in Alexandria (Va.) *Gazette,* January 3, 1860.

Bibliography

NEWSPAPERS

Abbeville (South Carolina) *Independent Press.*
Albany (Georgia) *Patriot.*
Alexandria (Louisiana) *Constitutional.*
Alexandria *Gazette and Virginia Advertiser.*
Alexandria *Louisiana Democrat.*
Anderson (South Carolina) *Intelligencer.*
Asheville (North Carolina) *News.*
Athens (Tennessee) *Post.*
Athens (Georgia) *Southern Banner.*
Atlanta (Georgia) *Daily Intelligencer.*
Atlanta (Georgia) *Gate-City Guardian.*
Atlanta (Georgia) *Southern Confederacy.*
Auburn (Alabama) *Sketch Book.*
Augusta (Georgia) *Chronicle and Sentinel.*
Augusta (Georgia) *Daily Constitutionalist.*
Austin (Texas) *Southern Intelligencer.*
Austin (Texas) *State Gazette.*
Baton Rouge (Louisiana) *Daily Advocate.*
Baton Rouge (Louisiana) *Weekly Gazette and Comet.*
Beaufort (South Carolina) *Enterprise.*
Bellevue (Louisiana) *Bossier Banner.*
Belton (Texas) *Democrat.*
Benton (Alabama) *Weekly Herald.*
Brandon (Mississippi) *Republican.*
Brenham *Texas Ranger.*
Camden (Alabama) *Republic.*
Camden (Arkansas) *Ouachita Herald.*
Camden (South Carolina) *Weekly Journal.*
Canton (Mississippi) *American Citizen.*
Carrollton *West Alabamian.*

Charleston (South Carolina) *Daily Courier.*
Charleston (South Carolina) *Mercury.*
Charleston (South Carolina) *Southern Baptist.*
Charlestown *Virginia Free Press.*
Charlotte *North Carolina Whig.*
Charlottesville (Virginia) *Review.*
Cincinnati (Ohio) *Daily Commercial.*
Claiborne (Alabama) *Southern Champion.*
Clarksville (Tennessee) *Chronicle.*
Clarksville (Tennessee) *Jeffersonian.*
Clarksville (Texas) *Northern Standard.*
Clarksville (Virginia) *Tobacco Plant.*
Columbia *Daily South Carolinian.*
Columbia (South Carolina) *Daily Southern Guardian.*
Columbia (Texas) *Democrat and Planter.*
Columbus (Texas) *Colorado Citizen.*
Columbus (Georgia) *Enquirer.*
Columbus *Mississippi Democrat.*
Corpus Christi (Texas) *Ranchero.*
Corsicana (Texas) *Navarro Express.*
Dallas (Texas) *Herald.*
Dallas (Texas) *Morning News.*
Des Arc (Arkansas) *Citizen.*
Des Arc (Arkansas) *Constitutional Union.*
Edgefield (South Carolina) *Advertiser.*
Fairmont *True Virginian.*
False River (Louisiana) *Pointe Coupée Democrat.*
Fayetteville *Arkansian.*
Fayetteville (Tennessee) *Lincoln Journal.*
Fayetteville *North Carolina Presbyterian.*
Fayetteville *North Carolinian.*
Fayetteville (North Carolina) *Observer.*
Fernandina *Weekly East Floridian.*
Florence (Alabama) *Gazette.*
Fort Smith (Arkansas) *Times.*
Gallatin (Tennessee) *Courier.*
Gallatin (Tennessee) *Examiner.*
Galveston (Texas) *Civilian and Gazette.*
Galveston (Texas) *Crisis.*
Galveston *Texas Christian Advocate.*
Galveston (Texas) *Weekly News.*
Greensboro *Alabama Beacon.*

Greensboro (North Carolina) *Times.*
Greenville *South Alabamian.*
Greenville (Alabama) *Southern Messenger.*
Grove Hill (Alabama) *Clarke County Democrat.*
Harrisonburg (Virginia) *Rockingham Register and Advertiser.*
Harrisonburg (Virginia) *Valley Democrat.*
Harrisonburg *Virginia Citizen.*
Hayneville (Alabama) *Chronicle.*
Hayneville (Alabama) *Watchman.*
Henderson (Texas) *Times.*
Hillsborough (North Carolina) *Recorder.*
Houston (Texas) *Telegraph.*
Indianola (Texas) *Courier.*
Jackson *Weekly Mississippian.*
Jacksonville (Alabama) *Republican.*
Jonesborough (Tennessee) *Express.*
Jonesborough (Tennessee) *Union.*
Kanawha (Virginia) *Valley Star.*
Knoxville (Tennessee) *Whig.*
Kosciusko (Mississippi) *Chronicle.*
La Grange (Texas) *True Issue.*
Leesburg (Virginia) *Democratic Mirror.*
Lexington (South Carolina) *Flag.*
Little Rock *Arkansas State Gazette.*
Little Rock (Arkansas) *Old-Line Democrat.*
Little Rock (Arkansas) *True Democrat.*
Lynchburg (Virginia) *Republican.*
Lynchburg *Virginian.*
Macon (Georgia) *Daily Telegraph.*
Marshall *Texas Republican.*
Matagorda (Texas) *Gazette.*
McKinney (Texas) *Messenger.*
Memphis, Arkansas and Ouachita *Christian Advocate.*
Memphis (Tennessee) *Avalanche.*
Memphis (Tennessee) *Daily Appeal.*
Milledgeville (Georgia) *Federal Union.*
Milledgeville (Georgia) *Southern Recorder.*
Montgomery (Alabama) *Confederation.*
Montgomery (Alabama) *Universalist Herald.*
Montgomery (Alabama) *Weekly Advertiser.*
Montgomery (Alabama) *Weekly Mail.*
Montgomery (Alabama) *Weekly Post.*

Murfreesboro (Tennessee) *News.*
Nashville (Tennessee) *Republican Banner.*
Nashville (Tennessee) *Union and American.*
Natchez (Mississippi) *Courier.*
Natchez *Mississippi Free Trader.*
Newbern (North Carolina) *Weekly Progress.*
Newberry (South Carolina) *Conservatist.*
Newberry (South Carolina) *Rising Sun.*
New Orleans (Louisiana) *Bee.*
New Orleans (Louisiana) *Daily Picayune.*
New Orleans (Louisiana) *Daily True Delta.*
New Orleans (Louisiana) *Daily Delta.*
New York *Times.*
New York *Daily Tribune.*
Norfolk (Virginia) *Southern Argus.*
Opelika (Alabama) *Weekly Southern Era.*
Opelousas (Louisiana) *Courier.*
Oxford (Mississippi) *Mercury.*
Palestine (Texas) *Trinity Advocate.*
Paris (Tennessee) *Sentinel.*
Paulding (Mississippi) *Eastern Clarion.*
Petersburg (Virginia) *Daily Express.*
Petersburg (Virginia) *Intelligencer.*
Plaquemine (Louisiana) *Gazette and Sentinel.*
Prattville (Alabama) *Autauga Citizen.*
Prattville (Alabama) *Southern Statesman.*
Raleigh (North Carolina) *Church Intelligencer.*
Raleigh (North Carolina) *Daily Ad Valorem Banner.*
Raleigh (North Carolina) *Democratic Press.*
Raleigh (North Carolina) *National Democrat.*
Raleigh *North Carolina Christian Advocate.*
Raleigh *North Carolina Standard.*
Raleigh (North Carolina) *Register.*
Raleigh (North Carolina) *Spirit of the Age.*
Raleigh (North Carolina) *State Journal.*
Raymond (Mississippi) *Hinds County Gazette.*
Richmond (Virginia) *Central Presbyterian.*
Richmond (Virginia) *Christian Advocate.*
Richmond (Virginia) *Dispatch.*
Richmond (Virginia) *Enquirer.*
Richmond (Virginia) *Examiner.*
Richmond (Virginia) *Religious Herald.*

Richmond (Virginia) *Whig.*
Ripley (Mississippi) *Advertiser.*
Rome (Georgia) *Weekly Courier.*
St. Augustine (Florida) *Examiner.*
Salem (North Carolina) *People's Press.*
Salisbury (North Carolina) *Carolina Watchman.*
San Antonio (Texas) *Alamo Express.*
San Antonio (Texas) *Daily Herald.*
San Antonio (Texas) *Ledger and Texan.*
San Augustine (Texas) *Red Land Express.*
Sandersville *Central Georgian.*
Savannah (Georgia) *Daily Morning News.*
Selma *Alabama State Sentinel.*
Shepherdstown (Virginia) *Register.*
Shreveport (Louisiana) *South-Western.*
Spartanburg (South Carolina) *Carolina Spartan.*
Staunton (Virginia) *Spectator.*
Staunton (Virginia) *Vindicator.*
Sulphur Springs (Texas) *Independent Monitor.*
Talladega *Alabama Reporter.*
Tallahassee *Floridian and Journal.*
Trenton (Tennessee) *Southern Standard.*
Tuscumbia (Alabama) *Constitution.*
Tuscumbia (Alabama) *States' Rights Democrat.*
Tuskegee (Alabama) *South Western Baptist.*
Tyler (Texas) *Reporter.*
Van Buren (Arkansas) *Press.*
Vicksburg (Mississippi) *Weekly Vicksburg Whig.*
Waco (Texas) *South West.*
Wadesborough *North Carolina Argus.*
Washington (D.C.) *Constitution.*
Washington (D.C.) *Daily National Intelligencer.*
Washington (North Carolina) *Dispatch.*
Weatherford (Texas) *White Man.*
Wellsburg (Virginia) *Herald.*
West Baton Rouge (Louisiana) *Sugar Planter.*
Wheeling (Virginia) *Daily Intelligencer.*
Wilmington (North Carolina) *Daily Journal.*
Wilmington (North Carolina) *Herald.*
Wilson (North Carolina) *Ledger.*

OTHER SOURCES

Addington, Wendell G. "Slave Insurrections in Texas, 1835–63," *Journal of Negro History,* XXXV (October 1950), 408–434.

Alexander, Thomas B. "Persistent Whiggery in Alabama and the Lower South, 1860–1867," *Alabama Review,* XII (January 1959), 35–52.

Aptheker, Herbert. *American Negro Slave Revolts.* New York: Columbia University Press, 1944.

Barron, S. B. *The Lone Star Defenders.* New York: The Neale Publishing Company, 1908.

Basler, Roy P., ed. *The Collected Works of Abraham Lincoln.* 8 vols. New Brunswick, New Jersey: Princeton University Press, 1953.

Bates, Edmond F. *History and Reminiscences of Denton County.* Denton, Texas: McNitzky Printing Co., 1918.

Bates, William M. "The Last Stand for the Union of Georgia," *Georgia Review,* VI (Winter 1953), 455–467.

Bond, Donovan H. "How the Wheeling Intelligencer Became a Republican Organ (1856–1860)," *West Virginia History,* XI (April 1950), 160–184.

Boyd, William K. "North Carolina on the Eve of Secession," *American Historical Association Report for the Year 1910,* (1912), 165–177.

Brantley, William H. Jr. "Alabama Secedes," *Alabama Review* VII (July 1954), 165–185.

Brown, John. "Diary of John Brown." Photocopy of the original, University of Texas Archives, Austin, Texas.

Brownlow, William G. *Sketches of the Rise, Progress, and Decline of Secession.* Philadelphia: G. W. Childs, 1862.

Bryan, T. C. "The Secession of Georgia," *Georgia Historical Quarterly,* XXXI (June 1947), 89–111.

Campbell Papers. University of Texas Archives. Austin, Texas.

Capers, Gerald M. *Stephen A. Douglas: Defender of the Union.* Boston: Little, Brown and Company, 1959.

Caskey, Willie M. *Secession and Restoration of Louisiana.* Baton Rouge: Louisiana State University Press, 1938.

Cauthen, Charles E. "South Carolina's Decision to Lead the Secession Movement," *North Carolina Historical Review,* XVIII (October 1941) 360–372.

———. *South Carolina Goes to War, 1860–1865.* Vol. XXXII of

The James Sprunt Studies in History and Political Science. Chapel Hill: The University of North Carolina Press, 1905.

Cotterill, Robert S. *The Old South.* Glendale, California: Arthur H. Clark Company, 1936.

Coulter, Ellis M. *William G. Brownlow: Fighting Parson of the Southern Highlands.* Chapel Hill, North Carolina: University of North Carolina Press, 1937.

Craven, Avery O. *The Growth of Southern Nationalism, 1848–1861.* Baton Rouge: Louisiana State University Press, 1953.

Crenshaw, Ollinger. *The Slave States in the Presidential Election of 1860.* Vol. LXIII of *The Johns Hopkins University Studies in Historical and Political Science.* Baltimore: The Johns Hopkins Press, 1945.

————. "The Speakership Contest of 1859–1860," *Mississippi Valley Historical Review,* XXIX (December 1942), 323–338.

Dabney, Thomas E. *One Hundred Great Years: The Story of the Times-Picayune from its Founding to 1940.* Baton Rouge: Louisiana State University Press, 1944.

Davis, Horace G. Jr. "Pensacola Newspapers, 1821–1900," *Florida Historical Quarterly,* XXXVII (January–April 1959), 419–445.

Denman, Clarence P. *The Secession Movement in Alabama.* Montgomery: Alabama State Department of Archives and History, 1933.

Donald, David. *Charles Sumner and the Coming of the Civil War.* New York: Alfred A. Knopf, 1960.

Du Bose, John W. *The Life and Times of William Lowndes Yancey.* 2 vols. New York: Peter Smith, 1942.

Dumond, Dwight L. *The Secession Movement, 1860–1861.* New York: The Macmillan Company, 1931.

————, ed. *Southern Editorials on Secession.* New York: The Century Company, 1931.

Eaton, Clement. *The Freedom-of-Thought Struggle in the Old South.* New York: Harper and Row, 1964.

————. *The Growth of Southern Civilization, 1790–1860.* New York: Harper and Brothers, 1961.

————. *A History of the Southern Confederacy.* New York: The Free Press, 1965.

Elliott, Robert N. Jr. *The Raleigh Register, 1799–1863.* Vol. XXXVI of *The James Sprunt Studies in History and Political Science.* Chapel Hill: The University of North Carolina Press, 1955.

Fertig, James W. *The Secession and Reconstruction of Tennessee.* Chicago: The University of Chicago Press, 1898.

Fite, Emerson D. *The Presidential Campaign of 1860.* New York: The Macmillan Company, 1911.

Fornel, Earl W. *The Galveston Era: The Texas Crescent on the Eve of Secession.* Austin: University of Texas Press, 1961.

Gage, Larry J. "The Texas Road to Secession and War: John Marshall and the *Texas State Gazette,* 1860–1861," *Southwestern Historical Quarterly,* LXII (October 1958), 191–226.

Gammel, H. N. P., comp. *The Laws of Texas, 1822–1897.* 10 vols. Austin: The Gammel Book Co., 1898.

Hesseltine, William B., ed. *Three Against Lincoln: Murat Halstead Reports the Caucuses of 1860.* Baton Rouge: Louisiana State University Press, 1960.

Holden, William W. *Memoirs of W. W. Holden.* Durham, North Carolina: The Seeman Printery, 1911.

Johnson, Gerald W. *The Secession of the Southern States.* New York: G. P. Putnam's Sons, 1933.

Kennedy, Joseph C. G. *Preliminary Report on the Eighth Census.* Washington, D.C.: Government Printing Office, 1862.

Kibler, Lillian A. "Unionist Sentiments in South Carolina in 1860," *Journal of Southern History,* IV (August 1938), 346–366.

Knight, Oliver. *Fort Worth: Outpost on the Trinity.* Norman, Oklahoma: University of Oklahoma Press, 1953.

Lanman, Charles. *Dictionary of the United States Congress, Containing Biographical Sketches of its Members from the Foundation of the Government.* Philadelphia: J. B. Lippincott and Company, 1859.

Lee, James M. *History of American Journalism.* Garden City, New York: The Garden City Publishing Company, Incorporated, 1923.

Luthin, Reinhard H. *The First Lincoln Campaign.* Cambridge, Massachusetts: Harvard University Press, 1944.

Malone, Henry T. "The *Weekly Atlanta Intelligencer* as a Secessionist Journal (1860–1861)," *Georgia Historical Quarterly,* XXXVII (December 1953), 278–286.

A Memorial and Biographical History of Ellis County, Texas. Chicago: The Lewis Publishing Company, 1892.

Milton, George F. *The Eve of Conflict: Stephen A. Douglas and the Needless War.* New York: Houghton Mifflin Company, 1934.

Monroe, Haskell. "Southern Presbyterians and the Secession Crisis," *Civil War History*, VI (December 1960), 351–360.

Mott, Frank L. *American Journalism*. New York: The Macmillan Company, 1941.

Nevins, Allan. *The Emergence of Lincoln*. Vol. II. New York: Charles Scribner's Sons, 1951.

Newcomb, Pearson. "That Man from Texas, A Minority of One: The Story of James P. Newcomb." Microfilm copy of typescript in possession of Dale A. Somers, Department of History, Georgia State University; original in possession of Pearson Newcomb, San Antonio, Texas.

Nichols, Roy F. *The Disruption of American Democracy*. New York: Collier Books, 1962.

Patton, James W. *Unionism and Reconstruction in Tennessee, 1860–1869*. Chapel Hill: The University of North Carolina Press, 1934.

Pease Papers. Austin Public Library, Austin, Texas.

Perkins, Howard C., ed. *Northern Editorials on Secession*. 2 vols. New York: D. Appleton-Century Company, 1942.

Potter, David M. *Lincoln and His Party in the Secession Crisis*. New Haven, Connecticut: Yale University Press, 1942.

Rainwater, Percy L. "An Analysis of the Secession Controversy in Mississippi, 1854–61," *Mississippi Valley Historical Review*, XXIV (June 1937), 35–42.

———. *Mississippi, Storm Center of Secession, 1856–1861*. Baton Rouge, Louisiana: O. Claitor, 1938.

Randall, James G. and David, Donald. *The Civil War and Reconstruction*. Second edition. Boston: D. C. Heath and Company, 1961.

Raper, Horace W. "William W. Holden and the Peace Movement in North Carolina," *North Carolina Historical Review*, XXXI (October 1954), 493–516.

Roach, Hattie. *A History of Cherokee County*. Dallas: Southwest Press, 1934.

Roberts, De Witt C. *Southern Sketches: or, Eleven Years Down South, Including Three in Dixie*. Jacksonville, Florida: D. W. Roberts, 1865.

Rogers, William W., ed. "Florida on the Eve of the Civil War as seen by a Southern Reporter, *Florida Historical Quarterly*, XXXIX (October 1960), 145–158.

Roland, Charles P. *The Confederacy*. Chicago: The University of Chicago Press, 1960.

Sandbo, Anna I. "Beginnings of the Secession Movement in Texas," *Southwestern Historical Quarterly,* XVIII (July 1914), 41–73.

———. "The First Session of the Secession Convention of Texas," *Southwestern Historical Quarterly,* XVIII (October 1914), 162–194.

Schultz, Harold S. *Nationalism and Sectionalism in South Carolina, 1852–1860.* Durham, North Carolina: Duke University Press, 1950.

Scroggs, Jack B. "Arkansas in the Secession Crisis (1860–61)," *Arkansas Historical Quarterly,* XII (Autumn 1953), 179–224.

Shanks, Henry T. *The Secession Movement in Virginia, 1847–1861.* Richmond: Garrett and Massie, 1934.

Shugg, Roger W. *Origins of the Class Struggle in Louisiana, 1845–1875.* University, Louisiana: Louisiana State University Press, 1939.

Sitterson, J. C. *The Secession Movement in North Carolina.* Chapel Hill: The University of North Carolina Press, 1939.

Smith, Edward C. *The Borderland in the Civil War.* New York: The Macmillan Company, 1927.

Steen, Ralph W. "Texas Newspapers and Lincoln, 1860–1946," *Southwestern Historical Quarterly,* LI (January 1948), 199–212.

Swanberg, W. A. *First Blood: The Story of Fort Sumter.* New York: Charles Scribner's Sons, 1957.

Thomas, David Y. *Arkansas in War and Reconstruction, 1861–1874.* Little Rock: Arkansas Division, United Daughters of the Confederacy, 1926.

U.S. Census Office. *Population of the United States in 1860; Compiled from the Original Returns of the Eighth Census under the Direction of the Secretary of the Interior.* Washington, D.C.: Government Printing Office, 1862.

———. *The Seventh Census of the United States: 1850.* Washington, D.C.: Government Printing Office, 1853.

Walmsley, James E., ed. "The Change of Secession Sentiment in Virginia in 1861," *American Historical Review,* XXXI (October 1925), 82–101.

White, William W. "The Texas Slave Insurrection of 1860," *Southwestern Historical Quarterly,* LII (January 1949), 259–285.

Woodward, C. V. *The Burden of Southern History.* New York: Vintage Books, 1961.

Wooster, Ralph A. *The Secession Conventions of the South.* Princeton, New Jersey: Princeton University Press, 1962.

Wortham, Louis J. *A History of Texas, from Wilderness to Commonwealth.* 5 vols. Fort Worth, Texas: Wortham-Molyneaux Company, 1924.

Index